The Guru is You

Yoga for Self-Discovery and Purposeful Living

Part I of the Fusion Yoga method

By Charmion O'Day Harris

Living True Works
3710 Farnum Creek Rd
Milford, KS 66514
www.wildsukha.com

Library of Congress Cataloging-in-Publication-Data
The Guru is You: Yoga for Self-Discovery and Purposeful Living
ISBN: 979-8-9940836-2-8

Other Living True Works:

Body as Teacher: *Yoga's Physical Practices for All* is an on-the-mat resource with almost 200 poses and pose variations for all bodies, including Kundalini kriyas, Qigong and Yin, breathing techniques, meditations, mudras, mantras, and Indigenous practices.

Sources

Some perspectives in this book were informed by the following sources.

Alexander, Eben. *Proof of Heaven*. Simon & Schuster.

Easwaran, Eknath (trans.). *The Upanishads*. Nilgiri Press.

Foxen, Anya, and Christa Kuberry. *Is This Yoga?* Routledge.

Frankl, Viktor. *Man's Search for Meaning*. Beacon Press.

Jaya the Trust Coach. *Scooch: Edging into a Friendly Universe*.

Judith, Anodea. *Eastern Mind, Western Body*. Celestial Arts.

Katie, Byron. *Loving What Is*. Harmony Books.

Kapur, Kamla K. *Ganesha Goes to Lunch*. Mandala Publishing.

Lad, Vasant. *Yoga & Ayurveda*. Ayurvedic Press.

Mallinson, James. *The History and Practices of Hatha Yoga*.

Nayaran, R.K. *The Ramayana: A Shortened Modern Prose Version of the Indian Epic*. Penguin Classics.

O'Day Harris, Charmion, *Body as Teacher: Yoga's Physical Practices for All*, Living True Works

Sarno, John E., MD. *Healing Back Pain*. Warner Books.

Satchidananda, Sri Swami. *The Yoga Sutras of Patanjali*. Integral Yoga Publications.

Anonymous. *The Rig Veda*. Various editions.

The Guru is You

Backstory and Dedication

My teenage parents left their childhood homes to become parents, farmers, and ranchers in Freedhem, Minnesota. By the time I was 7, I could do farm chores, saddle my own horse, pray the rosary, and move quickly between states and divorced parents. And by the time I was 18, being a soldier seemed like a good way to ease into adult life.

I became tougher than I dreamed possible. Unfortunately this new outer fortitude brought with it an inner numbness. After a few years, motherhood and college softened my edges. But still, something remained amiss between my head, heart, and body. So, the kids and I headed for the last frontier where I laid my problems on Mother Nature's alter by hiking straight up mountains and steering directly into the sea.

It worked; the dam broke as tidal waves of emotion met me every day and most nights. But without the tools to embrace both grit and vulnerability, I set out again searching for wholeness through adventures that put survival to the test. This time my body wasn't as forgiving.

So I cuddled up with my dog and read several books about yoga, employing multiple-colored highlighters to brightly expose life-changing revelations. Soon I was teaching yoga and volunteering around the world to learn about love through service. Still, it felt like I was in a video game where the avatar moves down a well-worn path lined with beautiful scenery, only to face shockingly repetitive obstacles.

I wanted out of the game.

I wanted to know what I was alive for.

That seeking led to Sacramento, California, where I took my spot at a yoga studio to practice with my favorite yoga teacher whose classes included fused techniques and philosophies that left students glowing from a complete physical, mental, and emotional workout. The only thing better I could imagine than experiencing Buck's class was having the ability to do the same for myself whenever I wanted.

For the next decade, I set out on new paths that are fused together in this book of mostly "off-the-mat" yogic work with real-life stories laced throughout in the hopes of sparking fresh insight and application into your own life. I believe that each of us holds the wisdom to reveal what we need for "living true" - the practice of awareness, feeling, knowing, and acting on what is true in our lives.

This book's companion, **Body as Teacher**: *Yoga's Physical Practices for All*, offers "on-the-mat" poses with variations for all bodies, along with breathing techniques, subtle energy practices, meditation, and movements from multiple lineages to help you fuse physical and energetic practices into ways that are the most potent for you on any given day.

Together, these books offer a combination of wellness, creativity, awareness, and inner evolution called the Fusion Yoga Method.

> *Life is not a game.*
> *You are not an avatar.*
> *You are the Guru.*

Boundless gratitude to my teachers, in person, virtual and historical, for shining light through collective wisdom.

A thousand sincere salutations to fellow students, past, current, and future, for the gifts you bestow along your authentic journeys.

Infinite gratitude to my children and husband, who encourage me to continue navigating wellness and purpose, and to my other families around the world that inspire me to continue living true.

Part 1 - The Ground

Hallowed out and done with the stale,
the winds of change arrive as a gale.
Not past an overdone fork in the road,
But into a gentle vibrant tornado.
Where mind, body, and spirit merge
to feel, be and know.

Atha yoga anushasanam.
Now, the teachings of yoga.
—Yoga Sutra 1.1

1. Foundation

For most of yoga's 5000 years of history, students of yoga in India began practicing at a young age to allow for a natural unfolding of helpful life practices. But over time and across many countries, a shift towards external productivity and streamlining processes grew, even in yoga. While this modern simplification can make yoga easier to approach, it can render absorption of it in everyday life more difficult.

For example, when I became a self-led student of yoga at age 40, I felt a swift boost to my life. But attempting to maintain that positive shift felt like pulling a train uphill. I hoped that formal training in a California yoga studio school would make things easier. And though my training was good, I graduated still unprepared to develop physically beneficial sequences, let alone understand and apply mental and spiritual tools that could soothe the greatest suffering within myself.

So I dove into the deep end to sink or swim by teaching others. Sharing yoga meant I had to research, learn, practice, process, apply and adjust over countless hours. In this way, little by little, the breadth and depth of yoga I dreamed of at last became reality. Best of all, yoga keeps teaching me. Before yoga, I dove headlong into almost everything that perplexed, scared, or otherwise enticed me. And I walked out of those same things when I felt adequately challenged, proficient or knew that I'd defied death enough that I should feel fulfilled. But not with yoga. Yoga has consistently shed light on my life for nearly two decades now.

When it was my turn to introduce others to yoga in teacher training, I dreamed of delivering a good foundation of yoga's totality but found the application of that desire to be of the highest challenge. It's one thing to offer a variety of learning and practice techniques that can feel like drinking from a fire hose, and yet another to make material meaningful, accessible, and possible to apply in one's life.

Over years of working with this challenge, my vision expanded to include not only yoga teachers, but also people practicing at home who may not attend teacher training or yoga classes due to mobility, health, or cultural barriers; teachers seeking quick reference; self-help programs; and health professionals needing accessible yoga resources.

In the hopes that understanding and applying principles in this book will feel like taking in fresh air and not like drowning, most chapters will fuse bite-size elements of learning, practice and self-study relating to something in each of the areas below.

Hatha tools *(pose categories, breathing techniques, energetic aids)*

Mantra *(tools for the mind)*

Yogic roots *(history, philosophy, culture)*

Anatomy basics *(physiology)*

Teaching tools *(methodology, professional development)*

Self-study *(integration)*

This book encourages sharing what you learn with others, not in an attempt to force yoga on others, but rather to integrate what you learn. If you are unable to share what you learn with others for any reason, try recording yourself "teaching" the practice exercises and then listen to your recording as a student of yourself to gain new insight.

When the term yoga teacher is used in this book, it can refer to teaching yourself or someone else. The term yoga instructor is not used as I have not found it possible to instruct self-discovery in a meaningful way.

And when the term student or practitioner is used, it can refer to anyone practicing yoga. While some in the yoga industry use the word client, I have also not found it possible to buy what being a student of yourself through the practice of yoga can offer.

Welcoming Exiled Bodies

There are 8 limbs of yoga, or areas of practice, according to the sage Patanjali's writings in the *Yoga Sutras*. One of these limbs focuses on poses, and the rest are practices of breath regulation, mental wellness, and yoga off-the-mat. The one limb about poses is called asana, which Patanjali said was a steady comfortable posture.

In 2025, an estimated 40 million people in the U.S. and around 300 million people worldwide were practicing yoga. About 16% of people have significant challenges to mobility according to the World Health Organization, so group yoga classes emphasizing poses and sequences for able-bodies are often not accessible for many people. And, depending on where you live, group classes that offer a holistic focus on the system of yoga, rather than one or two limbs, can be difficult for anyone to locate.

As a new studio owner years ago, many people came seeking relief . . .

"My doctor said yoga can help me. Will it?"

Conditions ranged from pregnancy, insomnia, back and knee issues, arthritis, obesity, osteoporosis, amputations, memory loss, fibromyalgia, PTSD, anxiety, depression and more. My answer was,

"It is best to seek out a yoga teacher who specializes in that."

Recommendations for such teachers were then requested, so I pointed to google which didn't expose any nearby options, and people persisted,

"Can I come to class anyway?"

My responses were laced with hope and hesitancy,

"Okay, but listen to your body and do what feels good."

Yoga teachers may not receive training in pose risks and modifications. Meanwhile, doctors may advise patients to do yoga for their condition unaware of differing practices that may be contrary to a patient's condition. So often people that need yoga show up to their first class and receive negative reinforcement of their fears and their suffering.

The result is often "I tried it and yoga's not for me."

For me, it didn't feel right to place responsibility on the person suffering for their wellness in a practice they may know little to nothing about. And even though I entered yoga with my body in exile, I had thought others found mind-body connection easier. But the more I taught, the more I realized how difficult this relationship is for many students . . . including those who can easily do all the poses.

Human mind body paradoxical relationships present some of our greatest challenges in life. Your body includes your mind, yet your thoughts can be in discord with your physical characteristics, actions, or sensations. Your body is your best friend, yet at times you might barely recognize it. Everything that happens to you is recorded by your body, yet your genius body can unlearn and gather new information each day.

So, I sought out seasoned yogis, people with health conditions, and more training. My own chronic pain also offered valuable insight from chiropractors, massage therapists, acupuncturists, surgeons, physical and mental health therapists, personal trainers, pain doctors, functional health doctors, internet gurus, and Alexander Technique experts.

Every person who develops a life-long physical yoga practice will need to one day adjust their practice for continued benefit. Gentle yoga practice uses gradual steps and low-intensity poses in mindfully sequenced movements while eliminating or limiting up and down transitions. However, due to prevalent messaging of what constitutes effort, gentle yoga can be a more difficult practice for those conditioned to do more, even though benefits can be the same, similar, and possibly beyond in some cases, as those requiring more outwardly visible effort.

Early on, I thought it strange that advanced yoga practitioners continuously signed up for classes labeled as "Gentle." Then one day a visiting friend asked if we could attend a gentle yoga class together, and I begrudgingly agreed. The amount of presence and focused mind-body connection that it took to be more still while still completely engaged provoked profuse sweating for me during the class – though many other practitioners seemed to be in comfortable bliss.

5

After class, I experienced effortless stamina and a grounded sense of being that shifted my perspective on everything within and around me. Now I often turn to my gentle yoga physical practice to carry me through physically and mentally tough seasons of life.

Gentle yoga can be a great option on any day, on its own or fused with other mind-body practices. In addition to Gentle practices, this book also introduces the following physical practices that can be fused together or done separately.

Part *1* - Ashtanga Series categories, Iyengar alignment principles
Part *2* - Backbends, balances, Yin, Qigong, Ayurvedic based principles
Part *3* - Inversions, revolved poses, Kundalini, Indigenous Practices

This book can be partnered with *Body as Teacher, Yoga's Physical Practices for All,* which is referred to throughout this book simply as *Body as Teacher.* This partner book explains and illustrates how all bodies can explore poses referenced here in choices of gentle, standing, supported, reclining and advanced variations. Being your own guru means having options that offer the freedom to discover what most serves you on any given day.

The notion that one must be well to practice wellness limits everyone.

Conscious Vitality

If breathing techniques were pharmaceuticals, they would be practiced at least once per day.

Another limb of yoga is Pranayama, the practice of breath regulation to impact the directional flow of energy, called Vayus in Sanskrit, within our bodies. In yoga, prana is considered vital life force, so conscious regulation of prana can directly impact all human functions.

Though asana (poses) is often synonymous with yoga in modern times, when asana is combined with pranayama, poses take on new potency as the practitioner goes beyond dense matter into the energetics of multiple bodily systems. This combination can strengthen positive mind-body feedback loops and offer a new level of experienced wellness.

The practice of poses alone would not have sustained my interest in yoga. It was yoga's other wellness practices that really sustained my interest and dedication to practice. Yogic breathing techniques, for example, are something I never tire of because there are breaths to increase energy and clarity, reduce anxiety and insomnia, release emotions, strengthen the immune system, raise or lower body temperature, etc.

Yogic breathing techniques can be used on their own or combined with poses and other energetic aids, such as drishtis (eye gazes), bandhas (energetic locks), mudras (hand gestures), and meditation practices. Breathing techniques and energetic aids are introduced in later chapters of this book and are further illustrated in this book's companion.

Part *1* – Equal count, segmented and thermoregulating breaths
Part *2* – Open mouth exhales and vibrating breaths
Part *3* – Channel breathing and breaths for inner radiance

New Signals of Opportunity

Yogic mantras are not one of the 8 limbs of yoga, yet they are included in ancient *Vedas* as early as 1500 B.C.E., as an instrument to train the mind so present moment awareness and a sense of connection can arise.

Though my practice of poses, breathing and other yogic energetic techniques practices helped a great deal when I actively engaged in them, my brain left to its own devices was like a channel scanner automatically looking for the station called, "all your past shit."

From the beginning of my yoga journey, I had been drawn to mantra but feared chanting references to unknown religions. So in 2020, when the pandemic confined physical spaces and opened on-line options, I found a teacher who specialized in mantras, history, philosophy, and culture.

I quickly fell in love of this new view and understanding of mantra, which a profound addition to my on-the-mat and off-the-mat yogic practices. With mantra added to my yogic resources, my brain's channel scanner found a new station - one that at least momentarily didn't try to forgive, teach, change, or transform. And I could turn on this new feeling of existence beyond time and space anywhere at any time.

Yogic mantras can be used on their own or combined with poses and other energetic practices. This book intertwines many mantras through story-telling of Vedic gods that personify cosmic forces and qualities of humanity. Many more mantras are included in this book's companion.

Each chapter ending includes opportunities to try mantra for yourself, as well as self-study questions pertaining to the material covered within the chapter. Both of these opportunities can offer surprising new doors to wisdom within yourself.

Our minds deserve moments to travel beyond time and space.

What Yoga Is and Is Not

Years ago, in a dharma workshop led by a yoga teacher who was a devout Christian, a student asked the teacher to explain her belief system. The teacher smiled, "My beloved is in all forms." Another question quickly followed, "But how can you practice more than one religion?." The teacher shrugged, "I no longer need to know how, I just do."

Her beloved was beyond dogma. I hadn't known such a place existed.

But sincere practitioners of yoga often discover that practice can ignite knowing beyond rationalization. Religious yogis can become closer to their beloved, and yogis who don't know one other may come to a shared wisdom - yet will practice that wisdom in their own way.

Beginner yogis may wrestle with how religion and yoga are related. Some are concerned because they don't want religion, others because they have a religion and aren't seeking another, and others simply don't want to be involved in that which they don't understand. To grasp all intricacies of religion and spirituality in yoga involves 5,000 years of culture, history, theology, and mastery of Sanskrit. My synopsis is:

✓ Yoga was established long before any formalized religion.

✓ Spirituality is part of yoga because it includes your spirit.

✓ A leader did not found Hinduism; it a geographical term before British colonists used it to categorize people for a census.

✓ Ancient yoga acknowledges a divine unifying power. Vedic gods tell stories to help make sense of the world.

✓ Early Vedas express Samkhya philosophy, wherein Purusa (soul, highest self) is at play with Prakrti (nature, matter).

✓ Vedanta adds to Samkhya without separation of Purusa/Prakrti.

✓ Later texts introduce Dvaita Vedanta which embraces duality and are distinctive from ancient yoga in terms of religion and deities.

✓ Equal meaning cannot be expressed in translation from some Sanskrit words, so often the explanation for what yoga is to say what it is not. Ancient yoga is not a religion.

Yogic culture comes from thousands of years of texts and practices before it became the system that contributes to the wellbeing of millions of people around the world. Most western yoga practices currently stem from the 8 Limbs of yoga, also called Raja Yoga, the Royal Path . . . a system that includes Yamas (universal principles), Niyamas (self-disciplines), Asana (poses), Pranayama (regulation of breath), Pratyahara (mastering the external), Dharana (single pointed focus), Dhyana (meditation), and Samadhi (bliss).

Cultural appropriation is harm committed when people take something from another culture without giving credit to its origin, its history and meaning. Cultural harm comes in many forms, and throughout the course of humanity, it has led to more suffering.

For example, people often show up at their first yoga class because they heard that yoga has been proven effective in the reduction of physical and mental tension. These students may instead receive challenging poses, minimal breathing techniques, demonstration by a teacher not looking at students, and no yogic philosophy beyond closing with "Namaste."

Taking parts of yoga to make it easier to teach or more accessible to mixed populations can harm the power of holistic yoga that was tended to by people in India for thousands of years. So cultural harm occurs often in yoga classes, often due to lack of awareness and not intent to harm.

As far as saying Namaste in class, Namaha is Sanskrit for "to bow" and Namaskar is Sanskrit for offering a salutation. When I asked people in India about the western debate regarding saying Namaste after yoga class, all said it was a non-issue assuming teachers are offering a salutation.

Whether something incurs harm or not becomes clearer after study of historically factual resources and interaction with those with culturally relevant lived experiences. Sometimes the best lessons are honest mistakes that teach us what not to do so that our future efforts are genuinely more empowering to ourselves and others.

Sometimes the best explanation is "Not this, not that."

10

Empowering Resilience

Our actions are always teaching others, either as an example or a warning.

Even though some students would like to think that yoga teachers represent some ideal, like a mirror of samadhi (another limb of yoga referring to transcendence or bliss), that is not likely. Everyone alive is still human, and not all yoga teachers have received training in yoga.

The yoga teacher-student relationship can be tricky to navigate. In fact, new students may hope that a yoga teacher can fix their health condition, that their teacher can fix their relationship problems, that their teacher can help with thoughts of suicide or violence, and that their teacher can change their life.

Yoga teachers offer space for self-discovery in mind, body and spirit that often feel unique, and students' feelings of being seen, accepted, cared about, and connected with are usually true. However, in a healthy student-teacher relationship, these feelings are attributed to what the student has done for themselves through practice, and the student knows they can continue those good experiences, even without their teacher.

On the other hand, if a yoga teacher takes on an elevated status and abuses students, their actions are not aligned with yoga. In fact, yoga teachers such as Sri K. Pattabhi Jois (Ashtanga), Bikram Choudhury (Bikram Yoga), and Yogi Bhajan (Kundalini) did abuse their students.

Even though some of these atrocities occurred many years ago, it can remain a conundrum for teachers or students as to whether or not to teach or practice anything offered by these abusers. Some yoga teachers, including myself, see these teachers as a reminder of what not to do while sharing practices associated with their lineages in alignment with both yoga and voluntary yoga industry standards and ethics.

Yoga studios have offered yoga classes in the United States since the 1940s, but the industry of yoga is not regulated in this country, so training is not a requirement to teach yoga. For those who choose to go through training, trainings can differ significantly in education and experience.

In 1997, Yoga Alliance formed as a non-profit to create voluntary standards for yoga teachers and yoga schools to reduce harm in the yoga industry. Core competencies for 200-hour yoga training programs for Yoga Alliance registered schools have remained relatively consistent . . .

✓ 30 hours, Yoga Humanities (history, philosophy, ethics)
✓ 50 hours, Professional Essentials (methodology, practice teaching)
✓ 30 hours, Anatomy/Physiology (anatomy, physiology, biomechanics)
✓ 75 hours, Techniques/Practice (asana, pranayama, meditation)
✓ 15 hours, Electives

Many yoga studios and resiliency programs will not hire a teacher unless they have graduated from a Yoga Alliance registered school, as that certification provides some assurance that students have adequate preparation and awareness of ethics – including being responsible for a class space free from false representation, unlawful acts, discrimination, harassment, restricting those in need of reasonable accommodations, violations of non-consent, and more.

There are other voluntary yoga industry organizations with standards, but this book and its companion book, along with both book's practice exercises, together meet the Yoga Alliance competencies listed above.

AUM and OM

Humans can develop ways to navigate the world based upon life experiences. Some tools we may have learned in the past helped us endure challenges, but over time those same tools can pose new challenges.

My survive equals thrive method of navigating life was very helpful during certain times of my life, but that method became engrained somewhere in my subconscious to the point that distress became a constant state. For decades, I assumed that the constant tension in my pelvis, back and leg was a result of physical stress and so systematically worked through every conceivable fix. But none of the things that should have fixed me provided long-term relief. So, I finally asked myself what else might be left to uncover and enrolled in mental health therapy.

Living with trauma is a reality for many people, whether harm occurred or whether the threat of it was so great that the mind and body reacted as if it did indeed occur. Adverse previous experiences can be stored in our bodies to be triggered by present events as well as thoughts of the future.

Later this book delves into traumas that humans can experience during childhood or later in life, and how those can show up in our bodies, thoughts and actions or inactions. Awareness of triggered responses is important in yoga, so that practice itself is not also an adverse experience.

The Sanskrit syllable OM, or AUM, is found in the ancient texts of the Vedas and in virtually every text on the philosophy and science of yoga since. Yogic texts describe the syllable somewhat differently, but all have a similar essence . . . that OM is the primal sound of the universe.

The word trauma contains "AUM," the word for OM in the *Mandukya* Upanishad. All humans experience suffering, and OM can feel like salve for mind, body, and spirit. Many yoga classes begin and/or end with chanting of OM for self-alignment and connection.

When the sages turned within, they heard OM, the sound that pervades the heart.
(Mandukya Upanishad)

Self-Study

1. What paths of yours brought you to this path now?
2. What is yoga without its philosophy?
3. What potential harm might exist without some standards in yoga?
4. Chant, say or sing the OM mantra or another affirmation for yourself and the heart of all beings. Try this for at least 3 minutes.

OM (or AUM)
Meaning: Primal sound of the universe.

2. Salutations

Yoga History Primer

"To understand a science, it is necessary to know its history" — *August Comte.*

Yoga is the first written mental health science, written in the oldest written language of Sanskrit. Throughout history, the science and philosophy of yoga is expanded upon and/or streamlined by different authors as a reflection of differing periods. Historical perspectives vary based on the lens of those studying yoga, such as scholars, historians, anthropologists, theologians, etc.

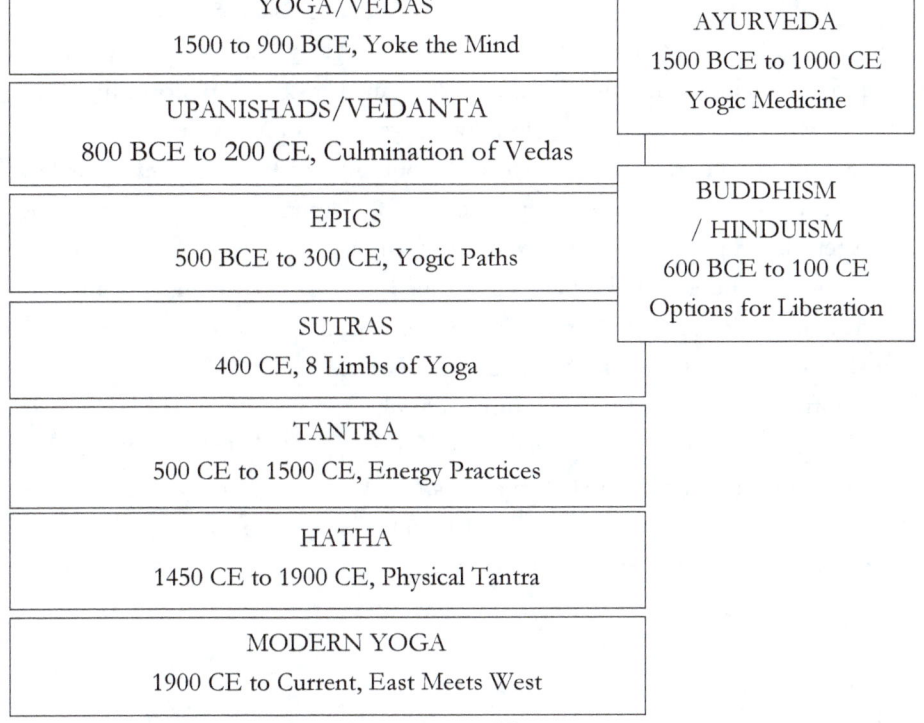

YOGA/VEDAS
1500 to 900 BCE, Yoke the Mind

AYURVEDA
1500 BCE to 1000 CE
Yogic Medicine

UPANISHADS/VEDANTA
800 BCE to 200 CE, Culmination of Vedas

BUDDHISM
/ HINDUISM
600 BCE to 100 CE
Options for Liberation

EPICS
500 BCE to 300 CE, Yogic Paths

SUTRAS
400 CE, 8 Limbs of Yoga

TANTRA
500 CE to 1500 CE, Energy Practices

HATHA
1450 CE to 1900 CE, Physical Tantra

MODERN YOGA
1900 CE to Current, East Meets West

3000 BCE-900 BCE - Ancient Vedas

Early on this period, the Indus-Sarasvati civilization in India (and what is now Pakistan) was the largest structured society in the ancient world and included citadels, roads, multi-story buildings, indoor bathrooms, sewers, baked bricks for construction, and thriving international trade.

A people known as the Harappans called this area home, as did later immigrant Nomadic Aryan tribes from Central Asia. Excavations at Mohenjo-Daro and Harappa uncovered soapstone engravings that resembled what we now know as a yoga pose. However, no engraving depicted a battle, a captive, or a victor. Weapons found were for self-protection and hunting. Around 2000 BCE, the region's water source – the Saraswati river – began drying up and people eventually left the area.

The oldest Vedic texts, the *Rig, Sama, Yajur,* and *Atharva* Vedas, were composed by Indo-Aryan speaking sages between 1500 BCE and 900 BCE. The Rig Veda is the first text to mention yoga or "Yuj." Collectively, the texts included rituals, commentaries, mantras, and philosophical narratives that later are blended into Samkhya philosophy.

Samkhya views consciousness (soul/purusa/highest self) as independent, free, and impossible to describe; and nature (matter/prakriti/unconscious) as cyclical, subject to states of change called gunas and affected by elements called tattvas. Consciousness and nature interact through human experience, which leads to suffering; however, one can transcend suffering in the world.

During this period, Indian culture grew around 33+ Vedic gods that personified cosmic forces, such as wind and fire, to tell stories about cosmic order and nature, alongside a unilateral Brahman, a gender-neutral transcendent unchanging reality.

Transcendence of suffering while alive is possible.

1500 BCE–1000 CE - Ayurveda

Sources of mind/body dis-ease can be traced to stressors on one's most natural state.

Ayurveda is yoga's sister science of medicine mentioned in the Rig and Atharva Vedas, making Ayurveda one of the first written medical sciences.

According to Ayurveda, dis-ease stems from subtle blockages in the body between one's natural constitution (most authentic state since birth) and current imbalances (stressors to natural state). Three dosha types are used to describe what shapes one's natural constitution, and each type shows up in differently in thoughts, emotions, and physical states of being.

Primary texts of this science are the *Sushruta Samhita* on surgery and *Charaka Samhita* on medicine. These texts outline the physician's role in prevention of disease, including pathology, diagnosis, anatomy, prognosis, pharmaceutics, and toxicology. They describe 1,120 illnesses, 700 medicinal plants, 64 medicinal minerals, 57 medicinal animal sources, and therapeutics that include exercise and hygiene. Protocols developed by Ayurveda over a thousand years ago, such as nasal surgery and skin grafts, are foundational practices of procedures currently in use.

Though Ayurveda's constitutions and expressions of imbalances are general categories, yoga's sister science emphasizes individualized wellness as each person has their own mixology of stressors to their natural state.

800 BCE–200 CE - Vedanta

In what is now northeast India on the Gangetic plain, spiritual seekers dwelling in forests gathered to study the Vedas and compile additional texts. With the Himalayan mountains as backdrop, they authored early Upanishads to define a perspective shift as foundational to what is now called Advaita philosophy. This philosophy is also referred to Vedanta, meaning culmination of the Vedas.

The Upanishads told stories from ancient sages to explain the hamster wheel of life and death called samsara, as well as the importance of truthfulness, self-control, tranquility, humaneness, breath control, mantra, sense withdrawal, concentration, and meditation.

The philosophy of Advaita builds upon Samkhya but distinguishes any sense of separation as an illusion because the soul's quest for liberation from suffering through one's actions are connected in a web of the divine (i.e., Brahman or infinite grace) . . . all that exists represents the divine.

One condensed story from the *Chandogya Upanishad* explains universal connection. "As by knowing one lump of clay, dear one, we come to know all things made out of clay. Like the rivers flowing east and west merge in the sea and become one with it, forgetting they were ever separate, so do all creatures lose their separateness when they merge into pure being.

You are that (Tat tvam asi)."

Another condensed story explains the mind-breath relationship.

"Take a bird that is tied with a string. It will fly off in every direction and, when it can't find a resting place anywhere else, it will alight back upon the very thing to which it is tied. Similarly, my son, the mind flies off, and when it cannot find a resting place, it alights back upon the breath itself; for the mind, my son is tied to the breath."

Separateness is an illusion. Truth, kindness, and self-regulation can remove the veil to infinite connection.

18

600 BCE–100 CE - Buddhism and Hinduism

One of the forest dwellers in 600 BCE was Siddhartha Gautama, who renounced wealth to find enlightenment via near starvation and other austere practices before at last sitting down under a pipal tree to meditate until enlightenment came. Eventually it did. Henceforth, he was called the Buddha (meaning awakened one).

Buddhism and yoga have a similar focus on the mind (manas), meditation, and the use of stories to explain the human quest for transcendence. Buddhism also shares three of yoga's kleshas (causes of suffering) of ignorance, attachment, and aversion, and has similar practices of universal morals and personal disciplines to yoga's Yamas and Niyamas.

Buddhism and yoga also have important differences in that ancient yoga teaches that transcendence can be found in a unifying principle beyond the mind, and Buddhism teaches that realization arises through emptiness. When both teachings are peeled back though, even this distinguishing difference between the two has commonality in the practitioner's lived experience of liberation from suffering.

Yoga and Buddhism are culturally connected to Hinduism due to geographical proximity. The term Hinduism came about to describe people with similar characteristics and was codified by British rule as a census category. But describing someone as Hindu does not delineate one religion as there are many religions under Hinduism.

Modern Hinduism and ancient yoga differ in that modern Hinduism can be associated with religious practices and ancient yoga is based upon spiritual practices. Ancient yoga holds that all can journey to their transcendence in the way that resonates most with them.

In yoga, meditation offers connection.
In Buddhism, meditation offers emptiness.

500 BCE–300 CE - The Epics

In the pre-current era in rural India, kings who inherited lands collected heavy taxes to became rich while citizens struggled. Many stories were written of elaborate dramas of heroes rising above difficult influences. These stories, referred to as Epics, include the *Ramayana, Mahabharata,* and a poem within the *Mahabharata* - the *Bhagavad Gita,* also called the *Gita.*

The *Ramayana*, written around 500-300 BCE, mentions ascetic positions that some historians link as precursors to modern yoga poses such as Hanumanasana (splits), Surya Namaskara (Sun Salutations) and Sirsasana (headstand). But the big lesson of the *Ramayana* is that of Rama, a prince who is vanquished to the forest for 14 years and learns what it means to fulfill one's dharma or sacred duty.

The *Mahabharata's* stories are told in 18 books from 300 BCE to 400 CE. The *Gita* is one of those stories depicting a battle between families where the hero learns evenness of mind through paths of yoga: Jnana (Knowledge); Karma (Service); Bhakti (Devotion); and Raja (Meditation).

The thousand years that follow the writing of the *Gita* gave rise to many devotional texts in India, collectively known as the Puranas, which spark cultural shifts towards divine personification. Over time, a new philosophy known as Dvaita Vedanta emerges to distinguish separation between the divine and the soul - everything not the divine is the other.

Later translations of the *Gita,* around the medieval period, express this shift and outline a blending of religion with yoga. Copies of the *Gita* that arrive by boat in the U.S. in the 1800s often leaned towards divine personification of Krishna. And even now, *Gita* translations can be debated as early yogic philosophies are non-religious in nature and later philosophies increasingly are.

For millennia, the *Epics* have played out and continue on in some religions, many forms of art, on stage and screen. How each story is told depends upon the translation and version of it used.

"On this path, effort never goes to waste"
– Krishna.

Around 400 CE - The Yoga Sutras

Threads sew the practice of yoga together like a quilt for life.

The Golden Age of India (300-500 CE) boasted scientific discoveries, technology, engineering, literature, logic, and mathematics extending through societal fringes, inspiring the sage Patanjali to convert existing yogic philosophy and texts into a simplified system.

Patanjali outlined the system of Raja Yoga (yoga of meditation), calling it Ashtanga. He titled this work *The Yoga Sutras,* also called the *Sutras,* and insisted that it was a collective work of the sages. Sutra means thread in Sanskrit, and the book's 196 concise statements weave together how to live a more meaningful life through an 8-limbed path of yoga, which need not be linear as they are life practices.

Yamas (non-harming, truth, non-stealing, moderation, non-hoarding)

Niyamas (purity, contentment, discipline, surrender, self-study)

Asana (poses - steady, comfortable posture for meditation)

Pranayama (breath regulation)

Pratyahara (mastery of the external)

Dharana (focus)

Dhyana (meditation)

Samadhi (transcendence)

Though the term Isvara references God or consciousness, the *Sutras* retain the infinite oneness from ancient Vedas and Vedanta and leaves out incarnations found in the *Epics*. Now most yoga taught in the U.S. is rooted, often unknowingly, in this 8-limbed foundation.

500 CE-1500 CE - Tantra

The caste system impacted Indian life and politics for much of yoga's history. Initially, this hierarchal system was introduced as "Varna" to describe societal roles that were: Brahmins (priests, scholars), Kshatriyas (rulers, warriors), Vaishyas (merchants, farmers), and Shudras (laborers, service workers). Over time, the caste system melded into social groups that dictated one's life. For example, those born outside of the recognized hierarchy were cast out of civilized society as "untouchables."

Accepted gender roles in India have also varied, beginning with women having significant roles in philosophy and equal partnerships with men. Later, with the rise of religious law, child marriage and female educational limitations became mainstream, and women were viewed as extensions of men rather than equals . . . all while being considered spiritually sacred.

After India's Golden Age, innovators across all castes and genders from India and Tibet came together to form a new embodied framework for yoga using Tantra. Tantra means to weave something together for expansion, so this involved using philosophies and practices from earlier Vedic texts, such as the *Taittirīya* Upanishad's koshas (physical, energetic, mental, wisdom and bliss layers of being), the *Yoga Sutras*, and Indigenous practices. Tantra evolved to include subtle energy practices including chakras, kundalini, poses, mantras, mudras and more to move energy throughout one's koshas to support the goal of yoga.

Tantra also represents a feminine aspect of the divine as Shakti, that which makes change possible through form and ability to manifest. Shakti's counterpart is Shiva, the formless and unmanifest masculine. In Tantra, masculine and feminine together represent totality in life. But Tantra does not dictate methodologies as it sees transcendence available everywhere in everything we do. From Tantra emerged Laya (Kundalini) and Hatha Yoga, physical practices to purposely direct energy.

Energy to thrive is meant for everyone.

22

1450 CE to 1900 CE - Hatha

The *Hatha Yoga Pradipika*, written by Swami Svatmarama in 1450 CE expanded Tantra to include intense personal disciplines to create a new school of yoga called Hatha, meaning force or the union of opposites in Sanskrit. Hatha became known as any physical practice including the following tools to prepare the body for Raja yoga (yoga of meditation).

Disciplines, Poses, Breath Regulation, Purifications
Energetic locks, Mudras, and Subtle Energy Management

When the Mughals invaded India in the 1500s, some Indian men trained in martial arts, weaponry, yogic poses, breathing techniques and other energetic practices to maintain their culture, physical and mental health, and to defend themselves. In this way, Hatha yoga became part of survival and inspired more Hatha yoga texts that reflect political eras, including the *Shiva Samhita* which combined Hatha and Tantra yoga through 84 poses, prana, tantric practices, mudras, and meditation; and the *Gheranda Samhita* which detailed purifications, 32 poses, mudras, focus, breath regulation, meditation, and transcendence.

Around 1750, the British East India company ruled large areas of India with private armies until the rebellion of 1857 resulted in British rule over all of India, and the marginalization of Hatha yoga as "black magic".

Hatha grew nonetheless and is the primary type of yoga now practiced. Many teachers label it as slower yoga or yoga without the philosophies; however, Hatha texts include tools mentioned in previous Vedic texts. And Hatha could be slower paced or faster as forms of physical asana fall under it. Vinyasa, Power, Anusara, Gentle, Bikram, Ashtanga, etc., are all styles of Hatha that came out of Tantric philosophy.

Hatha grew out of Tantra yoga (embodiment).
That evolved alongside Raja yoga (meditation).
Tantra and Raja are rooted in ancient wisdom (vedas).

1900 CE to Current - Modern Yoga

Awareness of yoga is easy. Finding the right fit can be a challenge.

Yoga in the U.S. began in New England in the late 1800s with Ralph Waldo Emerson and Henry David Thoreau reading the Epics. It expanded inland in 1893 as Swami Vivekananda spoke of self-realization at the Parliament of Religions in Chicago and Yogananda shared Kriya yoga in Boston in 1920.

The expansion of yoga from East to West inspired doctors, scientists, and psychologists to study yoga's science and philosophy. So, when Asian immigration to the U.S. was restricted in the 1920s -1940s, westerners traveled to India to continue learning about and publishing studies on yogic techniques. Psychiatrist Carl G. Jung even lectured with European scientists and doctors regarding the psychology of Kundalini yoga.

Tirumalai Krishnamacharya opened a Hatha school in Mysore during this expansion of yoga, and taught students who initiated styles of yoga still practiced today (Indra Devi, T.K.V. Desikachar, Sri K. Patthabi Jois and B.K.S. Iyengar). Devi opened the first yoga studio in Hollywood in 1947, and soon Richard Hittleman broadcasted poses on U.S. television.

After 50 years of yoga in the U.S., Yoga Alliance was founded in 1997 as a non-profit registry for yoga schools and yoga teachers meeting certain standards. As of 2022, there were almost 50,000 yoga studios and 100,000 yoga teachers registered with Yoga Alliance, another 100,000 unregistered teachers, and nearly 40 million Americans practicing various yoga styles. Many classes include breathing techniques, mudras, and eye gazes, and some include yogic philosophy, mantra, and meditation.

Though yoga classes have been fairly mainstream for 75 years, beginners often wonder where to start since class names may reflect various styles of asana and/or include levels of physical difficulty. Regardless, the practice of yoga continues to expand since most people are aware that it can somehow improve their lives.

Flying Straight into the Sun

Primary Series In the 1920s in Mysore, India, student Patthabi Jois needed a demanding physical practice to channel his energy, so Krishnamacharya designed a sequence for him. Jois then added poses to the sequence and named it Ashtanga, a sequence that continues around the world.

Traditional Ashtanga practice is a set sequence that can be led either by a teacher (who does not practice) or in the Mysore method (an open practice where students do the sequence from memory without the teacher calling poses, breath, or cues). From the Ashtanga sequence, vinyasa or flow, and power yoga were born. Unfortunately, Jois' also harmed students with sexual and physical violence. Because brave students shared painful experiences publicly, most yoga teachers and students now look out for these unacceptable atrocities in actions and words, and the benefits of Ashtanga Primary Series continue being shared.

The Ashtanga series can be practiced as a Primary Series (which includes Sun Salutation A, Sun Salutation B, Standing Series, Seated and Finishing Series). The Ashtanga series also includes Ujjayi (breath); Drishti (eye focus); Vinyasa (placing things in a special way and breath to movement); and Bandhas (energetic locks).

Ujjayi Ujjayi breath is breathing evenly, deeply, and strongly in and out through your nose while slightly constricting the back of your throat to create breaths that sound like the ocean. My teacher, AMK, explained if you lose your Ujjayi breath (miss an inhale or exhale) during Ashtanga, you are done practicing.

Prior to that Ashtanga class, I'd only figured out how to NOT breathe well and how NOT to place my body parts in special ways. So, I told AMK that I would sit out the practice then as combining breath and poses was impossible for me. Undeterred, she asked a fellow student to practice next to me. Within minutes of Celeste breathing a few feet from me, I was able to move with near perfection in and out of each pose.

25

Many yogis that are challenged with Ujjayi breathing quickly become loud nose breathers after experiencing the benefits of Ujjayi themselves. These benefits include increased cardiovascular health, vagus nerve stimulation, and an unlocking of one of the most symbiotic relationships – the one between the nervous system and musculoskeletal system.

Salutations & Hanuman

Prior to Jois' sequence, the Raja of Aundh published sunrise practice honoring Surya (solar principle of energy and light) as Surya Namaskar, which in the Ashtanga Primary Series is called Sun Salutation A (often shortened to Sun A). This first part of the Ashtanga Primary Series includes Ujjayi breath to movement through 7 poses in 5 repetitions. This book's companion, *Body as Teacher*, provides cues, images, and variations of Sun Salutation A poses for all bodies.

Even before the Raja's sunrise sequence, Hanuman (a mythical and storied monkey being) was rumored to have created Sun Salutations as a gift to his teacher, Surya. The *Ramayana* and *Mahabharata* contain stories of Hanuman's heart full of service, and his strength and ability to make good choices by first understanding the problem.

*Breath has the power
to carry the body
while it learns to fly.*

Musculoskeletal Health and Yoga

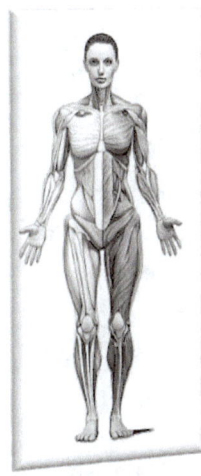

Yoga's 3500-year written history reveals the foundation of yoga, as well as how informed perspectives over the years have built upon physical practice theories.

Pose history begins as broadly esoteric to something necessary for sitting in meditation to a focused field of scientific and medical studies. Now, in recent years, some yoga teachers and practitioners are becoming more aware of how the practice of poses can help or harm physical functioning needed for life . . . but as a whole, functional practice of yoga has a long way to go.

Understanding musculoskeletal system basics (bones, muscles, tendons, ligaments, other connective tissues that keep us upright and able to function) in the practice of poses is crucial in maximizing the physical benefits of practice, while minimizing injury risks.

Bone health plays a key role in musculoskeletal wellness. Bone density refers the amount of mineral content in your bones. The denser one's bones are the less likely bones are to fracture under load or in response to falls or other injuries. Bone strength is typically established around 20 years old and stabilizes for another decade before gradually decreasing. Genetically, males average 35% more bone mass than females. Bone density also varies by race, nutrition, activity, frame size, and body weight.

We have 206 bones in our bodies for structure and mobility, and most are in our hands and feet. Osteopenia (less than normal bone density) and osteoporosis (much lower bone density with higher fracture risk) occur in high rates in women over 50, many of whom don't realize it.

Yoga poses done safely, along with strength training, balanced hormones, and nutrition support bone health at any age.

Bones come together at joints that include cartilage, ligaments, and tendons. Cartilage cushions shock, reduces friction and maintains healthy joint spaces. Ligaments connect bones and keep joints together by limiting movement to safe ranges, and tendons connect muscle to bone and help bones move without skeletal shock.

Joint conditions like arthritis and osteoarthritis impact many older adults, but hypermobility, repetitive and/or unstable movements, accidents, obesity, and lack of mobility can impact joints in people of all ages. Cartilage deteriorates with age, injuries, diabetes, obesity, or repeated stress on joints. Ligaments lose integrity with age, repetitive movements, overstretching, hypermobility, and unstable movement patterns. Tendon elasticity weakens with age, injury, sedentary lifestyle, and from trying to hold things together when ligaments are weak.

Joint, cartilage, ligament and tendon health benefit from stable movement, muscle strength, good posture, nutrition, balanced hormones, limiting repetitive stressors, and targeted warm up and cool downs.

Fascia is a connective tissue that encases and binds body parts in layers of tissue just under the skin. It resembles the white stringy covering of an orange after the peel is off and holds everything together, while also stretching during movement. Fascia injuries, such as plantar fasciitis, stress fascia's binding capacity. Like a tear in panty hose, fascia stress creates issues in other areas that must work differently to perform, resulting in localized pain or pain in other body parts. Fascia benefits from nutrition, stretching, yoga, acupuncture, massage, and heat therapy.

Yoga poses generally support joint health.
However, force and lack of control can shear tissues,
hyperextension can over stretch ligaments, and
joint misalignment can load tendons rather than muscles.

No Bypass on the Anatomy Freeway

Joints have varying motions and healthy ranges of motions, so sequencing that somewhat balances joint actions helps to decrease injury risk, increase stability, and balance bone, ligament, tendon, and fascia health. This book encourages intentional sequencing for joint wellness and to counter daily repetitive joint actions (like prolonged sitting).

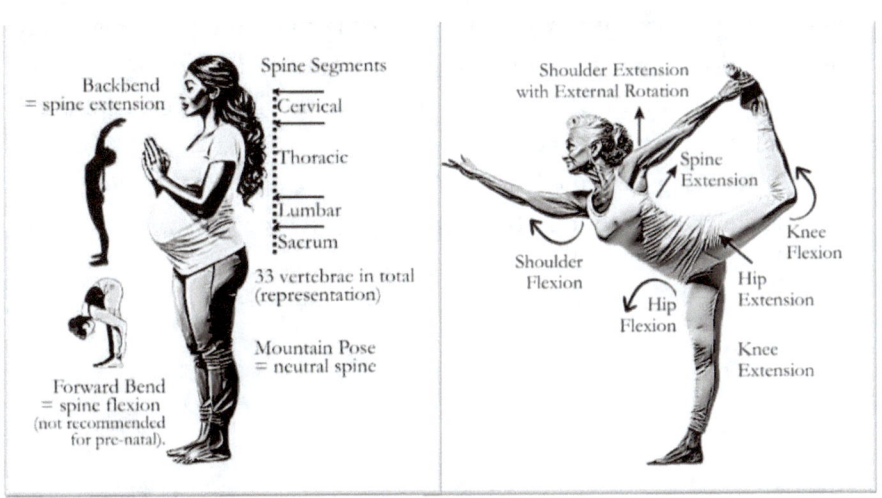

Joint Action Types

Rotation.	Around (internal, external).
Flexion.	Decreasing angle.
Extension.	Increasing angle.
Abduction.	Away from midline.
Adduction.	Towards midline.

Major Joints (*not all*)

Spine.	Flexion, extension, and rotation (except for lumbar).
Shoulders.	Flexion, extension, abduction, adduction, and rotation.
Hips.	Flexion, extension, abduction, adduction, and rotation.
Knees.	Flexion, extension, and some rotation in flexion.

Yoga can open the door for people to beneficial connections with their bodies they didn't know existed, and within those connections can lie untapped inner wisdom waiting to drive your most meaningful life. Some teachers and practitioners embrace that wisdom in intuitive sequencing of poses, without awareness of whether or not their sequences cover physical basics needed for functional wellness.

But Purusa (soul) always comes up against limits of Prakriti (matter) while you are alive, and there is no bypassing the finite times that body parts can do certain things or experience unbalanced actions without needing repairs that may not allow the same previous level of physical freedom. So practicing poses using sequencing informed by musculoskeletal basics can be most liberating for the longest time.

The greatest vehicle ever made, a body to serve your spirit.

Self-Study

1. Summarize each era in yoga in a simple sentence that could explain that period to someone unfamiliar with yoga's history.
2. Create an image of a person sitting in a chair working on a computer. Point to joints used in your image and label them.
3. If a person sits for an average of 6 hours per day in a similar position as above, what joint actions might counter those seated joint actions?
4. Chant, say or sing a Hanuman mantra or another affirmation of service of the heart, strength, and right understanding within.
Try for 3 minutes.

Hanuman bolo, Hanuman bolo; Jai Sita Ram, Jai Jaya Hanuman
Translation: *Hanuman, sing! Victorious Sita/Ram/Hanuman.*
Meaning: *Victory to the strong heart of service and understanding within ourselves.*

3. Eight Limbs

Yamas

Universal Ethics

Non-violence, truthfulness,
non-stealing, moderation,
non-hoarding

Niyamas

Inner disciplines

Cleanliness, contentment,
self-discipline, self-study,
celebration of spirit

Samadhi

Transcendence

Liberation from mind
fluctuations / bliss

Dhyana

Meditation

Keen awareness
without focus.
Being rather than doing

Asana

Physical Postures

Body readiness to sit
in meditation

Dharana

Deep Concentration

Single-pointed focus

Pranayama

Regulation of Life Force

Control of breath for
self-regulation

Pratyahara

Mastering the External

Consciously drawing awareness
from the external to the internal

Timeless Threads

After yoga's origin in the *Rig* Veda, the philosophy and practices of yoga went through periods of streamlining (Upanishads) and expansion (Epics). And nearly 2,000 years after the first mention of Yuj, yoga became even further streamlined when Sage Patanjali complied *The Yoga Sutras* on palm leaves to explain the 8-limbed path of Raja Yoga, the yoga of meditation, in a practical manner usable by anyone. Though the *Sutras* were written around 400 CE, they were not widely available until the 19th century. A basic summary of the *Sutras* is:

Purusa (*soul*, inner witness, highest self) views the world of

Prakriti (external, *everything else*) through Citta (layers of the *mind*).

Citta has grooves that can make things unclear, such as:

Samskaras (impressions/*conditioning*), and

Samsara (*cycle of existence*/wheel of life)

Vrittis (*surfaced thoughts*) from grooves promote actions/inactions.

Practice of the 8 Limbs can clear the citta for a more meaningful life.

Ashta is Sanskrit for 8, anga is limb, and sutra is thread. The 8 limbs of the *Yoga Sutras* in 196 threads weave together a path for practices towards your best life. The Sutras are comprised of 4 chapters (padas) that outline yogic practice concisely while explaining the 8 limbs of practice.

Sutras Pada 1 – Yoga Defined

Practice includes work and surrender, equally.

Pada (chapter) 1 of the *Yoga Sutras* defines yoga, the obstacles, purpose, and the importance of practice.

Sutra 1.02. Yoga is the cessation of the fluctuations of the mind (thoughts not of your true essential nature). The *Rig* Veda's philosophy of yoking something together is defined here - the mind back is yoked back to clarity that extends to all life experiences.

Sutras 1.05 – 1.11. There are five kinds of mental modifications, Vrittis, which are either painful or painless. The *Rig* Veda and Upanishads discussed these, but Patanjali simplifies the Vrittis we face as humans as:

Pramana, *knowledge* that reflects reality

Viparyaya, *misconception* or wrong judgement

Vikalpa, *delusional thoughts* conceived with other than facts

Nidra, mind state in *sleep*

Smriti, *memory* (mind storage of past experiences)

Sutras 1.12 – 1.13. Vrittis are mastered (controlled) through abhyasa (surrender) and vairagya (effort). Abhyasa and vairagya are like bird's wings in that both are required for flight. Ancient Vedic texts cited the importance of willful and sustained practice as well as turning inward as necessary for evolution. Patanjali adds that practice includes work and surrender, equally.

Sutras 1.14. Consistent practice over a long period strengthens samskaras (mental impressions) by improving positive thought processes and responses to stress and can remodel samsara (hamster wheel). Patanjali wrangles the preceding texts into a summation and offers awareness of choice here. If you wonder why results aren't coming then consider your practice time.

Sutras 1.15-1.16. Freeing the colors (desires) of the mind allows non-attachment, which promotes infinite abundance. Non-attachment doesn't mean not caring or acting, it means not acting or feeling out of obligation or longing. When there is true non-attachment, perspective shifts to knowing beyond matter/events to greater understanding. When Patanjali scribed this sutra on a palm leaf, the colors of the mind people experienced were vast discoveries in science, engineering, technology, logic, and mathematics after the Golden Age. While these developments were good, people may have been overwhelmed with the totality.

Sutras 1.17-1.18. The science of yoga results in predictable outcomes. Moments of Samadhi, or transcending to pure connection and joy, may occur often in yoga practice; however, enjoying Samadhi in life comes after consistent practice of all limbs for an indeterminate time. The ancient Vedas referred to it as Samana (balance and harmony), and early Upanishads refer to it as natural occurring bliss after mental modifications are stilled.

Sutras 1.19-1.22. Some people will not experience Samadhi before their bodies die, so the cycle begins again until liberation from suffering is experienced. The likelihood of experiencing lasting Samadhi while alive depends upon whether practice is mild, medium, or intense. The *Rig* Veda's view on multiple lives or heavenly/cosmic abode after death varies. It's not until the Upanishads of the Vedanta period that discussion of recycling life due to karma is mentioned. Either way, these sutras can refer to what your belief system views as transcendence.

Sutras 1.23-1.32. Another option to transcendence is total surrender to Isvara, a name that reflects the omniscient, unchanging, unaffected by human desires, the teacher of all teachers, and expressed by the word "OM." Patanjali uses Isvara rather than Brahman, to include all faith or nonfaith forms free of reference to avatars and is clear that bliss can also be experienced through faith – whatever that is for someone.

35

Sutras 1.33-1.40. Other people and events may disturb you. To remain undisturbed, cultivate differing responses towards other's (or your own) behaviors. In addition to cultivating your responses, also practice controlling your inhales and exhales to regulate the mind and focusing on subtle sensory perceptions (your image of the divine, someone dear to you, a dream, or the peace of deep sleep. Patanjali's brilliance here is perhaps a life's work in its own right, and it applies across millennia and cultures.

The four differing responses are:

1. Be *happy* for those who are happy.

   Jealousy or judgement robs your peace and does not affect them.

2. Be *compassionate* to those who are sad.

   Compassion may not ease their sadness, but mercy can help you.

3. Be *inspired* by virtuous people.

   Those of high integrity and hearts of service can open discovery of qualities within.

4. Be *indifferent* to the wicked/mean-spirited.

   You can lose your peace trying to advise those intent on suffering.

Sutras 1.41-1.51. When the mind becomes elevated and clear, without deliberation it can know the knower, knowledge, and the unknowable, and the soul becomes guide. These Sutras remind yogis that knowledge is finite to what one has accumulated thus far, and often knowledge we hold as truth limits inner wisdom from surfacing while also limiting self-knowing. Patanjali also plants a possibility that the unknowable is more accessible than one thinks.

The Equanimity of an Elephant

E$qual Breaths$ Yogic breathing techniques can support balance through conscious awareness and control to an otherwise automatic process.

Ujjayi breathing was introduced in the last chapter, and now a similar technique called Equal Count (Sama Vritti) focuses breath in and out through the nose without Ujjayi's throat constriction. Equal Count is often equated to Box Breathing, 4 counts in and 4 counts out – but you can equalize any number of counts.

Durga breathing is also done through the nose in equal counts by inhaling 3 counts and exhaling 3 counts. The inhale moves first in the lower abdomen, then the center of the torso, then into the lower chest. The exhale of 3 counts is done in reverse, first in lower chest, then middle torso, then back to lower abdomen. Both Equal Count and Durga breathing promote nervous system balance, clarity, present moment awareness, and mind-body connection.

Pranayama can be especially challenging for those accustomed to not breathing fully due to learned shallow breathing patterns. Durga can be a great start in reprogramming patterns of chest breathing for more optimum health. Ujjayi, Equal Count, and Durga breathing also increase symbiotic function of respiratory muscles and have a balancing effect on the sympathetic (fight or flight) and parasympathetic nervous system (rest and digest,), offering resilience in real life events.

Segmented breathing techniques also use ratioing of inhales and exhales to result in differing outcomes. Depending upon the ratio of those parts, within minutes you can adjust your felt level of energy, clarity, centering, focus, and calmness. For example, inhaling through your nose for a count of 4 and exhaling through your nose for a count of 8 can promote a quick sense of calmness, and conversely, inhaling for 8 and exhaling for 4 can provide a quick sense of increased energy.

37

Pranayama also supports conscious awareness of posture as most methods rely on length in the spine for completeness of breathing techniques, as well a strong diaphragm position and openness in the lungs and neck. While breathing techniques can be done sitting, standing, or laying down, most are more potent when seated with good posture.

$\mathcal{A}$ids to Energy

Other yogic techniques can improve physical equanimity by supporting the equalization of effort amongst your thoughts, musculoskeletal system, and breath. For example, pose transitions that look like advanced acrobatics can be possible by combining breath control, drishti (eye focus or gaze), and bandhas (energetic locks).

Drishti is gazing toward a specific direction that varies depending upon the pose and transition. When drishti is fixed, even momentarily, distractions can fall away to increase positive energy flow. While Drishti can appear easier than other yogic techniques . . . it can be quite a feat to steer your gaze away from other students, the teacher or to the mirror.

Bandhas are energy locks in your body (pelvic floor, core, neck) that you can activate to build, halt and release energy flow. Applying bandhas can help your body perform challenging transitions. They can also be used in breathing techniques, and as aids to meditation. Bandhas can be challenging, at first as they require present moment focus to engage.

In the Ashtanga Primary Series, after repeating the Sun A sequence 5 times, the series moves on to Sun Salutation B, continuing with the same poses of Sun A plus 2 new poses. Sun B is also performed in 5 repetitions. Together, Sun A and B provide about 15 minutes of a cardio and power workout. But one receives the most benefits of these salutations with the least injury risk by syncing and equalizing breath to movement, as well as engaging Bandhas and Drishtis.

Detailed explanation of how to perform breathing techniques, drishtis, energetic locks and Sun Salutations are in this book's companion, *Body as Teacher*.

Salutations & Ganesha

When I first learned Sun Salutations, my teacher repeated the cue "the only sound loud enough to hear is your inhale and exhale." I knew she wasn't talking to me . . . my feet landed in thuds much louder than my breath like I was an elephant amongst acrobats. It was the first time in my life that I couldn't simply fulfill what was being asked of me through pure will to accomplish it. Yet all around me people of varying sizes and ages seemed to float through transitions.

Before opening a yoga studio, my mind offered many reasons why I wasn't ready for such a challenge and how the decision might negatively impact my career, finances, and family. Determined to reverse my self-imposed negativity, I came across Ganesha, an elephant figure with origins in the hymns of the *Rig* Veda under the word Ganapati.

The story goes that a woman named Parvati created Ganesha out of a statue. He came to life with attributes of speech, writing, math, science, love, kindness, security, and stability as a remover of obstacles. Ganesha's lessons include removing self-negativity before beginning endeavors or the obstacles will be too great to overcome. When I opened my yoga studio, I adorned the entrance with an image of Ganesha to remind myself that bringing the "elephant in the room" into equanimity can dramatically lighten the load of challenging endeavors.

Yogis are control freaks when it comes to intentional energy toward equanimity.

Balancing Opposing Forces

A man rides his bicycle every day an average of 80 miles per day, many days over mountain passes, for 40 days enroute to Alaska. Each night he has dinner and sleeps at a hotel. When he finishes the 3200+ mile bike ride, he feels on top of the world and embarks on an Alaskan vacation of fishing and canoeing. However, within days, he cannot stand upright or move without pain, is hospitalized and requires rehabilitation.

Riding a bicycle day after day requires a leaning forward posture that contracts (shortens) muscles on the front of the body while stretching (lengthening) back muscles and buttocks, with little side to side muscular action. So, when the man arrives at his destination, his body lacks the stability necessary to do normal daily activities.

Muscles and connective tissues in this man's front body, including pelvic muscles, psoas, quadriceps, and other hip flexors were shortened the most during his bike trip and would have benefited from soothing stretches. His mid/upper back, low back, and buttocks were lengthened the most on his bike trip and could have retained stability through targeted strengthening exercises. His side stabilizers (outsides of upper legs/hips and insides of upper legs) could have also been targeted to retain overall balance. And since the body is so genius, all these specific counter movements may have taken about 15 minutes each day . . . during rest stops and/or in his hotel room each night.

Hindsight and pain are great teachers. And if an injury is severe enough, these teachers offer a lasting lesson that our bodies need evening out to function well in life. The basic principle of equalizing available joint actions also applies to equalizing muscle forces to promote long-term physical wellness. Sequencing yoga poses for equalization of joint actions and opposing muscles groups is foundational to teaching or practicing yoga in a way that improves health rather than diminishes it.

You don't need to be an anatomy buff to come up with smart pose sequences. Joint health in the last chapter explained how using joints evenly and in alignment leads to increased joint stability over time. Next we learn the basics of muscle health, that opposites attract wellness.

Muscles are tissues that attach to bones by tendons and work in pairs to move a joint. One muscle contracts (gets shorter to pull on a bone) while an opposing muscle stretches (gets longer to pull away from a bone). Muscle strains can occur with overuse, over-strengthening, or over-stretching one part of the muscle pair and not the other, or heavily tasking muscles without warm ups or cool downs. After about 40 years old, muscle mass naturally declines with the same input, but muscle health at all ages benefits from balanced hormones, nutrition, and balancing opposing (antagonistic) muscle pairs.

Opposing Muscle Pairs
1.   Mid/upper back and chest
2.   Low back (erector spinae) and stomach (abdominals)
3.   Hip outsides (abductors) and leg insides (adductors)
4.   Pelvic hip flexors (iliopsoas) and buttocks (glutes)
5.   Thigh fronts (quadriceps) and backs (hamstrings)
6.   Upper arm front (biceps) and backs (triceps)
7.   Shoulder fronts (pecs) and backs (trapezius)

Opposing Muscle Pairs Simplified
1.   Upper (superior) body: back (posterior) and front (anterior)
2.   Lower (inferior) body: back (posterior) and front (anterior)
3.   Side (medial) body: adductors and (lateral) abductors

Smart sequencing for opposing muscle groups not only provides opportunities to counter one-sided physical loads of certain poses, but also to counter basic life repetitive movements. For example, many people spend a good part of their day in flexion when driving a car, sitting, working at a computer, etc., so repetitive Forward Bends and Downward Dogs can further stress people's backs and hips.

Downward Facing Dog and Locust are examples as to how poses can be sequenced in pairs to increase physical resilience through the countering of major muscle pairs. Downward Dog shortens the upper and lower front body and lengthens the upper and lower back body, while Locust lengthens the upper and lower front body and shortens the upper and lower back body. An easy way to remember this is that when it comes to muscles, opposites attract long-term resilience.

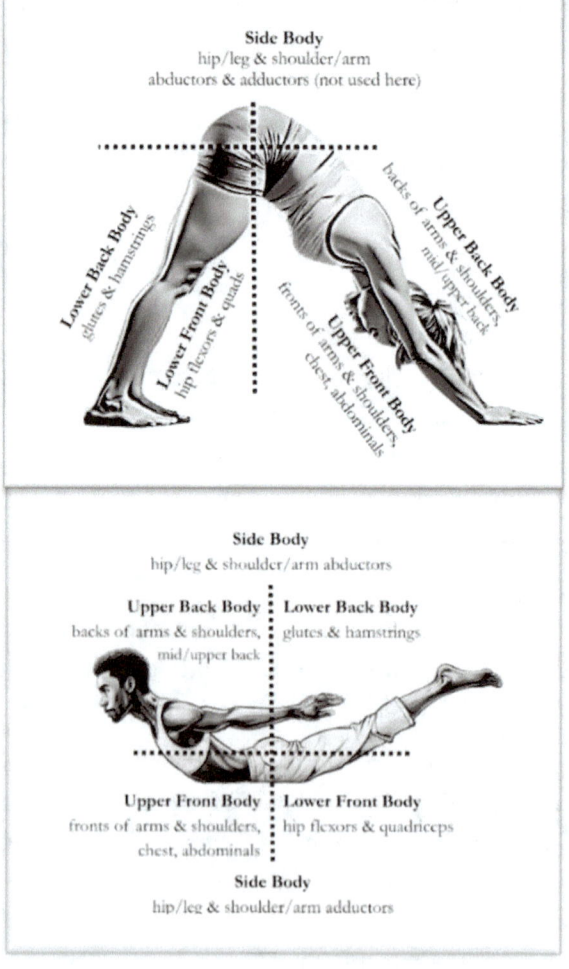

Equalizing major joint actions and opposing muscle groups can be life changing in terms of physical integrity.

Not equalizing joints and opposing muscles can also be life changing — not usually in good way.

1. Draw an image of purusa (soul) looking out at the world of prakriti (everything else) through your citta (layers of mind) grooved with samskaras (pre-conditioning) and samsara (wheel of life).

    a) Label each part in some way that makes sense to you.

    b) Name several of the vrittis you have experienced (surfaced thought grooves from actions or inactions).

2. Sitting, riding most bikes, and leaning forward or bending down are activities that place the spine and hips in flexion and contract/shorten muscles in the lower front and upper body.

    a) Brainstorm several yoga poses, exercises or movements that can counter sitting, riding, and bending down . . . ones that create extension in the spine and hip joints and contract and strengthen muscles in the lower back and lower front body.

3. Chant, say or sing the Ganesha mantra or another reminder to remove negativity before beginning something important. Try this for 3 minutes.

Om Gam Ganapataye Namaha

Translation: My salutations to Ganesha.

Meaning: Honoring the qualities within of strength, goodness, and prosperity.

4. Integrity

Yamas of Universal Ethics

Another of the 8 limbs of Patanjali's path of yoga is the Yamas. The Yamas are universal ethics or truths regarding one's relationship with others and to the world. Like all limbs of yoga, they are a practice.

Because we are all humans with differing life details, some Yamas will come easier than others, and some days it may feel difficult to practice any of them. Observing the Yamas can be humbling, but with consistent practice, each of these universal ethics returns priceless dividends into one's life and in the world.

#1 Ahimsa: Non-violence

"An eye for an eye will only make the whole world blind" — *Gandhi.*

Ahimsa means non-harm or non-violence. Physical violence, as well as harmful thoughts, behaviors, actions, and inactions, can all promote fear and separateness. The yogic view of Ahimsa includes not harming animals. If you do eat animals and animal products, you can still practice this Yama by choosing sources that ensure the quality of an animal's life and humane death. It can be challenging to find these sources at some supermarkets and restaurants but putting in the work to make choices that don't increase suffering is also an act of Ahimsa.

There are some professions, such as police or military, which require violence for protection and can make the practice of Ahimsa more challenging. While some choices remain out of our hands, there is never a moment void of personal choice to make small differences for good.

As a soldier, my job demanded a lot of physical strength to hold my own with mostly male soldiers, as well as to protect and defend my country using force if necessary. My greatest fear shifted from not knowing what college major to choose to not being ready every moment for anything. I managed this the only way my 18-year-old self knew how . . . by undereating, overexercising, and accepting every challenge.

Soon my physical fitness test scores were at the top of the chart, I led company running formations waving a flag and leading cadences of "Shoot, kill, mutilate!," drove 10,000 lb. forklifts and up to 9-ton trucks, dug deep holes in the darkness of German forests, mastered an M16, grenade launcher, M60, table saw and bander, and munitions loading on rail, truck, and aircraft. Counting the days until I could return to "normal" and smoking Marlboro Reds helped.

Then three years later, Desert Storm voided my contractual exit date while my platoon engaged in 24-7 downrange rail loading ammo throughout a cold German winter so ground troops could wage a winning offense. Frozen bottles of Jack Daniels were strewn about forklifts, trucks and on the table saw. One night I dropped a pallet of Multiple Launch Rocket Systems from a train, and no one raised an eyebrow. Fear had rendered us numb.

Desert Storm derailed my planned exit from the Army long enough to develop a new fear . . . what if "normal" was no longer possible? My new fear was so great that it no longer responded well to my vices, so I enlisted again to be officially unsafe as an Explosive Ordnance Specialist. Forevermore, I will understand how soldiers fight for a cause whether they understand it or not.

We all have experienced fear that has led to thoughts, behaviors and actions that separate us from ourselves and others. One impactful practice of Ahimsa is reducing violence towards ourselves. Many of us are conditioned to strive for improvement by beating ourselves up, but what feels wrong is a guide to what feels more in alignment with our being. The practice of Ahimsa is a return to the inner wisdom of our heart, where there is always an alternative approach to fear, which can be a great game changer in life.

#2 Satya: Truthfulness

"The least initial deviation from the truth is multiplied later a thousandfold" - *Aristotle.*

Satya is Sanskrit for truth, and Asat is the opposite, unreal. Great harm can grow from small lies as untruths lead to false perceptions and actions.

At times, speaking the truth can also feel like committing violence; however, there can be much more harm in avoiding the truth. Combining the practices of Ahimsa and Satya together can bridge what may appear in opposition. Untruths include not only lies, but also judgments, and once sewn into the fabric of an individual or a whole culture, they can be difficult to reveal. Telling only excerpts of truth and leaving out relevant data integral to what occurred turns into lies that future generations may base perceptions upon.

Some media platforms gain popularity via misinformation rather than unbiased details. And sometimes, the truth is not hidden, yet humans choose to avoid it – which is also a form of asat. For example, Adolph Hitler published a book about his intentions, yet verbally he told another story people wanted to hear. Hitler invaded multiple countries in accordance with his published plan before allied countries intervened.

Byron Katie's, *The Work*, offers truth inquiries that start with a bothersome thought. For example, "I am never going to find a job that I like and that pays me well." Next, ask yourself questions:

1. Is that statement true?
   I don't know, but it feels like it is.
2. Can I know it to be absolutely true?
   No. I haven't tried some things.
3. When I believe the thought, I feel?
   Disappointment, I want to give up.
4. If I did not have this thought, I might?
   Feel optimistic and in my own power to make a change.

#3 Asteya: Non-stealing

"Earth provides enough to satisfy every man's needs, but not every man's greed"
- Gandhi.

Asteya means non-stealing and includes not only not being a thief of things, but also not stealing in other ways. Life calls for choices, conscious or not, to contribute to abundance or steal from vitality.

Not stealing applies in many aspects of life. For example, in conversation with other people, we may have an urge to rob from what others say by preparing our answers while they are still communicating. Listening with an intent to hear, rather than an intent to respond, adds value to communication. Vice versa, when someone is speaking so much that others have less opportunity to speak, that person is stealing from others. Too much time on electronic devices can also steal from our wisdom and rob moments of contentment and enjoyment of our immediate surroundings.

And when we steal from nature by taking more than what we need in the name of short-term excess, we end up with less, not more. Demand for more meat at lower prices has resulted in an increase in large-scale beef production, decrease in small family ranches, environmental damage, and multiple health concerns and issues.

Stealing always creates a lack for the thief. Holding tightly to comfort takes away from our vitality. Stealing from the present moment means we don't experience the greatest treasure we will ever have, the abundance that exists around and within us.

#4 Brahmacharya: Moderation

"Everything in moderation, including moderation"
-Oscar Wilde.

Brahmacharya is behavior that leads to Brahman, a name in ancient yoga representing a gender-neutral, transcendent, ultimate unchanging force. Brahman is interchangeable with other names denoting the same principle. In early Vedic texts, Brahman binds the universe as one. In more modern philosophy, Brahman is separate (self reflects the divine but is not part of it).

Brahmacharya reminds us that excessive bodily pleasures can make us feel disconnected from our internal light and/or the unchanging infinite force, whatever name you give that.

In terms of the 8 limbs, the focus of Brahmacharya on celibacy or limits of sexual functions has shifted to a broader practice of moderating sensate pleasures. Brahmacharya can pertain to anything not practiced in moderation that reduces long-term vitality, such as addictions to sex, alcohol, nicotine, food, energy drinks, social media, gossiping, etc. Brahmacharya promotes vitality over short-term indulgence.

The human body is drawn to sensate indulgent pleasures; however, overfeeding our body's desire for short-term pleasure can take away from our vitality. Ojas is a Sanskrit term derived from Ayurveda, which means body's fluids that pertain to our physical, emotional, and spiritual vigor and vitality. Ojas are nourished through nutrition, yoga, and rest, and become toxic through Ama (Sanskrit for the opposite of nourishing). When Ojas contain toxic Ama, then we suffer more.

But can moderation also need to be moderated? We might also take away from our vital energy by focusing excessively on limiting pleasures (over exercising, over self-judgement, over restricting our diet, etc.). Brahmacharya can be practiced as a discovery of where abundance exists through following clues as to what our greatest individual obstacles to vitality are.

#5 Aparigraha: Non-Hoarding

*"If you have built a fortress,
and there is no longer a door to it
- what do you have?
A prison"
— Russ Hudson.*

Aparigraha means non-attachment or non-accumulation. This Yama was hard for me as I worried that if I didn't actively get and keep the things, roles, and relationships that I needed then I might die. After all, without them, who would I be and what reason for going on was there?

As humans, we all face some challenge in practicing non-attachment, but when we cling to things, people, or identities, we limit ourselves and our relationships. Aparigraha is the practice of releasing grips on things, labels, people, and feelings, and instead embracing without conditions. Less clinging allows more liberation, conscious decision making, trust in ourselves, and expansion of love. Patanjali also states that its practice can reveal a knowing of why we came to be in this life in this body.

Aparigraha can apply to everything, even to what we label as success in career, relationships, appearance, and wealth. While hard work and goals are necessary, if we focus on desires with tunnel vision on what we want to achieve, the result can be a life distracted from our true purpose.

Take the story of a man who works thirty years to build a business. Through sacrifice and hard work, the business expands to a great height of success. But then taxes increase, customer demand decreases, and staff turnover causes a decline in capable customer service and management. The potential loss of financial and energy investment, credibility and sense of self-worth is high. However, this perceived unraveling of success may offer the greatest pivotal opportunity in his life. Though failures can seem like obstacles separating us from what we most long for, these "failures" in our path of focus, or in our tunnel, are often our greatest blessings.

In yoga, Samsara is the hamster wheel of conditioned existence, which can include lessons from past lives or past experiences in this life that have created Samskaras (pre-conditioned grooves of thoughts/behaviors). Re-grooving Samskaras can pivot Samsara to add value to life's experiences, while also changing the type of Karma (consequences) faced in the future.

Outright blocks that arise wherein no amount of efforting will resolve them are opportunities for self-reflection and change, else we can easily revert to recycling karma. But when we remove attachments to wealth, labels, potential loss of a relationship or ideal, security, etc., and ask tough questions like "Is there something I'm clinging to that hinders a broader vision?," then the field of awareness and expansion can show itself. Aparigraha calls on us to notice how hoarding or clinging to any external validation results in limitations.

One way to practice Aparigraha is before going to sleep, try shifting your focus to a chosen beloved and internally wish that beloved freedom, happiness, and peace in their existence (without any extra language or conditions). A few minutes can lead to an uprising of joy.

Journaling the Yamas

My first yoga training required daily journaling of observations of the Yamas in our lives. I was concerned that the time this would require might be impossible while working full-time, but surprisingly it was one of the most transformative assignments I'd ever been given. I carried a pocket journal with me so I could note observations as they occurred rather than attempting to remember them every evening.

My reflections highlighted Yamas that felt foreign to me, as well as those that came naturally. The acknowledgment of both dramatically shifted my present moment experience— which in turn shifted much more. Practice observing the Yamas in life as a curious witness, and you may discover an interesting experience as well.

The Power of Words

Humans often seek validation in conditioned ways that show up in messaging. Practicing non-harming, truthfulness, non-stealing, moderation, and non-hoarding in every day conversations can powerfully shift the message's impact for both the speaker and listener.

For example, in what is said out loud by the teacher or internally in one's own thoughts during practice can add to or take away from mind and body connection. Read the cues below for Cobra or Upward Dog, assuming a practitioner is coming into Plank from Halfway Lift. Ask yourself what was likely experienced.

Now I want you to get ready to come to the floor.
You need to keep your arms close to your torso.
Before you lower to the floor, decide what to do next.
You can do Up Dog by coming closer to the floor.
Then lean forward over your hands a little bit,
and flip your feet until the tops of your feet are on the mat.
I want you to be strong in your arms and core,
that way your waist doesn't fall too low.
Look slightly upward and move your shoulders toward your waist.
OR decide maybe it's better to do cobra.
Instead of going part way down, go all the way down to the floor.
Your elbows point backwards and the tops of feet are on the mat.
Then press into hands to elevate your head and shoulders,
look up and lower your shoulders and broaden your chest.
Once you decide, then go ahead and inhale.

The cues above likely accomplished indecision, confusion, and holding of the breath. Statements like "don't do _____" may have led to evaluation of a negative, and repetitive permission likely created confusion rather than choice. Extra words can trap someone in transition while interrupting their positive energy.

Given the same transition, read the next example of going into Cobra using this more concise language that validate energy and focus. And while the option for Up Dog is important, hearing simplicity and feeling a heart opener in Cobra can set the stage for informed choice.

> Exhale and lower knees, torso, forehead to floor.
> Elbows hug ribs, tops of feet to mat.
> Inhale lift shoulders, chest, and gaze.
> Heart expands. Cobra.

When this pose repeats, further details could emerge, such as:

> Exhale lower for Cobra or hover for Up Dog, tops of feet to mat.
> Inhale backbend, strong lower body supports you, soft heart lifts you.

When this pose repeats again, a strong Ujjayi breath could present a somatic cue. Though it may feel difficult to trust what was said earlier does not need repeating, silence is when one can be self-taught.

Everyone will face difficulty with applying the Yamas in messaging. Most of us are pre-conditioned to unconsciously practice some or all barriers to powerful messaging: a fast-paced elevated tone that can transmit anxiety; a slow-paced quiet tone that can add to confusion; rigidness of body that can create more tension; speaking without listening that can steal time from everyone, and overusing words that promotes a lack of understanding.

Chanting a mantra, softening your jaw and shoulders, practicing equal count breathing, and asking questions with sincerity can empower your authentic message. One yoga teacher who struggled with anxiety stayed seated for an entire class without notes to teach authentically and see what others needed clearly. By doing this, she gifted students one of the best classes of their lives and gifted herself a sense of renewed authenticity and connection.

The heart's guarded justification is contrary to the very service of it.

52

Sustaining Your Integrity

Alignment   In this book, pose alignment does not mean placing your body parts in exact positions, it refers to using your body parts in ways that provide the most pose benefits. Pose alignment can be improved and pose benefits can be increased for most people by utilizing props such as dowels, straps, blocks, walls, chairs, bolsters, blankets, etc.

This perspective on supported alignment for maximum benefits can be traced back to B.K.S. Iyengar, who was a student of Tirumalai Krishnamacharya in the early 1900s in Mysore, India. Prior to coming to Krishnamacharya's Hatha school, Iyengar had lived through poverty, malnourishment, influenza, malaria, tuberculosis, and typhoid fever, so Krishnamacharya assumed Iyengar would do poorly physically.

Iyengar notes in his book, *Light on Yoga*, that he was mostly assigned chores around the school and received very little formal training; but that was enough to change his life. In fact, after his schooling, he went on to develop his own school of physical alignment in yoga and positively impacted many people, including the Queen of Belgium, Aldous Huxley, and many more. One of Iyengar's followers was Judith Lasater from San Francisco who helped to popularize Restorative Yoga.

Iyengar yoga focuses on reducing risks and maximizing benefits in poses by using props, functional sequencing, and precise cueing. A teacher of this type of yoga would not say to a student having trouble in any pose to "do what works for your body today" without also giving the options and supports to help someone investigate what that means for them.

Thermoregulation   Breathing techniques can also support a sense of alignment. For example, Sitali and the Caliber for Constant Authority techniques can adjust one's internal thermostat, or thermoregulation system, to a cooler setting while activating neutral thoughts not subject to external forces.

Sitali breath can reduce anger and anxiety, improve sleep, cool body temperature, and reduce tension and thirst. It is done by forming a straw with your curled tongue and inhaling through that straw, then exhaling through your nose. The Caliber for Constant Authority can do everything Sitali breath can, as well as aid in letting off steam from emotional or mental distress. This breath is done by inhaling through your nose, then exhaling through pursed lips, then inhaling through pursed lips, and completing one round by exhaling through your nose. Both breaths impact on blood pressure means that those with low blood pressure or poor circulation should limit its practice.

*S*tanding Poses and *R*ama

The Ashtanga Primary Series continues with the Standing Series after Sun A and B. While teaching Ashtanga, I notice a visible and felt shift occurring when practitioners arrive at the standing series. It's as if internal winds are harnessed after 10 salutations and creates the inner and outer alignment needed for the balancing poses in the Standing Series.

This new ground of standing poses also comes with the physical challenges of new body angles, folds, and twists in longer held poses. Sustaining the cooling effect on mind and body for inner calibration and temperature regulation in this part of the series can be easier when outer alignment has support.

This book's companion, *Body as Teacher*, provides cues, images, and variations of the Standing Series poses for all bodies, including the usage of blocks, blankets, and dowels for optimum alignment, as well as explanations of how to do these cooling breathing techniques.

In the *Ramayana*, the Indian epic written around the first years of the current era, Rama is the hero in a story of triumph over greed and adversity, ideal duty (dharma), and spiritual love. Rama's story starts with being born from a grain of rice and a Yagna (fire ceremony) initiated by a king in the hopes of conceiving sons. As time goes on and Rama grows up, is banished for 14 years to live a life similar to The Game of Thrones and uses his bow to restore balance in a forest threatened by destructive forces. An ongoing Indian festival called Diwali still celebrates Rama's return from exile.

Throughout the dramas that unfold in the Ramayana, Rama proves himself as a warrior but makes some questionable decisions before he becomes king. In the Iyengar influenced use of props throughout the Ashtanga Standing Series and in cooling breathing techniques, you can also put out fires, experiment with actions that contribute to your alignment, and come home to sustained integrity.

"Between us, we have the fire and the water. I'm quite sure that together, we can take on the wind."
— R.F. Kuang, The Dragon Republic.

Musculoskeletal Metaphysics

"Before I discovered the miracles of science,
magic ruled the world."
- William Kamkwamba.

Poses as we know them today are a relatively new phenomenon. There are only about 600 years of texts regarding the practice of poses as sequences. But ancient yogis seem to have understood the importance of energy movement. Early yogic views could be called metaphysical as they focused on the nature of energy, why certain forces exist and how to move them consciously for wellness.

In modern times, the metaphysical can be considered magic by some, however our anatomy has not changed much from those ancient yogis to now. What has changed are the forces upon our bodies. Ancient yogis were more physically active and often worked antagonist muscles and joint ranges as a natural part of daily life.

The term Vayu, Sanskrit for winds or flows of bodily energy, was found in early Vedic texts to tell stories, as well as to explain how to direct internal forces for increased alignment. Using vayus can be foundational for pose sequencing, just like muscle and joint actions. Vayus can also show you how to modify poses for similar benefits.

There are 5 main Vayus, which include:

Prana pulling energy *inward* (air/inspiration to head and heart).

Apana releasing energy *downward* (grounding).

Samana moving energy for *balancing* (stabilizing).

Udana pushing energy *upward* (expression and growth).

Vyana *expanding* energy outward (circulating and integrating).

Magic tricks, like pulling a rabbit out of a hat, are based in illusions. When faced with a physically challenging pose, or health condition that limits mobility, creating a beneficial modification for that pose can become easier when you remove the illusion that conformity is best.

Most of us are wired with preconceived notions that certain things will appear in a certain way. For example, many yoga teachers tell students to take Child's Pose whenever needed during practice. But believing that those physically challenged or exhausted could find benefit from Child's Pose is not reality for many people.

Applying metaphysical philosophy, on the other hand, can make a physics solution appear for actual wellness. Experiment with the case of a practitioner with PTSD or hip flexion limitations, and a teacher who wishes to offer this person Child's Pose as a resting option – but the practitioner cannot comfortably or safely rest in Child's Pose.

First, analyze the primary vayus at play in Child's Pose.
- ✓ Head below the heart is an inversion that increases blood flow to neck/head and pushes energy upward = Udana Vayu.
- ✓ Widening hips allows the torso to release downward for grounding = Apana Vayu.

Next, find a modification to Child's Pose that utilize these vayus.
- ✓ Udana Vayu (head below heart)
- ✓ Apana Vayu (releasing downward)

One option is lying face down with legs long to keep hips in a more neutral position. Widen hips slightly and place a narrow bolster under hip creases to elevate hips. Next, place something low and soft under your forehead for comfort, and a small, rolled blanket under ankle fronts to allow them to also soften downward.

Another option is lying face up with torso only on a folded blanket, back of head resting lower on mat, legs long and hips slightly widened with a larger bolster under knees. Both of these options provide Udana and Apana benefits, but there are many more options. In fact, when you understand Vayus, beneficial modifications appear like magic.

57

Self-Study

1. Using the Yamas in your language, brainstorm 4 concise cues for these poses: Downward Dog, Cobra, Upward Dog, Plank, Forward Bend.
2. What are the primary vayus/energy movements in these poses?
3. Use an example of someone who should not perform a forward fold/bend because they have back issues or are pregnant.
    a) What modifications could achieve similar Vayu benefits?
    b) Where could you use props in these modification to also achieve increased musculoskeletal benefits?
4. Journal the Yamas.
    Prepare two weeks of pages for the five Yamas to note observations of them in your thoughts, actions, and behaviors using short, simple statements. When finished, share your observations with others.

(prepare 14 lists like this)	Observations of my thoughts, actions & behaviors, and occurrences in the world
Ahimsa (Non-Harming)	
Satya (Truth)	
Asteya (Non-Stealing)	
Brachmacharya (Moderation)	
Aparigrapha (Non-Hoarding)	

5. Chant, say or sing a Rama mantra or another affirmation that reminds you to be present on your authentic journey beyond layers of ego, conditioning, or other's expectations. Try this for 3 minutes.

Sri Ram Jai Ram Jai Jai Ram
Translation: Auspicious Rama, Victory to you!
Meaning: Honoring qualities within of compassion, courage, authenticity.

5. Self-Care

Sutras Pada 2 – Obstacles

The Yoga Sutras refined yogic teachings into an 8-Limb science of methods one can use to live a more meaningful life. The Sutras are divided into 4 chapters or Padas. Pada 1 defined yoga, the obstacles, purpose, and the importance of practice. Pada 2 outlines Kriya yoga, causes of suffering, and 6 limbs.

Sutras 2.01 – 2.02 Kriya/Action toward a specific outcome. Patanjali offers a fast track kriya to move through challenges. Practitioners can use this kriya to minimize obstacles in life.

+ Tapas (*effort*)

+ Svadhyaya (self-*study* or study of spiritual books)

± Isvarapranidhana (*celebration* of spirit/surrender/grace)

= Fastest way through obstacles to *freedom*

Sutras 2.03 – 2.14 Kleshas/Causes of Suffering. Everyone faces obstacles that can be lumped into five causes of suffering. Fortunately, all can be tackled by tracing the suffering to its source (through effort, surrender and study) and then adding the practice of meditation.

Ignorance is the field for and *parent of all suffering.*

Egoism is the need for *external validation* of self-worth.

Attachment is *identifying self in another* person, thing, title.

Hatred/aversion comes from *previous pain* no longer present.

Clinging to life or *fear of death* can disrupt the joy of life.

Sutras 2.15 – 2.27 Gunas/Changes. Gunas are energetic forces that exist under the laws of alternation and continuity, meaning that everything with a cellular structure exists in a changing state. The Gunas are Tamas, Rajas, and Satva. Whichever force is present longest stabilizes until a conflict arises that calls for harmony of balance.

*T*amas is *negative* (dark, solid, clinging). It reinforces *stagnation.*

*R*ajas is *active* (productive, passionate, shaping). It initiates *change.*

*S*attva is *balancing* (light, flowing, virtuous). It sees/*evolves.*

Sutras 2.28-2.53 –The limbs are Yamas (ethics), Niyamas (disciplines), Asana (poses), Pranayama (breath regulation), Pratyahara (mastery of senses), Dharana (focus), Dyana (meditation, Samadhi (bliss). Steady comfortable posture allows controlled breathing, which improves the experience of life.

Harmony includes practicing through change
because everything with a cellular structure
is temporary and connected.

Niyamas of Self-Care

Self-adjustment may be our greatest power on the physical plane.

While the Yamas are practices to apply universally, the 5 Niyamas are self-disciplines or restraints. Applying Niyamas in life are akin to self-care rituals that can help you feel ready to show up in life in ways that matter to you.

#1 Saucha: Purity or Cleanliness

Saucha is uncluttering and purifying our insides and outsides. It applies to what we take in to digest, from our bodies and minds.

Consider walking into a yoga studio and you notice haphazardly folded blankets, scattered blocks, shoes strewn about the room, and dirt on the floor. When you get to the mats, they are partially rolled and appear dirty. You look towards the teacher, whose mat is surrounded by multiple personal items As class starts, you strangely feel more stressed than you did before you entered the studio for an hour of wellness.

Making small changes towards an uncluttered and clean living space – whether that be in a yoga studio, at home, in a hotel room, etc., is a great way to incorporate Saucha in life. For example, you can start by making your bed in the morning for an immediate boost similar to cleaning your car windshield. When you go from looking outward through bugs on your windshield to unclouded vision, clarity appears that wasn't evident before. The same applies to healthy fluids that your body uses for cleansing processes.

The intake of healthy fluids and clean food can promote clarity and energy. The practice of Saucha is not about perfection, it is about lightness like sun through a clear windowpane. In the gunas (states of change), Saucha contributes to a Sattvic state (flowing, evolving).

"If you want to change the world, start by making your bed"
– *William McRaven.*

61

#2 Santosha: Contentment

In each moment exists the capacity for evolution.

The space between nowhere and now here is contentment in the present moment, even in moments that are hard or mundane. Contentment doesn't mean not trying to better yourself or your circumstances. It means that in the present moment you can notice the treasures around you regardless of other details. Santosha also profoundly impacts future choices.

Years ago, I wanted to learn to rock climb and hired Tony as my teacher. On the last climb and at the 3rd pitch, separated from the ground by a sheer cliff of 600 ft, I froze. From his perch on a tiny ledge above me, Tony beckoned me up, but I was at the crux, the place that calls all rational and un-rational fears into the now. Tony promised there were good holds all around me, but he was lying. I could not identify a sliver of rock capable of wedging a fingernail onto. Tony continued unflustered, "Great·feet, Charmion, just above your waist to the right."

I moved my right foot and lost the wall. As I hung in the air by a man holding a rope high off the canyon floor, my body merged like a magnet to the rock face with legs and arms outstretched in a star. Then, I saw them, holds for the top centimeter of a finger and for a toe joint.

That last climb began with me judging how difficult the climb would be. Had I made it to the top without that humbling mid-air moment, the climb would have been temporarily celebrated as survival. The moment that changed everything is when I let go of control to be the softness and strength of the rock, the warmth of the sun, an encouraging friend, contentment that I could be still. As soon as I experienced all that was present, each moment offered opportunity.

Try Santosha by closing your eyes for a moment and when you open them, notice all of bounty of around you . . . example, "I have a body! There is light in this room! The floor below me is supportive!" Santosha is an evolutionary climb from human doer to human being.

62

#3 Tapas: Self-discipline

Tapas is effort towards change wherein we use our internal fire to burn through self-possessed limitations. For our efforts to yield fruit though, we must stay with the effort long enough to witness growth or new habits being formed. Tapas are about going to our edges, where internal monsters feed on that which seems impossible. Tapas can be used to burn through to the dras (the seer/witness) past pre-conditioning barriers.

While exercise is one way to do this, exercise alone doesn't burn limitations long enough for sustained mental and physical fortitude. For example, when sun salutations cues from a teacher include "option for vinyasa or take rest if needed," some practitioners may find it more difficult to take another vinyasa, and others may find it more challenging to choose rest. Similarly, choosing to take modifications in Sun Salutations can feel more mentally difficult than doing the "normal" version.

Tapas is acknowledging where your edges are waiting to teach you something new. For example, after my military service, I took a hiatus from exercise to focus on hiding who I was "before" – which surfaced embarrassing control issues for the world to see in full-blown adult acne. Then one day my cowgirl came back to life inside and would no longer be stifled, so I took my body on a wild ride to soothe my brain, yet for all my self-inflicted pain, pain remained.

Everyone has edges that can be cycled into perpetuity until they are burned through. But over time, other parts of life can become easier directly because of focused fires. Disciplined effort is necessary to experience a life of ease, but only you know your monsters and how to set them ablaze.

To slay the monster, take away what it feeds on. its embarrassing craving for the fulfillment of lies.

#4 Svadhyaya: Self Study

"I am not who you think I am.
I am not who I think I am.
I am who I think you think I am"
- Charles Horton Cooley.

Why do we show up the way we do in our thoughts and actions, in relationships and in the world? Svadhyaya is a study of oneself through self-observation, scriptures, poems, mantras, and philosophy, to discover inner truths, including where our work remains. Self-study can include completing assignments, journaling of the Yamas and Niyamas, other journaling, mental health therapy, brainstorming with others, etc.

The first time I read the *Gita*, I was angry about the battle and caste system, yet I knew the poem was revered by great philosophers – so I read it again. The 2nd time offered more wisdom, but alas it took reading the Gita twice more before I found value in it. My 4th time through is when I came to love the epic poem because I could at last absorb its timeless application without becoming lost in what offended me.

Years ago, I wrote a book about abandonment that led to battles and adventures. The first draft dripped with other's wrongdoings, hurt, loss, triumphs over death, and a desperate desire to feel safe and loved. When I reread my words in book form, it was obvious how I had hurt myself, over and over, and I knew my happy ending called for self-love.

That which we study is almost never the 100% true and correct answer as all human authors are biased in some form. Writing our own stories can provide overwhelming evidence of that. Our experiences and conditioning can obscure wisdom that we can be unaware until earnest study begins. For example, rereading scriptures from most any spiritual tradition can be like peeling back personal discovery of both conscious thoughts and awareness of unconscious motives. All methods of self-study can help to make more aligned life choices.

64

#5 Isvarapranidhana: Celebration of Spirit

In this Niyama, Patanjali offers a discipline to readers of the *Yoga Sutras* as either support for practice towards bliss, or the fast track to it. Although Isvara is referenced as a name for God, the *Yoga Sutras* are not a religious text as the book is not a system of faith, nor does it advocate for worship. Isvara is simply one name for the infinite, the divine, or universal power. Pranidhana means surrender, so Isvarapranidhana means surrendering to a force greater than yourself.

Our well-being in any given moment can be directly related to how much we try to control that which is not within our control. If we go through life feeling that the weight of the world rests squarely on our shoulders, then we will eventually crumble . . . maybe not like the heap of water the wicked witch of the west turns into in the Wizard of Oz, but we will feel an internal wasting away of connection to life. Regardless of your faith or beliefs, it is not possible for you to control other people, all of technology, and/or acts of nature.

Practicing this Niyama can start with checking yourself in stressful situations by asking another Byron Katie question,

"Whose lane am I in – mine, another's or God/universe's lane?."

When it comes to God's/universe's lane, you may as well surrender.

When the answer is other people's lane, you can get out of their car or in their passenger seat unless you want to drive their car for life.

When we surrender what is not meant for us to control, we regain the driver's seat for what IS within our power – and inexplicably even that which is heavy can feel lighter just knowing a greater force is at play. Surrendering what needs surrendering creates a lightness, like the bubble that Glenda the good witch travels in.

Surrender is not loss of control.   *"Jesus take the wheel"*
Surrender is celebration of support.   *– Carrie Underwood.*

65

Beloved Recalibration

Sequences of Stress

According to a study by the National Science Foundation, humans average 12,000 to 50,000 thoughts per day – most on replay and skewed negatively.

Once you've slayed the initial metaphorical demons of thoughts that aren't true, stressors continue to show up in new ways because life has a stockpile of them for our minds to process. Since stressors are part and parcel of life, resiliency is fundamental to enjoyment of life.

Some people suffer other triggers in addition to daily stress, such as trauma survivors who may experience automatic survival responses when no imminent danger is present. Most beginner yogis are aware that yoga practice can help with resilience to everyday stress and can help those coping with trauma responses. However, people may not be aware of how those with leading roles play a part in resilience, or lack of it.

Regardless of appearance, background, or identity, a teacher or leader who is internally dysregulated can subtly contribute to a heightened stress response in others. And those who have not yet practiced openness and authenticity in their own lives can transfer that lack of genuine acceptance unintentionally to others. These types of transferences can lead to more confusion rather than more resilience.

On the flip side, a teacher can most always create an environment of resilience for themselves and others by practicing the Niyamas of cleanliness, contentment, self-discipline, self-study, and celebration of spirit. This doesn't mean bypassing your own stress. It means using self-tools for your well-being that contribute to your ability to show up as an example of resilience, even when times are hard.

Stressors are like zombies coming back to life by stealing breath.

Breathing Fully   Yogic breathing techniques can help in countering everyday stress. They offer present moment awareness, mind-body connection, stimulation of the vagus nerve, improved circulatory and respiratory functions, increased clarity, and reduced anger and anxiety. They can also help reprogram previously engrained physical trigger responses wherein rigid neck, shoulder and chest muscles can learn to relax and the whole body can benefit from optimum oxygen levels

Conscious inhaling and exhaling fully can also increase physical strength in the body, as core muscles are continually activated, which can improve pelvic stability over time. The yogic philosophy of vayus can also promote further resilience in breathing practices. For example, "Inhale Expand" = inward fresh focused energy and "Exhale Let Go" = releasing stressors and surrendering burdens.

Breathing fully can become natural with practice, but it is almost never an easy practice. Previously wired patterns of breathing informed by our experiences thus far in life are ingrained patterns, so when attempting to integrate specific breathing techniques, the mind must continually be reminded that a variance from basic autonomic functions is desired. When I decided to recalibrate my breath to full capacity, I found it relatively easy during asana practice, but next to impossible in any other life thing. Without conscious correction, my brain reverted to its habit of chest breathing. So I set forth on a journey to practice fully breathing throughout the day and by doing so, breathing for resilience now comes more naturally.

While utilizing breathing techniques on and off-the-mat can first be challenging, the yogi who can breathe to their full capacity utilizing a variety of techniques, whether they are standing, seated or lying in stillness, is likely receiving more benefits in terms of overall resilience than a practitioner who can do all the poses but does not breathe fully.

Seated Folds   A category of poses referred to as bends or folds can provide practitioners with what can feel like a mini-vacation from stress. In the Ashtanga Primary Series, at approximately 30 minutes into the practice, after the 5 repetitions each of Sun Salutation A and Sun Salutation B, and the standing series, the sequence continues with moving energy downward in seated forward bends prior to backbends, inversions, and rest.

Modified Ashtanga Seated Series poses can stretch the spine and hamstrings, stimulate organ function, and decrease stress. And Ashtanga's transitions in the seated series is a sort of repetitive recalibration of meditative will and peace.

However, seated forward bends and transitions can also lead to more stress through misalignment and harmful momentum. When practitioners overly round their spines to deepen seated poses, this pattern can eventually show up as decreased stability – the opposite of resilience. And attempts at inward peace in a body that can't hold itself together result in a larger challenge than pausing for safe engagement and only folding as far forward as an aligned spine allows.

The finishing series of Ashtanga Primary Series also includes inversions, backbends and rest poses that are discussed later. This book's companion, *Body as Teacher*, provides cues, discussions on bending safely, images, and variations of the Seated and Finishing series of poses, as well as many more breathing techniques for resilience.

Sita   Archetypes can be another bridge to enhancing resilience in your practice and life. In the Indian epic, the *Ramayana*, Sita is Rama's beloved. While the hero Rama exemplifies duty, the heroine Sita exemplifies resilience.

As a teenager, Sita meets Rama and falls hard for him. But Sita's father wants his daughter to have an equal as husband and so has a requirement that Sita can only marry a man able to string the bow of Shiva – a bow so heavy that no man has yet lifted it even an inch. Sita's father knows Sita can move the table where the bow sits, so he see this test as the only way to know which man is worthy of his daughter's power.

When Rama accepts the challenge, he not only fastens the string - the bow breaks under his strength. Rama and Sita are married, but soon after, Rama is exiled to the forest. Sita chooses to go into exile with her husband and during this exile, she is captured by the demon-like Ravana who imprisons her in Lanka. During her imprisonment, Sita continually chooses inner peace above bargains to make her life temporarily easier.

Time goes on until there are mere hours left before Ravana forces Sita to be his wife. Since Rama has been unable to find Sita, he sends Hanuman, his best devotee, to find her. And that he does, accomplishing the splits in flight over the sea on his way.

When Hanuman arrives to save her, Sita turns her rescuer down, vowing to wait for her husband. At last, Rama saves Sita. But he questions her integrity and puts her through a trial by fire – which she passes through unharmed. Still uncertain about her integrity, Rama exiles Sita to give birth and raise twins in the forest . . . which she does heroically.

I have come to think of Sita's story as the embodiment of boundless resilience through strength and peace.

Walk through the proverbial fire in service of your natural resilience. For you, dear one, are the beloved.

Sequencing for Stress

My head could not take it in. So, my heart did.

When it comes to people that face high stress in daily life (i.e., firefighters, EMTs, therapists, etc.), some may think that sequencing should be less about strength and movement, and more about relaxation. But the idea that calming and slow sequences increase resilience for those under high stress calls for further examination.

Many close to daily trauma bake in numbness and avoidance as a recipe for continuing to function, and relaxation may equate to a temporary pretense. Add pandemics, polarization, and other threats, and higher stress now exists in many forms.

The theory that de-stressing involves relaxation is focused on countering the part of our nervous system that helps us prepare for battle or escape, as necessary. However, there are conclusive studies, namely from the Swami Vivekananda Yoga Research Foundation in India, which conclude combining active poses and breathing with relaxing poses and breathing is most effective for nervous system resilience.

Practitioners of the Ashtanga Primary Series experience this firsthand. If the sequence only contained Sun Salutations, or only the Standing Series, or only the Seated and Finishing Series, the sequence would likely not have continued around the world a hundred years after it was developed. But since the series contains a combination of those things, even though it is somewhat unbalanced in joint and muscle actions, it contains all vayus and nails it as an antidote to stress.

The Ashtanga Primary Series sequence, when modified for functional wellness, can consistently deliver a feeling of internal freedom, strength, and sanctuary. By understanding joint and muscle actions and vayus, you can create your own sequences for lasting resilience.

"The sanctuary is inside you" -Rumi.

70

Self-Study

1. Role Play. Take turns playing the teacher and student in a scenario where a student enters a yoga studio to prepare for a yoga class.
   The student actor is briefed only on the student details.
   The teacher actor is briefed only on the teacher actions.
   Others journal what I saw, what I heard, and what I felt (sensations).

   a. Role Play Scenario 1
      Student 1 works at a stressful job with a critical co-worker and has joint pain. Student 1 needs an hour to feel good.
      Teacher 1 is engaged in a distressing phone call, and bright lights blare over an empty and cold space.
      Student 1 enters without acknowledgement.

   b. Role Play Scenario 2
      Student 2 has a hard time socially but came out of their comfort zone to try yoga. Student 2 tried on many pairs of yoga pants and could not find any to help her feel like she will fit in.
      Teacher 2 is sitting on a mat laughing at what appears to be an inside joke with another student. Teacher 2 is still giggling as class begins without having made eye contact with Student 2.

   c. Role Play Scenario 3
      Student 3 comes to class for refuge from anxiety so enters the room 10 minutes early so as not to cause disruption. Student 3 sits down uncomfortably to wait for class to start.
      Teacher 3 is staring at notes as the class waits in awkward silence. 5 minutes after class is supposed to start, Teacher 3 gets on a mat and starts demonstrating class without looking at students.

   d. Role Play Scenario 4
      Student 4 feels like a failure and wants to feel like they matter.
      Teacher 4 sits at the front of the room and greets Student 4 before offering them a place for their mat where they feel most comfortable, as well as an affirmation card.

2. Which klesha (besides ignorance) do you find the most difficult?

3. Journal the Niyamas.

   Prepare two weeks of pages for the five Niyamas to note observations of them in your thoughts, actions, and behaviors using short, simple statements. When finished, share your observations.

(prepare 14 lists like this)	Observations of my thoughts, actions & behaviors, and occurrences in the world
Saucha (Purity or Cleanliness)	
Santosha (Contentment)	
Tapas (Self-discipline)	
Svadhyaya (Self Study)	
Isvarapranidhana (Celebration of Spirit)	

4. Chant, say or sing the Sita Ram mantra or another affirmation to remind you that caring for your resilience contributes to goodness in the world. Try this for at least 3 minutes.

   Sita Ram, Sita Ram, Sita Ram, Jaya Sita Ram
   Translation: Victory to Sita and Ram!
   Meaning: Honoring the qualities of both will and peace within you

6. Formation to Revelation

Sometimes people in our lives assume they know us and why we show up the way we do, physically, mentally, and spiritually. Those assumptions can be based on the form of our physical shape and condition, our family and financial status, our political beliefs and/or religion, the place we live in, the car we drive, our jobs and careers, our relationships, etc. We likely have some assumptions about our whys based on those things as well.

Form and the foundation of things are essential, or our lives might lack concrete meaning and purpose. Part 1 covered the form and foundation of yoga's history, the 8 limbs, Yamas, Niyamas, how to breathe fully and message clearly, practice resilience, direct internal energy, draw on supports for alignment and use basic musculoskeletal fundamentals for functional wellness. This is all a great start!

Foundational work in yoga and in life can then form a basis for further inquiries that can lead to new discoveries towards your most meaningful life. While going into the inner unknown threatens a pre-conditioned ego, which all humans have, it is a prerequisite to lasting growth. For example, a doctor has repeated his hypothesis countless times that some of my conditions stem from an incident I once mentioned about a canoe. I know differently. So, while what he knows about my body and that canoe story could be the start of inquiry, instead they have led nowhere new.

The same principle takes shape in yoga practice when outer work based on yoga's foundations reaches a limit that falls flat without deeper inquiry into the sources of why we show up the way we do, and what those forms are trying to show us what we really want and need. Part 2 takes you deep inside yourself to bring assumptions to the surface where they transform into revelations.

Why do you believe what you believe? Question everything. This is a universal test.

73

Part 2 – Inner Work

Sitting naked on a chair, she bows, "Mataji, we pray first". I close my eyes.

Herb satchels beat the darkness out of me,
then warm oil across my forehead renders me senseless.
At last, she cradles my head and whispers low, "I'm sorry".

In the night, canopies of monkeys witness as I find my way.
Arms wipe open, imperfect as f***, breaking rules against austerity.
I rest on airy dirt under the forest trees, cradled in love.

In the day I walk barefoot through busy streets.
Sacred cows nuzzle me as if saying, "Hello beloved!"
Holy orange robes draped over cobblestone meet our eyes with light.
If we are all avatars, who is doing the teaching then?

I climb a mountain to watch the sunrise over the Himalayas,
then scurry to the Ganges to soak in its pervading virtues.
Healing even in death, a family's beloved floats past me in fire.

Each day, dark eyes with tilaks stir spices of life into large pots
while I sit barefoot on thatch, eating soup with my hands,
for the guest is always God on our journey home.

In the rickshaw, horns announce
"Make a U-turn when needed. Rules make accidents.
It is enough to know that rage can kill us all."

Outside of the ashram, a stranger and I stare each other down.
"Come with me. We shall all die, but not today".
I gaze at fields of mustard merging into one as we speed by.
And tears fall out of the well of my heart.
He is returning to lay his head on the lap of his Mother.

Life is so much more than I dreamed it to be
and too often more of a dream than real.
Worth more money than a lifetime of chasing it,
our days on Earth are what we create.
May they always include more space for that which is unseen.

7. Chakra System

"What we have not conquered in the past returns again and again" — Satprem.

My Dad died of a cancer in 2010 after he fired a rifle shot near his heart, so I decided it was high time I figured out what spirituality meant. Though I knew little about yoga except it was rumored to connect mind, body, and spirit, it seemed the best place to start. However, there was so much under the umbrella of yoga that I didn't know where best to set forth on my journey until I discovered the Chakra System.

Chakras appealed to me in the simplicity of definable human needs similar to Maslow's Hierarchy. So, I rubbed my chakra beads while affirming basic rights and in a surprisingly short period of time, deep-rooted scars became less apparent. Unfortunately, as liberating as feeling less emotionally disfigured was, I strangely missed my scars.

This liminal place between freedom from emotional pain called for an unravelling of limitations as prerequisite to crossing the threshold to change. I didn't have the strength, so life unraveled them for me. My children graduated and went onto their lives, my husband wanted a divorce, my body began failing and toxicity at work left me cowering behind my office door. Soon thereafter, at a reunion, I noticed that many people were still clinging to their comfort zones with zeal and our "reconnection" efforts could not exceed a purely superficial level.

All along, I knew there were some crossroads leading toward pots of gold and some to no man's land, so I thought taking them all would at least lead somewhere new. Ironically, I ended up with the same. I had married an incarnation of my father and been abandoned again, had searched across foreign lands and mountains to find a box to get back into, and ascertained for myself that geographical cures aren't all one might give them credit for.

Fast forward several years to Sacramento, California, and halfway through a 200-hour yoga training where 44 other students and I arrive at the Edge weekend, a horrifying gut-wrenching blurting out to everyone the gravest scars we possess. Not one person in my life had been so blatantly honest about their demons as nearly every single other human in the room. For the first time in my life, I felt connected to all of humanity.

The Edge weekend included practice teaching to 50 people, and not only were we supposed to teach the correct sequence without notes or demonstrating, but we were also supposed to "speak to the spirit" . . . create a space for each individual to unravel their peace. You could not be in your own way and accomplish this. Thoughts of quitting were real, but other trainees rose to the challenge – many of whom had suffered things I could not imagine.

My teaching started strongly, but lost ground quickly – as if someone else was in the room robbing my authenticity. After several tortuous minutes, at last I reclaimed myself after my exhibition of internal despair. After it was over, a fellow trainee offered feedback.

"I didn't expect your voice, presence, and care to come through like it did at first. But then, you started pacing back and forth and acting like John Wayne - you kept grabbing your waistband and holding onto it. It was a relief when you came back from wherever you went."

Tears rolled down my cheeks as I explained,

"I used to wear a cowboy belt as a girl and an LBE (load bearing equipment) belt as a soldier. I held onto both for security. This time I found another way."

After our big reveals, we sat glowing in front of a guest teacher who explained chakras to us. At last, I had what was needed for the other side. For the next five years, I worked with the chakra system to create maps across my thresholds. This chapter's approach is the combined result of that internal mapping, research, practice, and training. It is not intended to be a substitute for mental health therapy.

Subtle Energy Anatomy

 Chakra means wheel in Sanskrit and each chakra is comprised of subtle energy that represents a natural development center. The Chakra system includes multiple chakras with differing properties moving through energy channels, called Nadis. Blockages in subtle energy arise through life events that can alter energy in our bodies, resulting in stored energy (creating an excess) or avoidant energy (creating a deficiency). Like Maslow's Hierarchy or Erikson's Psychosocial Stages, the chakra system represents previous experiences showing up in our thoughts, behaviors, and actions by spotlighting kleshas (causes of suffering), and what work can support positively changing cycles.

Chakras are traced back to the early Upanishads around 3,000 years ago. They show up in Ayurveda, the *Yoga Sutras*, Hinduism, and Buddhism. Here we focus on Tantra's school of Hatha yoga that includes 7 main chakras, with additional wisdom from Kundalini yoga wherein the 3 lowest chakras make up the lower triangle, comprised of dense, survival-based physical properties; the 4th chakra acts as a transformation point, where survival needs meet spiritual needs; and the 3 higher chakras constitute the upper triangle, a lighter and transformational form of energy. Kundalini also recognizes an 8th chakra as the aura, which radiates from our bodies representing our overall energy.

In the last 200 years, many scientists, psychologists, and ascetics have traced psychological systems and theories that seem to overlap with the Hatha yoga chakra system. For example, Anodea Judith's book, *Eastern Mind Western Body*, published in the 1990s, compares ancient and modern psychological insights inside of the chakra system. Her book, written from a clinical perspective, made the Chakra System useful to experts in the field of western psychology as well as lay persons. This book also overlaps chakras with psychological insights.

As you move through the chakras, difficult feelings may arise that may be directed at someone else, or yourself. Uncovering hurt may feel like assigning blame to others and/or self, but it is not. Bringing light, or perspective and awareness, to darkness, or what was hidden or perceived at the time that may not have reflected the whole picture, is a way to break negative cycles. Knowing what we are working with is essential in discovering how to help ourselves, so we don't have a future spent missing something we needed in the past. Consider someone who can provide space for listening or guidance, including mental health therapists, before you embark on this journey. A support system can improve one's ability to process unraveling of the past.

We develop behavior patterns throughout our lives that help us navigate the world. So, as you work through the chakras, you may uncover embedded behaviors you aren't ready to change as they feel essential to self-identification. Consider utilizing the Enneagram to support allowing your personality strengths to be part of your purpose.

When it comes to deficiency or excess chakra energy, one is not better than the other. What shows up is simply an indicator of what processing tools were most available to us at the time.

It is never too late to adjust energy as the very nature of it is fluid and can move; however, chakra energy is seldom isolated work, as energy builds upon energy. What has been shaped below also shows up above. And while most people are curious to know why they think, behave, and act the way we do, the mere awareness of it can bring more negative energy if not coupled with work to establish balance.

The methods listed at the end of each chakra description can assist with important balancing work. *Body as Teacher* also provides quizzes, poses and breathing practices for chakras.

Right to Exist

*"As the parent was to the child,
so the mind is to the body"* -
Anodea Judith.

Root chakra (muladhara) development occurs in the womb until about 1 year old in our first experiences of survival. This chakra is located near the tailbone, is associated with the color red and the element earth and basic needs of safety, nourishment and of feeling wanted.

If our first experiences of life included a relatively smooth entrance into the world, healthy bonding with at least one person, consistent nourishment, and shelter from the elements; and did NOT include major surgeries, violence, abuse, neglect, malnourishment, or caregivers living with inherited traumas or internal fear or sense of scarcity, then we generally can start out feeling safe in this world. A balanced root chakra shows up in life as knowing you can feed and shelter yourself and shows up as physical and financial health, abundant energy, groundedness, and satisfaction with life.

However, a sense of "I should feel safe, but don't" can pervade the child's first experience of life if the child instead experienced digestive problems, surgeries or lengthy hospital stays, threatening environments including substance abuse and war, or if their caregiver lacked basic stability themselves. If there is fear on this level, then everything is built on this fear, forcing energy into upper chakras to bypass basic needs. A child who does not feel safe can develop behaviors of constant trying to achieve that or a void of desiring it.

Deficient root chakra energy shows up as proving you don't much by not providing for your basic needs, such as undereating, passiveness, lethargy, poor focus, disorganization, poor boundaries, and lack of desire for change. Excess energy looks like a constant need to "fill up" like everything is necessary, hoarding, obsessive eating, rigid boundaries, dominant behavior, and activities that provoke fear. Imbalanced root chakra energy can also lead to conditions at or below the tailbone, such as bone disorders, lower back/buttocks/legs/knees and foot conditions, and constipation.

There are cultural and geographic differences when it comes to all chakras. For example, in 2014, I arrived in San Iglesia la Laguna, Guatemala, with a group of volunteers at a home building site for a Mayan woman named Catalina who was 58 years old, stood 4'10" and weighed about 90 pounds. Her dwelling previously consisted of stick and mud walls that fell short of meeting the scrap tin roof, leaving a gaping hole of security. The only item of financial value she claimed was a coffin, repurposed as a counter until the inevitable.

Sometimes Catalina arrived in the morning already having worked for hours collecting firewood in her traditional Mayan skirt, thick belt, and beautiful blouse. She put the machetes away for safekeeping, washed her hands in lake water, and greeted us with poise before working happily in the hot sun, seemingly with no need to eat, drink, or use the bathroom. Together, we scraped bamboo stalks clean, cut and wired them into place, mixing piles of mud and water by dragging and stomping it with bare feet, and then packed walls by throwing mud at bamboo and molding it with bare hands. Catalina was easily the most secure person in our group, even though her basic needs had far less physical substance than ours.

These methods promote healthy energy in your root chakra:
- Nature, walking, gardening, and growing plants.
- Root vegetables, proteins, and earthy spices.
- Poses and breathing techniques for the root chakra
- Ayurvedic self-massage.
- Seed sound "Lam."
- Anjali and Adi mudras.
- Cassia or patchouli oils.

Right to Feel

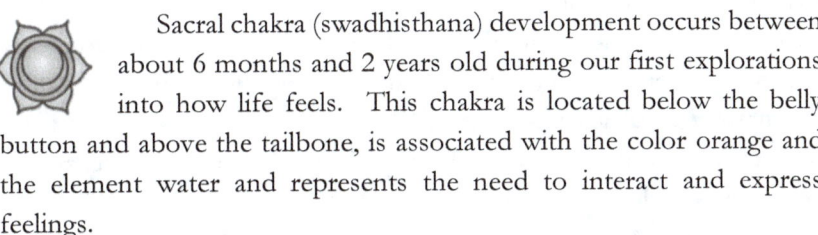Sacral chakra (swadhisthana) development occurs between about 6 months and 2 years old during our first explorations into how life feels. This chakra is located below the belly button and above the tailbone, is associated with the color orange and the element water and represents the need to interact and express feelings.

If we were encouraged safe separation during motor development, to experiment with touch and taste, to report on how things felt; and were NOT confined from movement for long periods, given messages that our feelings were unacceptable, were punished for curiosity, or consistently entertained by electronics, or were abused in ways that proved it was not ok to feel, then we can begin developing healthy authenticity. A balanced sacral chakra shows up as feeling ok to be yourself, express your feelings, have rhythm and graceful movement, be emotionally intelligent, enjoy pleasure and creative expression in life, and have relative ease in establishing healthy boundaries.

Some caregivers limit a child's exploratory movements to "keep them safe" or were conformed as children themselves and in turn find fault with a child who resists conformance. Toddlers who are punished for expressing feelings can be confused as to which aspects of their authenticity are acceptable and develop built-in guilt for feeling - impacting all chakras above.

If feelings aren't real, how is it ok to act, to love, to speak or to trust?

A child who grows up without the ability to feel for themselves can develop adult behaviors that reflect either a constant seeking of validation from others or a desire to not feel at all. Deficient sacral chakra energy shows up as lack of emotion, guardedness and rigidity, excessive boundaries, resistance to change, lack or denial of desire, repressed intimacy, and poor social skills. Excess sacral chakra energy can present as sexual promiscuity beyond what is safe, overly strong emotions, a lack of healthy boundaries and invasion of other's boundaries, co-dependence, pleasure addictions, over sensitivity, seductive manipulation, emotional dependency, obsessive attachment, and compulsive behavior. If we don't learn to depend upon our own healthy feelings for feedback in the world, we may later develop reproductive and sexual conditions, menstrual issues, rigidness in body, urinary system problems, and low back pain.

As a parent myself I wanted my toddler to behave in a certain way since I thought his behavior reflected upon how well I was doing as a Mom, but definitions I associated with correct behavior interfered with my child's development. Sure, there was concern for his safety, but looking back it is easy to see that it was more about my safety.

Not until my 30s did I realize that not everyone was as rigid as I was, and in fact some people went far outside the lines I considered safe and were still responsible people. I became drawn to friendships with those who felt freer in expressing their emotions and bodies than I did. With their examples and self-imposed solo dancing in the park to a Tom Petty cover band on weekends one summer, I felt some guilt lose its grip.

The originality of you is not meant to be guilted into some false standard supposedly applicable to all humans.

These methods promote healthy energy in your sacral chakra:

- Water, dancing, movement therapy, emotional release therapy, and inner child work.
- Fruits, nuts, and sweet spices.
- Poses and breathing techniques for the sacral chakra.
- Seed sound "Vam."
- Dhyana mudra.
- Cinnamon or grapefruit oils.

Right to Act

Solar Plexus (manipura) development occurs between about 2 and 4 years old when we begin to build our self-esteem. This chakra is located just above the navel, is associated with the color yellow and the element of fire and is the need of self-empowerment.

Appropriate adult guidance can support understanding how actions can be helpful or hurtful but harming or shaming a child for empowering themselves is not beneficial for learning parameters. If our early environment encouraged self-motivated actions such as cleaning up after ourselves, pouring our own juice, independent play, etc., and did NOT include narrowly defined behavior (in general, culturally, religiously), being a caregiver to an adult or being shamed for innocent mistakes, then willpower, self-esteem, and resilience skills develop in balance and show up as a healthy ego that exhibits capability, confidence, reliability, playfulness, appropriate self-discipline, and personal power.

Unfortunately, many caregivers were pressured to succeed, punished for innocent mistakes, or weren't allowed to do for themselves, and so don't exhibit confident actions themselves. Children unsure of what and how to do for themselves can develop an ego fused with shame that leads to shallowness of action. Deficient solar plexus chakra energy shows up as poor self-discipline, low self-esteem, coldness, poor digestion, stimulant addiction, blaming others, unreliability, passive aggressive manipulation, and avoidance of confrontation. Excess energy shows up in behaviors that are controlling, stubborn, manipulative, lacking in mind-body connection, and in deceit to self and others as unconscious fronts to cover up self-doubt. Imbalances can show up as chronic fatigue, high blood pressure, eating disorders, hypertension, stomach, pancreas, gall bladder, and liver disorders. And further efforts to love, speak, trust, and connect can feel superficial because decisions seem to lack value.

Perceived barriers to action can be superficial and failure is paramount to resilience. For example, years ago, a friend and I stood in the mountains of Nicaragua and negotiated with a driver for transport over the land border at Los Manos to the then homicide capital of the world, Tegucigalpa, Honduras. Our driver, Roberto, was 40 years old, tall, stout, with thick black hair and wide smile. Upon our approach to the inner city, beaded sweat ran down his furrowed brow, and he veered to the curb of what felt like a war zone and stepped into oncoming traffic while men drank gasoline and breathed fire at us.

The next morning our small plane violently took off for a 5000-foot climb over the mountains to La Ceiba, a jungle town that met us with heavy sheets of rain that left us sloshing through streets of sewage in search of a man named Mino, who would soon warn us,

"What we encounter in Mosquita is only for the adventurous."

Come morning, Mino threw our bags into the back of a truck to a small barefoot boy standing atop a giant mound of building supplies. Our little house on wheels then crossed swollen creeks until the road turned to the beach of the raging Atlantic Ocean. Hours later, at a large lagoon, two young boys with dugout boats attached to pallets waved us onto their "raft," but a tire slipped, perching us on imminent disaster. The boys quickly stabilized it all before pulling us across a lagoon in a dead tree. Though it seemed impossible, those boys found a way.

"Go confidently in the direction of your dreams"
- Henry David Thoreau.

These methods promote healthy energy in your solar plexus chakra:

- Take risks for action or opportunities for relaxing, core stability.
- Digestive spices like turmeric, cumin, fennel, mint, and ginger.
- Poses and breathing techniques for the solar plexus chakra.
- Seed sound "Ram."
- Rudra mudra or Surya mudra.
- Bergamot or wintergreen oils.

Right to Love

 Heart (anahata) chakra development occurs between about 4 and 7 years old when we experience feelings of compassion. Anahata, the Sanskrit word for the heart chakra is translated to unstruck, unbroken, and unhurt. This chakra is located at the level of the heart, is associated the color light green and the element of air and is a pivotal developmental need for love to include compassion, empathy, forgiveness, altruism, and unconditional self-love.

Since our experiences thus far in life show up at the door of our heart chakra, who we need love from the most depends upon on previous experiences. Our heart's natural warmth begins to expand from the inside when we receive love from who we most need it from that is steadfast, caring, compassionate, forgiving and kind, which is not conditional, indifferent, jealous, or sacrificial, and doesn't involve abandonment (perceived or real),

Often, we seek love from adults that cannot genuinely love themselves. Perhaps a parent said the words "I love you" and provided gifts of that love, yet a sense of indifference or lack of inner quality permeated the child/parent's relationship because the parent was experiencing their own heart imbalance. The unheard message transmits to a child perhaps more profoundly than what is said and done. Children cannot process cognitively like adults and so the missing pieces get integrated into the child's developing perceived worthiness of love.

The heart is a balancing point between the dense energy of the right to be here, to feel and to act, and the lighter energy in the right to speak, to trust and to be connected. When conditions are tied to love, such as "I love you if you do ____," then energy is pushed downward to the solar plexus and actions become intertwined with love. But true self-love cannot develop through external validation. Deficient heart chakra energy shows up as isolation and loneliness whereas excess shows up as poor boundaries, jealousy, compulsive "helping," and self-identification through relationships with others. Imbalances of the heart chakra in development may represent as a sunken area around the heart, pain between the shoulder blades (an area of "armor" to protect the heart), heart conditions, including circulatory issues, and asthma.

Perceived limitations to genuine love counteract the natural lightness of the heart, as well as impact the chakras downward and/or upward. But it is never too late to go the child within and bestow love within. Take the story of a girl named Mercy who lives in Gulu, Uganda, where less than a decade ago, almost half of the children were missing both parents, owing to the atrocities waged by the Lord's Resistance Army and the HIV and Aids epidemic. Grandmothers, aunts, cousins, and strangers stepped forward to care for and love these children.

One of these adults was Sally, 62-year-old homemaker from Indiana who arranged donations through her church for school, medical care, and food. But she felt something was missing, so she went to Uganda to find orphans and talk with them about their lives. After a few of Sally's visits, Mercy's heart seemed to grow larger. The day I met Mercy outside of a small earthen hut, she squeezed my hand while presenting her drawings of Sally and other sponsors in a story of love and forgiveness. With joy radiating from her small frame, she explained "Love and joy belong to everyone, even those in different tribes."

When I fall in love with me,
Then I feel love in the world
and see mercy everywhere.

These methods promote healthy energy in your heart chakra:
- Relationship therapy, journaling, and massage.
- Green foods, herbs, and teas (soothing for your dosha).
- Poses and breathing techniques for the heart chakra.
- Seed sound "Yam."
- Lotus mudra.
- Geranium or melaleuca oils.

Right to Truth

*"Three things cannot long be hidden:
the sun, the moon, and the truth"* - Confucius.

Throat (vishuddha) chakra development occurs between about 7 and 12 years old when we learn to discern and share messages. This chakra is located at the level of the throat, associated with the color sky blue and the element of ether or space, and represents our need to express ourselves, speak and hear the truth.

If messages around us were open, transparent, and based in objective views encouraging independent research and validation rather than perceived illusions, then our voices and ears can be tuned like a musical instrument that can communicate clearly and listen well with internal resonance. On the other hand, mixed messages and those that threaten our basic rights, as well as outright lies, threats for telling the truth, and deliberate hiding of the truth counteract the fluidity and spaciousness of listening and speaking. Questionable merits of what we learn through external messages makes discernment difficult. Smart phones show countless claims of truth at our fingertips and determining which are correct can be overwhelming and result in more uncertainty, thus shaping perspectives that hinder upper chakra trust and connection.

Deficient throat chakra energy demonstrates an unconscious effort to not be heard such as introversion, fear of speaking, weakness of voice, difficulty expressing our thoughts, shyness, and poor tone and rhythm. Conversely, excess energy shows up as too much talking, talking over others, poor comprehension, lack of awareness of how interrupting is disruptive, gossiping, and a dominating voice. Imbalanced throat chakra energy may show up as disorders of throat, ears, voice, neck, and jaw.

While practicing listening and hearing can improve our expressive abilities, we cannot fully develop the potentiality of our message if lies are part of that message. Denying fundamental truths about ourselves to achieve acceptance takes away from our message's potency, regardless of how loud and well it is shared. For example, my brother, Wyatt, earned a full-ride scholarship to college and became a successful medical doctor. His efforts earned him widespread respect and a platform for important messages. But he mostly hid the truth that he was gay until coming out in his early 30s. When he felt ready to face possible loss so that he could feel whole, his act of liberation resulted in some saying his "lifestyle" was a sin and abomination that would condemn him to Hell.

Soon thereafter, on a cold winter morning in the Spearfish Canyon of South Dakota, my brother tried to jumpstart his Porsche with his Land Rover but ice patched asphalt in his steep driveway caused his car to roll backwards. Wyatt rushed to stop the car, but instead the Porsche ran him over and drug him into a ravine, where he lay pinned. Wyatt's partner dialed 911 and set the phone next to Wyatt under the car before heroically lifting the car just enough to allow the air Wyatt needed to explain what would need to happen if he had any chance of survival.

Wyatt's accident and recovery offered a way into freedom of truth in all areas of his life and even catapulted a new professional path that aligns fully with his gifts, talents, and education. Many in his family experienced his accident and recovery as eye and heart opening as well. While some family members remain trapped in their own prisons of judgement, Wyatt has been a force of love, freedom, and truth for countless others. Each of our truths holds a message that needs to be heard, as there is no lasting relief of suffering in the world possible until it is so.

These methods promote healthy energy in your throat chakra:
- Quiet time, singing, mantra, talk therapy, and listening.
- Juices, teas, and water.
- Poses and breathing techniques for the throat chakra.
- Seed sound "Ham" and Hakini mudra.
- Lavender or oregano oils

Right to Trust

3rd Eye (ajna) chakra development occurs between about 13 and 18 years old when we want to trust we can make good life decisions. This chakra is located just above the center of the eyebrows, is associated with the color indigo (like a night sky) and the element of light and is our developmental need of inner wisdom to guide us in a world that is anything but concrete.

Balance in this chakra shows up as trusting that our 6th sense and intuition are inspiring us to action toward our purpose or away from what is adharmic (not a good fit for our harmony), as well as an openness to visualization, memories, dreams, and symbolism. However, experiencing betrayals or hidden truths can interfere with trust in ourselves. Deficient 3rd Eye chakra energy makes it difficult to imagine outcomes, remember details or dreams, and expand beyond self-delusion, leaving denial and rigid belief systems in place as guides rather than actual wisdom. Excessive energy shows up as difficulty concentrating, hallucinations, obsessions, and frequent nightmares. Imbalances can lead to headaches, vision issues, and impeded memory.

Problems trusting our inner guide or compass cannot be fixed with rationale as higher levels of awareness and consciousness are outside of normal thought processes. However, what feels wrong or unfulfilling often is clearly showing us a different direction that is right for us. For example, a woman named Donna was on horseback in the Sierra Madre foothills of Mexico when she came across a mirage of bones with fur. She rode nearer to the vision and, discovering it was a horse, wheeled her mount around and galloped into town for help. George and his wife Loretta, a couple from California living in Mexico, loaded their jeep with feed and headed into the mountains to find the starving horse.

As the would-be rescuers neared the lone horse with life-saving oats, the young adult appaloosa walked away from them. Within minutes, the starving horse emerged from the trees again, this time with 6 other horses, including a young colt whose mother was dead. Next came a flurry of decisions – what and how much to feed the horses until they could get further care, how to pay for the horse's veterinary care, how to convince the horse's owner to release his animals, etc. And how would they get the horses to refuge as they were too weak to walk?

Miracles of life sustaining food, water, needed funds and permission came through, and soon George stood in front of the horses that hadn't been handled in a long time, if ever. Most would not survive the stress of being roped and forced into what appeared to be a metal cage, so George simply opened the back door of the trailer and waited. The horse from Donna's earlier vision walked slowly toward George and directly into the trailer. The other 6 horses followed. After they arrived at their new home and the trailer door opened, all horses walked knowingly out and into the care of those rallying for their survival. The horse's leader came out last, taking one step before falling - never to rise again.

The horse was named Chance for his heroic actions. George and Loretta erected a permanent refuge with the help of locals, foreign travelers, and retirees. Teenage Mexican boys trained the horses to work with special-needs children. The refuge continues to this day, with a beaded horse skull made by the Huichol people announcing the horse cemetery, in an ongoing vision and meaning of life.

Our internal compass always knows the way to miracles of chance.

These methods promote healthy energy in your 3rd Eye chakra:
- Mandalas, symbolism, imaginative writing, time in natural light.
- Nightshade berries and red wine or grape juice.
- Meditation, poses, and breathing techniques for the 3rd Eye.
- Seed sound "Aum."
- Gyan mudra.
- Clary sage or lavender oils.

90

Right to Connect

 Crown (sahasrara) chakra development occurs in adulthood when we begin to expand our thoughts, actions, and behaviors to include a bigger picture. This chakra is located on top of the head, is associated with the colors of violet or white and the element of thought and represents our need to experience universal connection. Energy in the crown chakra reflects all chakras below it and is integral to a meaningful adult life.

Religion, or lack of one, can prove to be either an obstacle or pathway to grace. Seeking attunement in a world of matter can either deliver more rigidity or expand universal connection – which one prevails depends upon whether there is a basis of spiritual freedom or condemnation of self and others. Forced spiritual dogma, denied education, blind obedience, and misinformation stifle awareness, rather than support it.

A balanced crown chakra shows up as outward radiance, heightened awareness and analysis capabilities, and an openness to new ideas. Deficient energy shows up as rigid belief systems, spiritual cynicism, learning difficulties, indifference to suffering outside of an "acceptable" group of people, and condemnation of, or imposing force to obtain compliance from, those with new ideas or other beliefs. Excess energy shows up as spiritual addiction, over-intellectualization, confusion, and dissociation from one's body. If crown chakra energy does not develop fully by mid-life, energy can be forced downward for storage; however, events in one's life that cause significant suffering can elevate awareness in soul-opening ways. Whether those glimpses develop into sustained liberation, or flicker on and off, depends upon the level of suffering and the unraveling work that one is willing to do.

On the Salkantay route trek to Machu Picchu, I had already survived a snowcapped mountain of 16,000 ft, giardia, and landslides, so I added a bonus hike up Huayna Picchu, the mountain towering 1100 feet over

Machu Picchu. The recorded death toll on this hike was around 20 people, but there was no way to know. My group of friends hiked steadily up the engineering miracle of a route, a mile long trail adorned with steel cables for survival, and a foot path carved into a granite face, stark against the sky with nothing but sheer drop offs for viewing pleasures, snaking its way up to a complex of boulders requires contortionist skills for admittance.

Near the top, fear overcame me, and I fixed my gaze to my feet. Within short order, I was alone – and lost. My group had turned to stay on the trail while I had walked into the death trap of a 100-foot-high incline fashioned for ancient Incas with faith in gods I knew nothing about. Behind me existed a deadly steep rock face not conducive to the continuance of life. I yelled as loudly as I could. No one came.

Suspended 2 miles above safety on about a 170-degree incline, I prayed for intervention from Jesus, God, Pachamama and all Incan Gods of all times. Almost instantly, peace enveloped me and carried me upward over a giant boulder and through a crevasse where my friends were happily taking selfies. The seen of this world were oblivious to my struggle, while the unseen saved my life.

Vulnerability can reveal vistas of connecting trails that were previously invisible, and higher connections can light the way through all paths, and to all as one.

An untethered soul sees all paths.

These methods promote healthy energy in your crown chakra:
- Prayer or meditation, chanting with a mala or rosary.
- Cleanses and fasting.
- Poses and breathing techniques for the crown chakra.
- Seed sound "Aum."
- Hakini mudra.
- Melissa or rosemary oils.
- Sage, copal, myrrh, frankincense, and juniper incenses.

Self-Study

This exercise is to support the breaking of negative cycles. Mental health support is encouraged.

1. Chakra Reflection. For questions #1-#5, first try to provide answers relevant to the ages shown for each chakra. If you know of a relevant event later in life, include that answer as well.

2. Chakra Map. Answers for #6 go on the image (see example). If you are uncertain as to #6. e., review the final paragraph of each chakra in this chapter.

Chakra Map

Root Chakra (Womb to 1 year old)
1. What do you know about your birth?
2. In your first year, were there big challenges you know of (adoptions, mental or health issues, family addictions, poverty, other traumas)?
3. What kind of nurturing do you think came from your mother or caregiver (breastfeeding, holding, caring for needs)?
4. Was my mother or caregiver comfortable in their own body?
5. Did an event occur that ripped the rug out from under you (significant accident or disease, loss of shelter, food insecurity, war, violence, etc.)?
6. Answer the questions below on your chakra map next to the Root Chakra (use one word or very short responses).
    a. My feet feel_____.
    b. My stomach feels_____.
    c. My head feels_____.
    d. This person offered me consistent nurturing_____.
    e. Changes available to me for self-nurture are_____.

Sacral Chakra (6 months to 2 years old)
1. What kind of freedom did you likely have to explore as a toddler?
2. Are you aware of any family emotional or substance dependency in your early years? If so, what?
3. What was my parent(s)/caregivers' attitude toward intimacy/openness?
4. What types of play were you drawn to in your early life?
5. Did an event occur that made you feel that it wasn't ok to feel (rejection of authenticity, religious dogma, assault, etc.)?
6. Answer the questions below on your chakra map next to the Sacral Chakra (use one word or very short responses).
    a. My nervous habit exaggerated looks like _____.
    b. I do that nervous habit because_____.
    c. If I didn't do that habit, this might happen_____.
    d. This person honored my feelings_____.
    e. Changes available to me for expression are_____.

Solar Plexus Chakra (2 to 4 years old)

1. What kind of behavior was ok in your early home or community?
2. How were you disciplined for behavior outside of the "norm"?
3. Were you a caregiver at an early age? To whom?
4. What types of play/exploration were encouraged during toddler years?
5. Did an event break your will (significant failure, bullying, etc.)?
6. Answer the questions below on your chakra map next to the Solar Plexus Chakra (use one word or very short responses).

    a. When I need to take the lead, I feel_____.
    b. In a group, I play this role_____.
    c. I feel like this when I make a mistake_____.
    d. This person supported my genuine actions (even when they didn't turn out well) _____.
    e. Change(s) towards developing a healthy ego (faithful servant to heart) are _____.

Heart Chakra (4 to 7 years old)

1. What does love mean to you?
2. In elementary school, did you feel deep rejection, heartache, or grief?
3. Before age 8, who did you need the most love from and why?
4. What role does your own self-love play in your relationships with others?
5. Did an event break your heart in a way that felt irreparable (deep rejection or loss of a loved one)?
6. Answer the questions below on your chakra map next to the Heart Chakra (use one word or very short responses).

    a. My heart feels_____.
    b. Other people's love towards me feels like_____.
    c. I want my love to be felt in this way_____.
    d. This person was an example of unconditional love _____.
    e. Change(s) I could make towards unconditional self-love are_____.

95

Throat Chakra (7 to 12 years old)

1. What message did you speak in middle school?
2. What would happen if you got up and presented in front of a group of strangers right now? Why?
3. In what ways have you learned to use your voice so that it is heard?
4. To whom do you speak your truths?
5. Did an event take away your voice in a way that you couldn't say what mattered to you (legal, abuse, threats, etc.)?
6. Answer the questions below on your chakra map next to the Throat Chakra (use one word or very short responses).
   a. I hear this around me most of the time_____.
   b. I hear this within me most of the time_____.
   c. The word(s) I am hold back on saying is _____.
   d. This person consistently asked to hear my thoughts (even when they didn't flow easily) _____.
   e. Change(s) towards speaking my truth are_____.

3rd Eye Chakra (13 to 18 years old)

1. Do you remember recurring or unique dreams? If so, describe?
2. What are some basic symbols of this dream?
3. As an older teenager, what external messages were given to you that reinforced you don't know what is right?
4. In what big ways has your ability to trust impacted your life?
5. Did unforeseeable events make you rethink what you thought you knew?
6. Answer the questions below on your chakra map next to the 3rd Eye Chakra (use one word or very short responses).
   a. My favorite myth is_____.
   b. I know this to be true about myself_____.
   c. When my mind wanders, it often sees_____.
   d. This person allowed me to discuss my options without telling me what to do_____.
   e. Change(s) towards trusting my intuition and vision are
   _____.

Crown Chakra (adulthood)

1. Name one recurring situation in your life that troubles you.
2. Write down the same situation in 3rd person.
3. What do you think or feel often that promotes a sense of separateness?
4. What do you think or feel often that promotes a sense of unity?
5. Has an event occurred that felt like your spirit must deserve punishment and/or the universe/God hates you?
6. Answer the questions below on your chakra map next to the Crown Chakra (use one word or very short responses).
   a. My divine looks like (a picture or a word) _____.
   b. If I could ask one question of my divine, it would be_____.
   c. I think my divine's answer might be_____.
   d. I am most interested in learning about now is_____.
   e. Change(s) I can see towards spiritual connection are
   _____.

3. Mantra

Experiment for yourself chanting the Bija mantras and the Ho'opononopo mantra. Try each for at least 3 minutes.

Lam, Vam, Ram, Yam, Ham, Om, Aum
Meaning: Syllables resonates with internal energy and a body part or region.

I'm sorry. Please forgive me. Thank you. I love you.
Meaning: Forgiveness prayer to support release of internal hurts to heighten self-love and compassion for others.

8. Enneagram Wisdom

"Every person is perfect, there is no conflict between head, heart, and stomach or between the person and others. Then the ego begins to develop, karma accumulates (and) man falls from essence into personality "- Ichazo.

Adding the wisdom of the Enneagram into yogic layers of inner work is not part of approved yoga teacher curriculum. But like Chakras, the Enneagram can help explain behaviors that drive personality, and how suffering can positively drive our purpose in this life.

Enneagram wisdom differs from other personality tests in that it is based upon psychology, cosmology, metaphysics, spirituality, symbolism, numerology, human consciousness theories, and holy orders of an array of religious wisdom. Parts of the Enneagram structure are ancient, but some parts date only back to the early 1900s when George Gurdjieff used its symbolism along with mindfulness and sacred movements built around basic ego structures to help people to not suffocate in their own shallowness.

Fast forward to the 1960s and Oscar Ichazo established the Arica School in Chile, building on Gurdjieff's work and further linking essence to personality/ego utilizing philosophy from Judaism, Christianity, Islam, Taoism, Buddhism, and ancient Greek philosophy (Socrates, Plato, and the Neo-Platonists). Psychologists Claudio Naranjo and John Lilly then studied with Ichazo and contributed to the modern Enneagram.

When the Jesuit order learned that the Enneagram could identify the sins people were most likely to be confronted with, Roman Catholic institutions in North America adopted the Enneagram in churches. But then Don Riso, a Jesuit in Toronto, left the seminary in 1975 to develop the Enneagram's nine levels of development (liberated or healthy to pathologically unhealthy) and publish a book on personality types in 1987. Riso, along with Russ Hudson, then founded the Enneagram Institute in New York to offer Enneagram resources to the public.

When I attended my first Enneagram training years ago, it felt like when the Chakra system and Ayurveda clicked for me . . . an awareness that universal puzzle pieces were concrete tools for life choices, relationships, self-study, and inner and outer work through the maze of human construction on the path to spiritual liberation. I incorporated wisdom of the Enneagram in daily life by frequently practicing Kundalini kriyas specifically for my Enneagram type, fusing Enneagram kriyas for all types into group yoga classes, following my ups and downs on the 9 levels of my type, incorporating Enneagram coaching into my offerings and leading retreats that included Enneagram work. Later, I trained under Russ Hudson to learn the Enneagram on a new level, which overlapped even more with ancient yoga, including a 7-minute daily meditation of mindfulness to tune into body, mind, and spirit – or the gut (instincts), body (feeling), and mind (thinking).

In a nutshell, the Enneagram has nine types of personality with differing strengths, weaknesses, fears, desires, predictable evolution and spiraling paths, arrows pointing to alignment and arrows pointing away from it. It also offers the insight of wings (types closest to our number on either side). In addition to a basic type and a leaning wing, a person also falls somewhere on the spectrum of favoring one of three basic human needs (survival, intimacy, social belonging). All information can spotlight where someone can benefit from self-development, and what tools can provide maximum benefit.

The 9 types of personality and wing combinations together result in over 45 ways individual personality may express itself. To find out your Enneagram type combination, you can take an on-line quiz through various sources such as Eclectic Energies or the Enneagram Institute. However, simply taking the quiz does not ensure a valid result. If your answers to questions are too vague (like answering a lot of "somewhat")

99

or are self-deceptive (threatened ego answers) or are lacking awareness (reflecting what others would say to do and think), then results may not be valuable. Answering questions truthfully and as decisively as possible while considering long spans of time in life rather than isolated incidents will lead to meaningful quiz results. It can also help to take multiple quizzes, read Enneagram books, listen to podcasts, etc. Working with a mental health therapist certified in Enneagram wisdom may be necessary for those with significant trauma that has impacted baseline behaviors.

Landing on your correct Enneagram combination can feel like a much-needed embrace that also reveals issues to face. When you've got your match, you realize you are not alone in your struggles, that you can improve relationships and experiences, and that suddenly even confusing parts of you make remarkable sense. On the other hand, Enneagram wisdom can be worthless if it is used only as theory.

There is no Enneagram type or combination that is best, and we all have aspects of each of the 9 types. In fact, similarities between types are prevalent in all type's healthiest levels. The average and unhealthy levels are where more distinct differences between types show up. The practice of consistent awareness of where your behavior is on the continuum of your type's levels can help you consciously evaluate choices to stay where you are, spiral downward, or uplevel. Upleveling can occur by making choices towards healthy behaviors of the type in the direction of your growth area, and spiraling can occur by fixating on unhealthy behaviors of the type in the direction of your stress direction.

As an Enneagram 7, Wing 8, who favors Self-Preservation instinct, I can look at both Enneagram 7 and 8's lists of behaviors. When I ask myself where I'm showing up, I might recognize my 7 showing up at level 2, as me being responsive, enthusiastic, resilient, and cheerful; and my 8 showing up at level 4 as enterprising, pragmatic, risk-taking, and hardworking but denying my own emotional needs. And while all that sounds exciting, I'm doing most of it by myself because my self-preservation boundaries are nearly concrete.

100

If I want to continue a trajectory of wellness, the directional lines of stress and growth and my instinctual blind spot can show me the way. In this case, continued goodness means using my resources to deal with destructive thoughts and actions of unhealthy 1s (punitive and depressive) or unhealthy 5s (reclusive and isolated); and I can encourage thoughts or take actions in the direction of growth towards healthy 5s (practice skills and learn something) and healthy 2s (practice empathy and compassion).

Finally, finding ways to get out of my self-imposed bubble of self-preservation to work on one-on-one relationships with people I vibe with will add to my well-being. Simplicity unfolds once you are within the wisdom, or rather the wisdom is within you.

Theory without practice doesn't work.

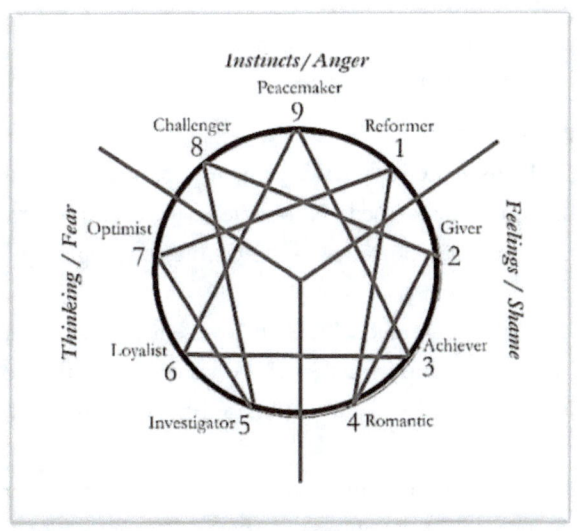

Reformer (1)

Gifts	Principled, purposeful, organized, self-controlled, ethical, teachers, crusaders, and advocates for change.
Challenges	Critical, perfectionistic, resentful, and impatient.
Wings	1w9 – Idealist / 1 w2 – Advocate
Basic Fears	Being corrupt/evil, defective
Basic Desire	Goodness, integrity, balance
In stress	Moody and irrational like unhealthy Fours
In growth	Spontaneous and joyful, like healthy Sevens

Childhood Message Heard	It's not okay to make mistakes.
Childhood Message Not Heard	You are ok even if you "fail."
Child Learned he/she is good IF	You do what is right.

Summary of the 1

- ✓ Have a strong sense of purpose but also feel a strong need for justification.
- ✓ Their convictions/judgments can drain them of their good instincts/drive.
- ✓ Concerned about expressing concerns, leading to resistance and rigidity.

I could change the world tomorrow, as long as it is the exact right thing.

Healthy Levels

- ✓ Level 1: Transcendentally wise, humane, inspiring, truthful.
- ✓ Level 2: Spiritually focused, reasonable, mature, and moderate.
- ✓ Level 3: Principled, objective, sense of integrity/higher purpose.

Average Levels

- ✓ Level 4: Idealist, feels uniquely able to problem solve, won't take criticism.
- ✓ Level 5: Orderly/impersonal workaholics driven by fears of mistakes.
- ✓ Level 6: Critical, judgmental, perfectionistic, scolding, and impatient.

Unhealthy Levels

- ✓ Level 7: Self-righteous, intolerant, absolute (only they know the truth).
- ✓ Level 8: Hypocritically obsessive of other's imperfection/wrongdoing.
- ✓ Level 9: Punitive, cruel, obsessive-compulsive, and depressive.

Giver (2)

Gifts	Loving, helpful, generous, considerate, appreciative.
Challenges	Pride, self-deception, selfishness, manipulation
Wings	2w1 – Servant / 2w3 – Host/Hostess
Basic Fears	Of being unwanted, unworthy of being loved
Basic Desire	To feel loved
In stress	Aggressive and dominating like unhealthy Eights
In growth	Self-nurturing and emotionally aware like healthy Fours

Childhood Message Heard	It's not ok to have own needs.
Childhood Message Not Heard	You are wanted.
Child Learned he/she is good IF	You are loving/giving to others.

Summary of the 2

- ✓ Generosity to others can feel paramount.
- ✓ Either genuinely helpful or highly invested in seeing themselves as helpful.
- ✓ Lack of validation of their worth can reinforce lack of value within, resulting in a hiding of silent emotional needs.

I will do everything you need, besides what I don't think you need.

Healthy Levels

- ✓ Level 1: Unselfish and grateful, humble, altruistic, unconditional love.
- ✓ Level 2: Empathetic, compassionate, thoughtful, forgiving, and sincere.
- ✓ Level 3: Encouraging, appreciative, service-oriented, nurturing.

Average Levels

- ✓ Level 4: People pleasing, seductive with attention, love is the goal.
- ✓ Level 5: Overly intimate, intrusive, co-dependent, controlling.
- ✓ Level 6: Self-important martyr who is overbearing and patronizing.

Unhealthy Levels

- ✓ Level 7: Self-serving/deceptive about motives, casting others as guilty.
- ✓ Level 8: Domineering, coercive and entitled, using intimacy as threat.
- ✓ Level 9: Self-victimization for being too much, resents others.

Achiever (3)

Gifts	Ambitious, capable, adaptable, charming, inspiring.
Challenges	Overly competitive, superficial, and inauthentic.
Wings	3w2 – Star / 3w4 – Professional
Basic Fears	Feeling worthless
Basic Desire	To be valued
In stress	Disengaged and apathetic like unhealthy Nines
In growth	Cooperative, committed to others, like healthy Sixes

Childhood Message Heard	It's not ok to have own feelings.
Childhood Message Not Heard	You are loved, have inner worth.
Child Learned he/she is good IF	Your success is seen by others.

Summary of the 3

✓ Often equates worth with attractiveness, activities, and achievements.

✓ Success is easy as feeling "less than" can feel intolerable.

✓ Stifled feelings, workaholism or stimulants can over-stress body/mind.

Feelings hinder success, so why do relationships require them?

Healthy Levels

✓ Level 1 (At Best): Self-accepting, authentic, modest, charitable, loving.

✓ Level 2: High self-esteem, competent, charming, and gracious.

✓ Level 3: Ambition and effective actions motivate others positively.

Average Levels

✓ Level 4: Driven to prove self-worth, comparison used for ranking.

✓ Level 5: Perform for success, issues with intimacy and credibility.

✓ Level 6: Arrogant/jealous focus on impressing to promote themselves.

Unhealthy Levels

✓ Level 7: Exploitative and opportunistic in quest for superiority.

✓ Level 8: Deceives others to hide issues, betrays self/others for triumph.

✓ Level 9: Vindictive, relentless, obsessive, and narcissistic.

Individualist (4)

Gifts	Self-awareness, unique sensitivity to other's needs, honesty, creativity, can inspire diverse groups.
Challenges	Moody, self-conscious, melancholy, self-pity
Wings	4w5 – Bohemian / 4w3 – Aristocrat
Basic Fears	Having no identity or personal significance
Basic Desire	Finding themselves and significance (for identity)
In stress	Over-involved and clinging like unhealthy Twos
In growth	More objective and principled like healthy Ones

Childhood Message Heard	It's not ok to be happy/practical.
Childhood Message Not Heard	You are seen for who you are.
Child Learned he/she is good IF	You are uniquely unique.

Summary of the 4

✓ Deep emotions allow painful experiences that overwhelm others.

✓ Feels uniquely flawed, missing something needed to be happy or to fit in.

✓ Seeks others who understand their hurts, attracts a cycle of rescuers.

Why is the big picture so clear, but my unique talents and flaws don't fit in it?

Healthy Levels

✓ Level 1: Profoundly creative, inspired, self-renewing, regenerating.

✓ Level 2: Self-aware, intuitive to self and others, tactful, compassionate.

✓ Level 3: Individualistic, humane, shows strength via vulnerability/irony.

Average Levels

✓ Level 4: Artistic, romantically oriented, high imagination and passion.

✓ Level 5: Self-conscious/absorbed, introverted, moody, withdraws.

✓ Level 6: Impractical/unproductive fantasy world with self-pity and envy.

Unhealthy Levels

✓ Level 7: Dreams fail, depression, alienation, self-shame, loses function.

✓ Level 8: Self-contempt, self-hatred, blaming others to avoid help.

✓ Level 9: Despair, self-destruction, and emotional breakdown.

Investigator (5)

Gifts	Perceptive, innovative, insightful, curious, independent, able to concentrate/focus on the complex.
Challenges	Isolated, imaginary constructs, detached, eccentric.
Wings	5w4 – Iconoclast / 5 w6 – Problem Solver
Basic Fears	Being useless, helpless, or incapable
Basic Desire	To be capable and competent
In stress	Hyperactive and scattered like unhealthy Sevens.
In growth	Self-confident and decisive, like healthy Eights

Childhood Message Heard	It's not ok to be comfortable.
Childhood Message Not Heard	Your needs are not a problem.
Child Learned he/she is good IF	You know or master things.

Summary of the 5
- ✓ Convince themselves they have few needs but pursue knowledge in spades.
- ✓ Observe and contemplate to internalize knowledge/gain self-confidence.
- ✓ Social, emotional, and physical health suffer as self-care distracts from plans.

I can master anything. So why would I waste time on self-care?

Healthy Levels
- ✓ Level 1: Visionary, pioneering new ways with great impact.
- ✓ Level 2: Observant, inquisitive, able to predict, engaged with others.
- ✓ Level 3: Excited by knowledge, industry experts, creates original works.

Average Levels
- ✓ Level 4: Conceptualizes before action, studious, specialized, intellectual.
- ✓ Level 5: Detached, intense, preoccupied, lack of mind-body connection.
- ✓ Level 6: Opposes interference, abrasive, cynical/argumentative.

Unhealthy Levels
- ✓ Level 7: Reclusive, eccentric, fearful, repulsive towards relationships.
- ✓ Level 8: Obsessed with distortions, phobic, threatened by own ideas.
- ✓ Level 9: Self-destructive psychotic breaks with reality.

Loyalist (6)

Gifts	Committed, engaging, reliable, hard-working, foresees issues and fosters cooperation.
Challenges	Self-doubt, anxiety, suspicion, rebellion, overreaction.
Wings	6w7 - Buddy / 6w5 – Defender
Basic Fears	Being without support/guidance
Basic Desire	Security and support
In stress	Competitive and arrogant like unhealthy Threes
In growth	Relaxed and optimistic like healthy Nines

Childhood Message Heard	It's not ok to trust yourself.
Childhood Message Not Heard	You are safe.
Child Learned he/she is good IF	You are responsible, do the expected.

Summary of the 6

✓ Fights for beliefs, loved ones and alliances more fiercely than for themselves.

✓ Insecure about inner guide/resources, reliance on others' beliefs is easier.

✓ Attached to positions and react as either the bully or victim, or both.

If we work together, we'll be ok – unless something bad happens.

Healthy Levels

✓ Level 1: Self-affirming, trusting, positive, courageous leaders.

✓ Level 2: Appealing, endearing, affectionate, healthy relationships.

✓ Level 3: Secure, responsible, persevering, sacrificing, community builders.

Average Levels

✓ Level 4: Vigilant focus on safety and organization; expects issues.

✓ Level 5: Passive-aggressive procrastinating, indecision, overly negative.

✓ Level 6: Sarcastic, belligerent, blaming, conspiratorial, defensive.

Unhealthy Levels

✓ Level 7: Panicky, volatile, self-disparaging and berating others, divisive.

✓ Level 8: Fanatical, irrational, or violent acts to prove what their fears.

✓ Level 9: Hysterical and self-destructive paranoid escapist.

Optimist (7)

Gifts   Multi-talented, optimistic, versatile, playful, high-spirited, practical and can make things happen.

Challenges   Too blunt, overextended/exhausted by own impatience.

Wings   7w8 – Realist / 7w6 – Entertainer

Basic Fears   FOMO, pain and being controlled

Basic Desire   Contentment and feeling they are enough

In stress   Perfectionistic and critical like unhealthy Ones

In growth   More focused and fascinated by life like healthy Fives

Childhood Message Heard	It's not ok to depend on anyone.
Childhood Message Not Heard	You will be taken care of.
Child Learned he/she is good IF	You are happy and needs are met.

Summary of the 7

✓ Upbeat cheer pervades interactions to distract from negative feelings.

✓ Acts fast rather than with grounded decisions, leading to spent resources.

✓ Gluttony can lead to ruined health, relationships, and finances.

I can do anything but regret, so why can't I find someone to take care of me?

Healthy Levels

✓ Level 1: Grateful, awed by life, joyous, spiritual, connected, grounded.

✓ Level 2: Enthusiastic, vivacious, spontaneous, resilient, and cheerful.

✓ Level 3: Multi-talented achievers; productive in many interests.

Average Levels

✓ Level 4: Adventurous, worldly wise, always seeking new experiences.

✓ Level 5: Hyperactive, performative, unable to say no to themselves.

✓ Level 6: Self-centered, materialistic, greedy, demanding, hardened.

Unhealthy Levels

✓ Level 7: Anxious and impulsive addictive escapists.

✓ Level 8: Erratic mood swings and compulsive manic actions.

✓ Level 9: Claustrophobic, panic-stricken despair.

Challenger (8)

Gifts	Self-confident, decisive, strong, assertive, protective, charismatic, straight-talking – "The Cowboy"
Challenges	Willful, confrontational, ego-centric, domineering
Wings	8w9 – Bear / 8w7 – Maverick
Basic Fears	Of being harmed or controlled
Basic Desire	Protection and control of own life
In stress	Secretive and fearful like unhealthy Fives
In growth	More open-hearted and caring like healthy Twos

Childhood Message Heard	You cannot be vulnerable.
Childhood Message Not Heard	Trusting others is ok.
Child Learned he/she is good IF	You are strong and in control.

Summary of the 8

✓ Physically and psychologically capable of persuading others to follow them.

✓ To achieve big goals, they can develop fortitude while blockading their heart.

✓ Fear of disempowerment increases pain tolerance. Rejection can lead to shut-down.

If I'm in the lead, I can save us all. If needed, I can also destroy us all.

Healthy Levels

✓ Level 1: Calm, courageous, merciful, heroic, spiritual surrender.

✓ Level 2: Self-confident, resourceful, uplifting others with compassion.

✓ Level 3: Decisive, commanding, protective, honorable, a natural leader.

Average Levels

✓ Level 4: Pragmatic, risk-taking, hardworking, denies own needs.

✓ Level 5: Dominating, boastful, egocentric, sees weakness in others.

✓ Level 6: Intimidating, confrontational, belligerent, adversarial, unjust.

Unhealthy Levels

✓ Level 7: Defiant, ruthless, dictatorial, criminal, immoral con-artist.

✓ Level 8: Delusional about their power, feeling invulnerable.

✓ Level 9: Antisocial, vengeful, destructive, and sociopathic.

Peacekeeper (9)

Gifts	Receptive, reassuring, accepting, trusting, stable, creative, optimistic, and supportive
Challenges	Complacent, stubborn, simplifying problems to minimize
Wings	9w8 – Comfort Seeker / 9w1 – Dreamer
Basic Fears	Loss and separation
Basic Desire	Inner stability/peace of mind
In stress	Anxious and worried like unhealthy Sixes
In growth	More self-developing and energetic like healthy Threes

Childhood Message Heard	It's not ok to assert yourself.
Childhood Message Not Heard	Your presence matters.
Child Learned he/she is good IF	Everyone around you is ok.

Summary of the 9
- ✓ Desires peace and connection.
- ✓ Can lack a sense of strong identity yet is grounded physically.
- ✓ Can bypass tension/suffering with false peace, denial, or daydreams.

I can be of great service to the world, as long as there isn't any conflict.

Healthy Levels
- ✓ Level 1: Autonomous, fulfilled, equanimous, profound relationships.
- ✓ Level 2: Receptive, accepting, emotionally stable, trusting and patient.
- ✓ Level 3: Optimistic, harmonizing, group mediator, good at synthesizing and communicating.

Average Levels
- ✓ Level 4: Self-effacing, accommodating, saying yes to deflect conflict.
- ✓ Level 5: Inattentive, complacent, tuning out, oblivious.
- ✓ Level 6: Stubborn, procrastinating, and unresponsive.

Unhealthy Levels
- ✓ Level 7: Repressed, neglectful, ineffectual, obstinate, denial.
- ✓ Level 8: Dissociates to the point of numbness and loss of function.
- ✓ Level 9: Catatonic dependence on false realities and others.

Self-Study

1. Take the free Enneagram quizzes on-line or elsewhere. One quiz recommended is https://www.eclecticenergies.com/enneagram/test (both the classical test and the test that includes instinctual variants). Screenshot or email your results to yourself.
2. Review your primary type and wing summaries and note all words that resonate with you.
3. Review the "in stress" unhealthy behaviors and "in growth" healthy behaviors of the types your personality moves to naturally in periods of stress and growth and note words that resonate with you.
4. Note what behaviors or actions you might exhibit when you are spiraling downward so you can catch yourself.
5. Note what activities or actions might help you uplevel on a given day.
6. Experiment for yourself for three consecutive days doing a self-guided 7-minute meditation in which you bring awareness to your gut (instincts), body (feeling), and mind (thinking).

9. Science of Ayurveda

When I reached my 40s and wanted to lessen my pain, one of the first things I did was clean up my diet. Removing coffee, gluten, meat, dairy, and processed foods promoted improvement in energy and mood, but didn't help my stress levels, stomach problems, or neck pain.

Medical tests confirmed that I was very fit . . . except for gallbladder disfunction, depleted hormones, chronic fecal stasis, early osteopenia, decaying teeth, and joint and muscle pain. Well-intentioned doctors offered prescriptions, pain management, and surgeries. When I sought mental health care, overwhelmed therapists said I didn't need it.

Years later without any improvement, I took an on-line Ayurvedic quiz to discover that my constitution was primarily Pitta, and imbalance was primarily Kapha. A yoga teacher, Luz, looked at my quiz, then at me with eyebrows raised "really?" She stood me next to another student who was a Pitta and told us to outstretch our arms. Luz asked the other students what they thought I was by my body presentation.

Everyone said Vata in unison.

With the help of Ayurveda, I at last had a frame in which to look at my body differently and begin to appreciate what it had done for me over the years. Soon thereafter, during formal Ayurveda training, my teacher pointed to the parts of a plant and seemed to stare straight at me. "All of the answers are easy when you understand the elements." Between tattvas (elements) and koshas (layers of being), Ayurveda offers fresh perspective that, combined with western medicine, fills in gaps that may not otherwise make sense.

Your Dosha (constitution at birth), also called Prakriti, includes some combination of the pancha mahabhutas, five elements of earth, water, fire, air, and space that exist in nature, which are fire (transforms), water (lubricates), earth (binds), air (shifts), ether (opens). Blockages to wellness can then be found by examining one's current imbalances, also called Vikruti (after creation). This book's companion, *Body as Teacher*, provides quizzes for your dosha and current imbalance.

Ayurveda includes treatment to restore harmony, including therapies, panchakarma (detoxification), natural pharmaceuticals, daily routine and nutrition, mudras, exercise, yoga, and psychology. To practice as a doctor of Ayurveda in India, Nepal, Pakistan, and Sri-Lanka requires an advanced medical degree and internship. Most other countries have no regulatory guidelines around Ayurveda. and many medical doctors lack training or experience in whole person individual approaches to wellness, so people may seek alternative practices like Functional Health.

The information presented here can be a fresh look at why the "one size fits all" perspectives don't seem to work. The animal associations used are to help make sense of each Dosha's gifts.

Vata *(bird)*   **Pitta** *(lion)*   **Kapha** *(bear)*

Lion, body ready, flames blazing in water,
Earth, air, and ether are offering cool change for progress.

Bird, head in the clouds, wind, and stars,
Earth, water, and fire are offering grounding to unite perspectives.

Bear, gentle heart of Earth and water,
Fire, air, and ether are offering power to heal the world.

Doshas

Doshas Overall	Vata (Bird) Air & Ether	Pitta (Lion) Fire & Water	Kapha (Bear) Earth & Water
Overall Qualities	Moving, expressing Inspiring, Uniting	Doing, organizing Transforming, Manifesting	Enduring, cohesion Stability, Healing
Balancing Food	Warm, moist Sweet, sour, salty High protein/fat	Cool, hearty Rough, sweet High in carbs	Warm, dry Light, spicy, Easy to digest
Aggravating	Cold, dry, bitter	Hot, spicy, salty	Oily, sweet, salty
Best Sleep Cycle	Sleep by 9pm Wake by 6am	Sleep by 10pm Wake by 7am	Sleep by 10pm Wake by 5am
Challenging Times of Day	2pm-6pm depleted 2am-6am insomnia	10am-2pm hunger/heat 10pm-2am active mind	6am-10am slow, sleep 6pm-10pm sluggish
Balancing Asanas	Heated space Slower, grounded Core engaging Balancing poses Moderate flexibility Pelvis/colon focus	Cooler space Nurturing, relaxing Yin with less tension Backbends Moderate poses Sm intestine/liver focus	Warmer space Energizing, fast-paced Challenging Emotional Releases Minimal slow/low Circulation focus
Balancing Pranayama (there are more)	Equal Count Abdominal Left Nostril Ujjayi, Breath of Fire	Sitali Alternate Nostril Balancing Opposite breaths	Breath of Fire Right Nostril Ujjayi Longer inhales
Aggravating Asanas	Yin or cold Fast moving Deep twists Forward bends	Hot yoga/heat Highly technical High intensity Short savasanas	Yin or cold space Restorative/savasana Forward bends Slow moving/holds
Balancing Exercises	Qigong, hiking, Weights, warm swims	Qigong, hiking, Cold water swims	Early group workouts like jogging, dancing
Overall Self-Care	Presences and rest Salt or steam baths Connect with body Sesame massage	Allow stillness Celebrate the process Practice forgiveness Coconut massage	Creative expression Loving self-care Clear clutter Sunflower massage
Optimum Digestion	Restrict iced drinks, processed and herbicide treated foods. Largest meal at lunch and last meal 2 hours before bed.		

Continuum of Change

In Ayurveda, states of change are called Gunas, and life is a continuum of alternation at play between 3 changing states:

*R*ajasic state: *productive*, motivating, aggressive and passionate

*T*amasic state: *depressive* qualities of dullness or lethargy

*S*attvic state: *virtuous* and balanced with heightened awareness

In life, we may get exhausted or sad about something and hunker down until something or some emotion such as anger or boredom sparks our motivation to make a change, and then we have an ah-ha wisdom experience and feel harmonious until we discover maybe we were wrong about something or there is more to do to achieve balance.

While we are in the predominant guna, we draw more of the same (same type of feelings, choices, people, etc.) and if we stay too long in a depression or aggression, it may feel impossible to get out as like draws like. Often, something unexpected happens to push us into another cycle.

Modern medicine often views of states of change as a need for correction. But Ayurveda says the answer is more complex and requires addressing the koshas, all layers of being. Identifying where the source problem is that is wreaking the most havoc and thus affecting all other koshas is part of Ayurvedic science. This book also uses this koshic approach to Fusion yoga sequencing in Part 3.

The 5 koshas currently used in Ayurveda and in most yoga:

*A*nnamaya/Physical	*tangible* aspect of ourselves
*P*ranamaya/Energetic	*subtle power* beyond physical body
*M*anomaya/Mental	*beliefs*, absorbed pre-conditioning
*V*ijnanamaya/Wisdom	*awareness*, intuition, observation
*A*nandamaya/Bliss	*essence*, natural goodness

Ayurveda also uses gunas as a prescriptive measure. For example, if you feel tamasic and ready for a change, you can support change through self-inquiry, rajasic or sattvic activities and limiting food that is tamasic.

	TAMAS	RAJAS	SATTVA
Overall	Dull	Extroverted	Calm
Awareness	Hidden	Limited	Heightened
Season	Winter	Summer	Fall / Spring
Emotion	Depression, laziness	Anger, anxiety, boredom	Happy, present
Action	Sluggish	Aggressive	Wise
Perspective	Fear colors experience	Desire colors experience	Truth
Upside	Rest	Motivation Accomplishments	Clarity Proper perception
Downside	Hinders self-inquiry	Hinders awareness	None
Overall qualities, types, and states of foods	Difficult to digest Acts as sedatives Low quality meat/fish White flour/sugar Excess starch/sugars Excess fats and oils Preservatives Artificial flavors Canned food Battered/fried food Tobacco Hard liquor Cold/processed dairy Food in distress	Mutable Acts as stimulants High quality meat/fish A lot of spice, salt, sour Jarred foods Overcooked sattvic foods Wines Soda Coffee Fried foods Chocolate Food as "fuel"	Pure Acts as harmonious Fresh, lightly cooked Rice, wheat and oats Legumes, mung dal Steamed greens Fresh fruits Toasted seeds/nuts Buttermilk, curd, ghee Ginger, cardamom, cinnamon, fennel, coriander, turmeric Honey, raw sugar Food with mindfulness

116

External forces can create imbalances in our natural constitution (Doshas) and disturb one or more of our layers of being (Koshas). Those disturbances can then affect how energy is directed in our bodies (Vayus) and contribute to a state of change in our lives (Gunas).

Part 1 of this book introduced how Vayus can be consciously directed as needed for increased wellness through poses, breathing techniques, energy locks, and mantras. Sound or music therapy can also impact vayus through vibrational frequencies that can resonate via like frequencies. Mudras, outward gestures of inward intention, are yet another yogic technique that can consciously impact vayu direction.

Mudras subtly impact the brain's autonomic nerve reflexes through energy circuits of the fingers, each of which represents an element that corresponds to a kosha and one or more vayus. Each finger may also represent a meridian. Kundalini kriyas often use mudras, further linking them to planetary connections.

Yet another method of impacting koshic balance in Ayurveda is mindful eating. Meals too often can feel like a thing to fuel our energy, a distraction from stress, a way to reward productivity or compliance, or as punishment for perceived transgressions – all of which impact digestion that is tied to mental processes and physical energy being experienced.

Meals can be a transformative place to practice union of mind and body for immediate benefits. Some mindfulness practices around meals that can support digestion and mindfulness are:

✓ Add present moment awareness to chopping, cooking, and seasoning.
✓ Sit where you feel content and awake (a table or designated space).
✓ Give thanks to those who planted, harvested, and prepared foods.
✓ Eat, see, smell, feel, taste, and chew each bite separately to notice sensations in your mouth, chest, and stomach.
✓ After meals, notice a feeling of fullness and satisfaction.

117

Another Ayurvedic principle of vitality around meals is the importance of assuring the quality of an animal's life before consuming its products. Many of the practices used in large scale animal production for food are not natural, nor are they caring. When an animal has lived artificially (including crowding, expedited extreme fattening, hormone additives, etc.) and/or has died in fear, consuming that animal does not promote vitality as those qualities are not conducive to harmony. Ayurveda recognizes that knowing an animal's quality of life matters as its vitality in life is directly linked to your vitality in life.

Cows are sacred to Hindus in India as they are thought to represent the divine and therefore, should be protected. In the *Rig* Veda, the milk cow is said to be unslayable in keeping with Ahimsa (non-harming), and the cow's association with motherhood and Mother Earth.

In the late 1900s, clashes between Hindus and Muslims over clow slaughter led to anti-Muslim riots and contributed to partitioning of India in 1947. Today in India, cows are venerated for their 5 healing products (Panchagavya) of milk, curd, butter, urine, and dung.

When I travelled in India, I loved visiting cow shalas where monks tenderly care for the herds. I also felt joyful when walking down streets with cows meandering at will. So, while some products of cows are considered essential to vitality, cows in India live a mostly blissful life.

The rest of this chapter includes additional Ayurvedic approaches to wellness regarding foods, cleanses, and daily routines. Please consider your foundation of the Yamas, Niyamas and musculoskeletal basics if applying these in your own life. Ayurveda is not meant to be rigid, forced, or prescriptive in all cases as those approaches may yield outcomes opposite of Ayurveda's overall goal of harmony. If Ayurveda offers you anything in support of your best life, I hope it is a greater sense of empowerment, as well as appreciation for your amazing body.

Food For Vitality

What we consume also impacts wellness. In Ayurveda, each Dosha type has 3 tastes that are soothing and 3 tastes that can be aggravating.

Dosha	Balancing Tastes	Balancing Qualities	Aggravating Tastes
Vata	sweet, sour, salty	warmer, grounding, moist	acidic, dry, overly spicy
Pitta	sweet, acidic, dry	cooler, airy, soothing	sour, salty, spicy
Kapha	dry, spicy, acidic	warmer, airy, light	sweet, sour, salty

However, using all 6 tastes in one meal, such as a Thali plate, can somewhat balance all Doshas if also applying geographic seasonal tastes. Thali is a traditional Indian plate of 6-10 tastes that are a visually appealing contrast of colors, texture and flavors that can be digested for optimum vitality. In India, regional plates vary, but most contain some variation of: khichdi (with lentils, vegetables and spices), chutney (cooked with fruit and spices), paneer (cheese dish), curry (spicy vegetable dish), aloo (potato dish), a pickle, a flatbread (such paratha, chapati, or naan), fresh ginger or chai tea (served warm), raita or lassi (yogurt), and a sweet dessert (such as ladoo or fruit cup).

The next several pages outline foods generally balancing or aggravating to each Dosha. Not all foods are included in the interest of outlining a general list that can provide a good starting point.

No one knows your body better than you, so experimentation helps determine if these hold true for you. Eating to soothe your constitution can increase vitality, but only if you've identified your primary dosha and current imbalance. For example, a Vata with a Pitta imbalance could avoid all Pitta aggravating foods for a week to see if there is a positive shift.

Like draws like,
For better or worse.

VATA BALANCING = WARM, COOKED, SWEET, SOUR, SALTY

FRUITS
- ✓ sweet, ripe, and juicy – best on an empty stomach, not with a meal
- ✓ apricots, sweet apples, peaches, oranges, grapefruit, lemons, limes, papaya
- ✓ dates, berries, coconut, pineapple, rhubarb, tamarind, plums, kiwi, raisins

VEGETABLES
- ✓ grown low to ground, have softer texture – best cooked, steamed, wilted
- ✓ asparagus, spinach, zucchini, green beans, leafy greens, chilies, cabbage
- ✓ carrots, pumpkin, cucumber, garlic, sweet potatoes, beets, yellow squash
- ✓ avocado, leeks, parsnip, okra, black olives, onions, cauliflower in moderation

MEAT
- ✓ animals who lived naturally; dark, easily digestible meat (not overcooked)
- ✓ eggs, dark poultry, duck, dense oily fish (trout, salmon, sardines, tuna)
- ✓ beef, buffalo, elk, venison that forage (not on corn/wheat/soy crops)

DAIRY
- ✓ separate from meals (except ghee), warm and in least processed form
- ✓ ghee, butter, buttermilk, goats' milk, cheese, fresh yogurt, cottage cheese

LEGUMES
- ✓ limited amounts: split, soak, cook thoroughly with oil and digestive spices
- ✓ red/black lentils, miso, mung beans, soy-based products (not beans)

NUTS AND SEEDS
- ✓ most all (except popped corn) in moderation (high amounts task digestion)

OILS
- ✓ those that are free of toxins, organic, heavy, and least complex
- ✓ sesame, ghee, olive, coconut, avocado, almond, castor, mustard, peanut

GRAINS
- ✓ quinoa, porridge, cooked oats, pancakes, rice (all kinds), sprouted wheat

BEVERAGES
- ✓ almond, rice and oat milk, aloe vera, miso broth, chai
- ✓ juices of sweet berries/apple, grapefruit, mango, orange, papaya, lemonade
- ✓ teas of chamomile, clove, eucalyptus, fennel, ginger, lavender, lemon grass, licorice, peppermint, rosehips, saffron, sage

SPICES
- ✓ all, but more pepper, ginger, mustard, less cayenne, chili, or horseradish

SWEETENERS
- ✓ dates, fruit concentrates, monk, raw honey, molasses, cane, maple syrup

VATA AGGRAVATING = RAW, COLD, BITTER (ACIDIC), ASTRINGENT (DRY), PUNGENT (SPICY)

FRUITS
- ☒ raw apples and bananas (unless completely ripe/warmed), dried fruits
- ☒ cranberries, pomegranate, pears, watermelon, persimmons

VEGETABLES
- ☒ most veggies can aggravate Vata if not cooked, steamed, or well-oiled
- ☒ beet and dandelion greens, broccoli, brussel sprouts
- ☒ kale and onions if warmed, cooked and/or massaged with oil
- ☒ tomatoes, celery, corn, lettuce, green olives, sprouts, mushrooms
- ☒ artichokes, white potatoes, winter squash, kohlrabi, eggplant

MEAT
- ☒ lamb, pork, rabbit, venison on wheat/corn crops, white turkey

DAIRY
- ☒ heavily processed or frozen, such as powdered milk and frozen yogurt

LEGUMES
- ☒ most legumes are too difficult for Vata to digest efficiently
- ☒ red mung, kidney, pinto, white, lima, navy, and black beans, black-eyed peas, chickpeas, brown lentils
- ☒ not soybeans or edamame, soy-based products in moderation

NUTS AND SEEDS
- ☒ popcorn

OILS
- ☒ canola, corn, flax seed, soy

GRAINS
- ☒ yeast breads, buckwheat, millet, corn, rye, spelt, tapioca, bran, pasta
- ☒ granola, cereals, couscous, crackers, granola, dry oats and rice, polenta

BEVERAGES
- ☒ cold dairy, soy milk, coffee, caffeine, black/iced tea, carbonated drinks
- ☒ juices of cranberry, pear, pomegranate, and tomato
- ☒ teas of alfalfa, barley, blackberry, dandelion, jasmine, nettle, yarrow, passionflower, limited hibiscus

SPICES
- ☒ Cayenne, Chili Pepper, Horseradish, Fenugreek

SWEETENERS
- ☒ cooked honey, artificial sweeteners, white sugar

PITTA BALANCING = COOL, SWEET, BITTER (ACIDIC), ASTRINGENT (DRY)

FRUITS
✓ sweet and dry – and best on an empty stomach, not with a meal
✓ berries, pineapple, plums, oranges, apricots, apples, mangos, grapes, pears
✓ limes, coconut, dates, figs, prunes, raisins, pomegranates, strawberries

VEGETABLES
✓ Pitta can tolerate raw vegetables the best of any Dosha
✓ kale, zucchini, spinach, broccoli, asparagus, brussels, cabbage, green beans
✓ avocado, sweet peppers, mushrooms, cilantro, parsley, sprouts, wheat grass
✓ cooked leeks, carrots, onions, leeks, radishes, pumpkin, sweet/white potato
✓ artichokes, cauliflower, celery, cucumber, olives, rutabaga, spaghetti squash

MEAT
✓ animals who lived as naturally as possible, meat is relatively sweet and dry
✓ buffalo, venison, rabbit, white poultry, egg whites, freshwater fish, shrimp

DAIRY
✓ separate from meals (except ghee) and in least processed form
✓ cow/goat's milk, fresh cheese/yogurt, plain butter, ghee, cottage cheese

LEGUMES
✓ most beans have a dry quality, so Pitta has many to choose from
✓ black, kidney, pinto, lima, mung, white, black-eyed/split peas, chickpeas
✓ soy-based products (except for soy sauce, meats, and miso)

NUTS AND SEEDS
✓ most contain a lot of oil, so Pitta is limited, but moderation for those below
✓ flax, sunflower/pumpkin seeds, unsalted popcorn, almonds (soaked/peeled)

OILS
✓ those that are free of toxins, organic and moderate in taste
✓ olive, soy, ghee, coconut, and flax oils

GRAINS
✓ wheat, barley, bran, amaranth, tapioca, pancakes, cooked oats, granola
✓ couscous, pasta, quinoa, rice (basmati, white, wild), rice cakes, crackers

BEVERAGES
✓ almond and rice milk, occasional black tea
✓ juices of apple, apricot, sweet berries
✓ teas of berries, chamomile, chicory, hibiscus, jasmine, lavender, licorice, nettle, peppermint, raspberry, sarsaparilla, spearmint, wintergreen

SPICES - turmeric, cardamom, coriander, cumin, dill, basil, saffron, vanilla, mint
SWEETENERS—maple/rice syrups, fruit juices, date sugar, sugar cane, turbinado

PITTA AGGRAVATING = SOUR, SALTY, AND SPICY

FRUITS
- ☒ sour apples, apricots, pineapples, oranges, plums, berries, and cherries
- ☒ lemons, bananas, cranberries, grapefruit, green grapes, kiwi, green mangoes, tamarind, persimmons, peaches

VEGETABLES
- ☒ raw varieties of beets, corn, leeks, onions, radishes
- ☒ tomatoes, green chilies, hot peppers, garlic, green olives, horseradish
- ☒ eggplant, kohlrabi, beet/mustard/turnip greens, green olives, turnips, cooked spinach

MEAT
- ☒ beef, dark chicken/turkey, duck, egg yolks, lamb, pork, saltwater fish, salmon, sardines, tuna

DAIRY
- ☒ salted butter, buttermilk, hard cheeses, sour cream, yogurt (frozen or with fruit)

NUTS AND SEEDS
- ☒ walnuts, cashews, peanuts, pecans, pistachios, sesame or chia seeds, tahini, Brazil, hazelnuts, macadamias, pine nuts

OILS
- ☒ sesame, almond, corn, and safflower oils

GRAINS
- ☒ yeast bread, corn, rye, buckwheat, millet, polenta, brown rice, muesli

SPICES
- ☒ cayenne, cloves, nutmeg, sage, fenugreek, garlic, dry ginger, marjoram, asafoetida, caraway, mustard seeds, oregano, paprika, rosemary, salt, thyme, dried basil, bay leaves

BEVERAGES
- ☒ apple cider, sour juice, caffeinated and carbonated
- ☒ teas of clove, eucalyptus, fenugreek, dry ginger, ginseng, hawthorne, juniper, sage, sassafras, yerba mate

SWEETENERS
- ☒ white sugar, honey, jaggery, molasses, artificial sweeteners

KAPHA BALANCING = LIGHT, WARM, DRY, SPICY, BITTER

FRUITS
- ✓ apples, apricots, pears, pomegranates, peaches, mangos, lemons, limes
- ✓ prunes, figs, raisins, strawberries, cranberries, berries, grapes (not green)
- ✓ dried fruits are very dense, so enjoy these in moderate quantities

VEGETABLES
- ✓ spinach, leafy greens, collard/mustard/beet/turnip/dandelion greens, kale
- ✓ green beans, asparagus, broccoli, brussels, cilantro, parsley, chilies, okra
- ✓ Cauliflower, celery, corn, radish, turnips, artichoke, kohlrabi, rutabaga
- ✓ white potatoes, winter and spaghetti squash, mushrooms, cooked tomatoes
- ✓ onions, fennel, garlic, horseradish, leeks, peppers (sweet/hot), watercress

MEAT
- ✓ animals that have lived as naturally as possible, meat is mostly light and dry
- ✓ white poultry, freshwater fish, shrimp, venison, eggs in limited amounts

DAIRY
- ✓ separate from meals (except ghee), while warm and in least processed form
- ✓ limited goat's milk and cheeses (unsalted), ghee, buttermilk, yogurt (diluted)

LEGUMES
- ✓ astringent/good for Kapha, like cooked tofu, tempeh, soy meats/milks
- ✓ white, black, black-eyed peas, chickpeas, lentils, pinto, navy, lima, mung dai

NUTS AND SEEDS
- ✓ most are very dense and oily, so best to limit quantities
- ✓ almonds, chia, pumpkin, sunflower, popcorn without salt or butter

OILS
- ✓ those that are free of toxins, organic and in limited quantities
- ✓ almond, sunflower, corn, flax, ghee

GRAINS
- ✓ most are heavy by nature, so best to limit quantities
- ✓ oats, corn, millet, rye, barley, buckwheat, spelt, seitan, tapioca, wheat bran
- ✓ unsweetened cereal, couscous, crackers, granola, muesli, polenta, quinoa, rice

BEVERAGES
- ✓ warmed soy milk, aloe vera, apple cider, spiced black tea
- ✓ juices of apple, berry, carrot, cherry, grape, mango, peach, prune, pear
- ✓ teas of blackberry, chicory, cinnamon, clove, dandelion, fennel, ginseng, hibiscus, jasmine, juniper, raspberry, peppermint, spearmint, wintergreen

SPICES - all except refined salt; best are garlic, black pepper, cayenne, chili
SWEETENERS - fruit juices, honey (raw) that is not cooked

KAPHA AGGRAVATING = WATERY, SWEET, SOUR, SALTY

FRUITS
- ⊠ cantaloupe, papaya, pineapple, watermelon, melons, grapefruit, kiwi, plums, rhubarb
- ⊠ avocado, oranges, bananas, coconut, dates, fresh figs, tamarind

VEGETABLES
- ⊠ raw tomatoes, cucumber, parsnips, olives, sweet potatoes, pumpkin, summer squash, zucchini

MEAT
- ⊠ beef, pork, lamb, dark parts of chicken/turkey, duck, buffalo, dense saltwater fish/seafood

DAIRY
- ⊠ cow's milk and creams, butter, cheese (other than goats), frozen yogurt, ice cream

LEGUMES
- ⊠ cold tofu, soy derivatives like sauces, flours, cheeses, and miso
- ⊠ black lentils, kidney beans

NUTS AND SEEDS
- ⊠ walnuts, Brazil, cashews, peanuts, sesame, tahini, macadamia, pecans, pine, pistachios

OILS
- ⊠ olive, avocado, soy, sesame, coconut, safflower, sesame

GRAINS
- ⊠ wheat, bread with yeast, pasta, cooked oats, pancakes, rice (brown/white)

SPICES
- ⊠ salt

BEVERAGES
- ⊠ coffee, cold drinks, iced tea, milks (except soy/goat's), carbonated beverages, miso
- ⊠ sour juices such as grapefruit, lemonade, orange, papaya, and tomato
- ⊠ limit teas such as licorice and marshmallow

SWEETENERS
- ⊠ white sugar, artificial sweeteners, turbinado, rice or maple syrup, molasses, jaggary, honey that is heated, date sugar

Spring Cleaning

According to Ayurveda, we face additional forces of imbalances during seasonal shifts. Spring is considered a time for cleansing, rejuvenation, transition and clearing excess heavy and cold qualities left over from winter like excess Kapha or Tamasic qualities (subdued and sluggish, poor digestion, seasonal colds, allergies, and excess weight).

This Spring cleanse nourishes rather than deprives, balancing to all constitutions, or doshas. The "cleanse" is of excess ama - undigested food, emotions, and experiences. This Spring seasonal shift is often recognized as 3 weeks before the Spring Equinox, but it may be beneficial to adjust the time so week 2 does not coincide with menstrual cycle if applicable. Consult your doctor if you have any health conditions or concerns.

WEEK 1 PREPARE

The first week includes adjustment to sleep cycle for your Dosha, adding more soothing food and drink for your Dosha, and limiting sugar, alcohol, and caffeine. Some nutrition ideas that are supportive for preparing the gut and lymphatic system are green vegetables, warm oatmeal or porridge, vegetable curries, and lots of water and teas.

WEEK 2 IGNITE

In the second week, introduce kitchari, ghee and CCF, and add self-massage and other self-care practices. Stored emotions from the release of ama may arise (i.e., headache, fatigue, irritability, low mood).

✓ Morning Ghee. Take in the morning on an empty stomach (1 Tbsp for 2 days, 2 Tbsp for next 3 days, 3 Tbsp for last 2 days). Suggest having on hand unrefrigerated ghee (organic, grass-fed, pasture-raised). Ghee contains butyric acid, omega-3 fatty acids; fat-soluble vitamins; short/medium/long-chain fatty acids; and helps bind and eliminate fat-soluble toxins. If ghee intake is difficult, add ghee to morning kitchari or oatmeal or porridge.

- ✓ Kitchari for 3 meals/day until satisfied. Kitchari contains essential macronutrients: carbs (rice), protein (mung dahl), and fat (ghee). If this feels too much, try oatmeal or porridge in the morning. Try not to snack between meals. If needed try fruit or nuts.
- ✓ CCF Tea. Whatever time feels best. To make CCF, mix 2 tbsp coriander seeds, 2 tbsp cumin seeds, and 2 tbsp fennel seeds and place mixture in an air-tight jar in a dry, dark place. To drink, combine 2 teaspoons of CCF Tea with 2 cups of water in a saucepan. Boil, reduce heat and simmer for 5-15 minutes (longer = stronger). Pour through a mesh sieve.

Lentil & Veg Khichari (also spelled Khichdi)
- o 1/2 C. split green moong lentils (or yellow) and 1/2 C. white rice (Kapha do less rice and more lentils)
- o 3 C. water
- o 1 Tbsp ghee (or oil if vegan) and 1/2 tsp cumin seeds (Jeera) and 1/8 tsp asafoetida (Hing)
- o 1/2 Tbsp ginger paste and 1/2 small onion, chopped
- o 1 potato, cut into 1" cubes
- o 3 carrots, cut into ½" chunks
- o 1 cup peas or green vegetable for your Dosha
- o 1/4 tsp turmeric (Haldi powder) and 1/4 tsp cayenne or red chili powder and 1 tsp salt

Start instapot on sauté and add ghee, cumin, and asafoetida, stir for 1 minute. Add onions and ginger to cook for another minute. Add all veggies and spices, stir well, add lentils, rice, and water. Stir well. Close lid, pressure cook for 10 min on high with vent in seal position, then 10 min release of pressure manually. Or cook lentils and veggies on stovetop according to lentil directions. Garnish with cilantro. Serve hot with additional ghee on top of it.

Oil Everywhere

At a Pancha Karma center outside of Mumbai, a woman told me to don paper underwear and sit on a chair next to a large wooden table that looked straight out of a horror film. The woman then chanted a prayer in Hindi which I didn't understand but felt reassured by nonetheless. On the table, she spread oil across my marma points without any real pressure, which felt disappointing as it is generally obvious to massage therapists that my tense body requires pressure to fix itself.

Just when I was certain this would be a waste of time, she hooked up a hot pot over my head, put cotton in my ears and a soft barrier across my eyebrows, and opened the spout on the pot. The pot contained warm oil and as it moved from side to side pouring oil on my forehead, my mind turned to butter. After about 20 min of bliss, she massaged more oil through my hair and placed a cap over it to preserve the moisture. Next was a shower and a steamy box with an opening for my head, which was awkward, but not stressful as I no longer felt stress anywhere. This combination was Abhyanga, Shirodhara, and Swedana.

At the reception desk, I pointed to the next massage on the list and was told to consult with an Ayurvedic doctor, a tall man whose head shook back and forth as he sat at a large desk peering at my intake form. I anticipated sticking out my tongue for evaluation as was customary, but he didn't find it necessary in my case. He wanted to know about my bones and job and shook his head aggressively as I shared the details.

His prescription included waking each day by 5am, self-massage, tongue scraping, oil pulling, breath regulation, and drinking lukewarm water before some brisk walking or yoga. For meals, he suggested porridge with nuts and fruits for breakfast; large portions of chappathis and sabji and lesser portions of rice and daal, as well as buttermilk for lunch; and for dinner, foods easy to digest like kichdi, kanji, vegetable soup, steamed vegetables, and warm milk. Between meals I should enjoy fruits, coconut water, or soaked nuts.

The doctor packed the things needed for my conditions, including oils to massage my joints, oils for internal use for hip pain and bloating, tablets for inflammation, tablets for stress and ashwagandha powder to add to warm milk. I stared at the large volume of items and thought of my intercountry flight to Dehradun that disallowed excessive baggage.

When I returned for my next massage, there was a hot plate with a pan on it filled with oil and items next to the table. After preparing and praying, a woman took large poultices from the pan and pressed them all over my body, while also rotating them in and out of the pan to stay hot. My body pains gave way to a feeling of youth under the hot herbals and oil called Podi kizhi. Now that I felt educated in Ayurvedic massage, I eagerly anticipated trying more.

At another Ayurvedic center in Rishikesh, I pointed to desired treatments and was directed to a small shack in a garden adorned with a propane tank hooked precariously to a steam box, next to another large wooden table. A woman who spoke Hindi completed preparatory steps but offered no chanting of prayers - which I very much missed. Then she started with body oil and kept going long past after forehead oil dripping should have begun, so I pointed to my forehead and motioned oil dripping that encouraged harsh movements that tore out my hair. I cried and pointed at the reception desk.

A man quickly appeared as I lay in my paper underwear and he directed the woman to beat me from head to toe and back and front. I feared for my bones but thought maybe this was necessary. We were both crying when she motioned to the steam box, where she left me, the door open to a cafe as a hose sprayed painfully hot water on my legs.

After wrestling with my emotions, I returned in the morning. The same woman placed a piece of rolled dough on my back and poured hot oil into it – allowing it to penetrate until pain dissolved in what was called Basti. Afterwards she cradled my head and said carefully, as though she had practiced it many times . . . "I am sorry." I said that I was sorry too. Massages are an exchange of energy, and we all need compassion.

Dinacharya at Home

Oil on the inside. Oil on the outside.

Ayurvedic daily routine, or Dinacharya, are self-care practices - like dry brushing (garshana), and oil massage (Abhyanga), and oil pulling (kavala). Basic items needed for home self-care routine are:

o   Ayurvedic body brushes
     One with hand strap, bristles, and massage nodules
     One with a longer handle that reaches your back
o   Body oils (see below for each Dosha)
o   Container for warming oil (for best absorption into tissues)
o   Tongue Scraper
o   Mouth Oil
o   Nasal Oil (Nasya)

The type of oil you use depends upon your Dosha as different oils have either warming or cooling properties to soothe your constitution. It is best to distinguish between cooking and massage oil in purchases.

For Vata, a base of untoasted sesame oil is warming. Other oils, such as ashwagandha, bala, shatavari, and mahanarayan oil also have properties beneficial to the nervous system and joints. Often Vata may not need to rinse the oil off as skin is often dry.

For Pitta, a base of sunflower or coconut oil is cooling. Other oils, such as brahmi, shatavari, and licorice can be beneficial for the nervous system, joints, and digestion. Neem oil added to a base oil can be beneficial for targeting inflamed skin.

For Kapha, a base of untoasted and refined sesame, almond and corn oils are warming. Kapha is typically oily, so certain oils help to absorb excess natural oil. Other oils can be added, such as Punarnava, chitrak, calamus, and rosemary for digestive and circulatory systems.

Perform dry brushing on torso and limbs prior to oil massage to help oil penetrate. The direction of brushing matters to get the most benefits for your circulatory system. Start by brushing the limbs from the furthest point away from heart toward your midline. Then move to your joints, using circular strokes on your ankles, knees, hips, shoulders,

130

elbows, wrists. Lastly, move to your abdomen in a clockwise circular motion the path of the colon. After dry brushing apply oil similarly.

In the morning before eating, use your tongue scraper to clean the tongue. Then do oil pulling (kavala) for dental health by placing 1 TBSP of ayurvedic mouth oil and gargling around teeth and gums for about 15 minutes. Spit out gargled oil (do not swallow oil), then rinse your mouth with warm water.

At bedtime, place Nasya oil (unless you have a sinus infection) in your nose by tipping head back for 1-3 drops of oil in each nostril. Nasya oil can help lubricate the nasal passages for easier nose breathing while you are sleeping to support respiratory health.

Once per week, try a scalp/head massage using bhringaraj (for hair loss, improved sleep) or brahmi (brain health). For hair massage, start at top of your head and go outward in circular motions.

Foot and face massages are also great for relaxation and rejuvenation. I add these during my Ayurvedic cleanses and sometimes as part of yoga practices, though they are beneficial anytime.

Feet. Use bhringari or brahmi oil (or oil for your Dosha).
✓ Use fingers to apply a Thai inspired type of massage:
✓ While seated, start with the sole of a foot. Apply a few drops of oil.
✓ Press thumbs from heel to toe pads, repeat.
✓ Above heel, use "pincher fingers" to kneed 2" up/down Achilles.
✓ With "pincher fingers," place fingers between toes and pull outward.
✓ One hand holds flexed. Other hand taps bottom of foot.
✓ Do the same routine on the other foot.

Face Marma Points. Mix base with tea tree, lavender, and frankincense.
✓ On clean face and neck, apply oil with 2 fingers in small circles.
✓ Massage center of brow to forehead (up/out), repeat a few times.
✓ With 2 fingers, massage from collarbone towards chin, repeat.
✓ Massage along jaw towards ears.
✓ Extra –Marma points with moderate pressure for 1 minute each. Chin center, between nose/upper lip, sinuses, above cheekbones, eyebrow lower ridges, temples, 3rd eye, crown.

Self-Study

1. What is your body's story throughout your life?
2. Review your Dosha's balancing and aggravating foods and try eating more balancing foods for a week and note your observations.
3. Practice dry brushing and self-massage with oil for your dosha for a week and note your observations.

10. War Within

The Gita - God's Song

"Everyone must come out of his exile in his own way"
- Martin Buber.

A poem about yoga called the Bhagavad Gita (translated as God's song) is part of the Mahabharata. This poem is often simply referred to as the *Gita* and has many translations and interpretations.

An important side note for readers not familiar with the term Brahman - in the *Gita*, Brahman is a godhead representing religious or non-religious tradition. In the Hindu belief systems of the Trimurti, Brahma is the creator. Brahma and Brahman are not the same thing as Brahman still pervades the whole system as consciousness itself. Furthermore, Brahma the creator, and Brahman the Godhead, should not be confused with Brahma, a type of cow venerated in India. Another similar word is Brahmin, referring to the highest class in the Indian caste system, who serve as priests and spiritual teachers.

The *Gita* is a dialogue between two main characters on a battlefield. One is Arjuna, an everyday hero who stands for all who face difficult circumstances and question what they should do. The other is Krishna, an incarnation of divine power who acts as Arjuna's counsel, representing transcendent wisdom. The poem's battle is waged between the Pandavas, Arjuna's family, and the Kauravas, his cousin's family.

The battle's backstory starts with Pandu, Arjuna's father, a king who went on holiday and asked his brother Dhritarashtra to cover down for him while he was out. Unfortunately, the king dies on vacation, and his wife returns home as a widow with 5 sons, one of them being Arjuna. Since his brother wasn't coming back, Dhritarashtra kept on being king, and children of both men grew up in the palace, trained and educated by the same teachers. But people in the kingdom began questioning the legitimacy of Dhritarashtra's reign because those with disabilities were supposed to be barred from the throne. Dhritarashtra was blind.

The question then was which brother's (one alive and blind, and one dead) sons would take his place. The blind king decides to crown his dead brother's eldest son Yudhishthira as king. Dhritarashtra's eldest son, Duryodhana, disagrees and so concocts a plan to send the Pandavas on vacation to a house built of flammable materials. The Pandavas discover the plan to burn them alive and dig a tunnel beneath the house before a party of villagers commences. When Duryodhana sets the fire, the Pandavas escape and charred bodies pass for dead Pandavas.

The Pandavas go into hiding and disguise themselves as a brahmin family who beg for daily alms (food offerings). But one day, there is a festival where princess Draupadi will be given in marriage to the winner of a contest which involves shooting arrows at a revolving fishing on top of a pole erected in water. Competitors must look down at the revolving fish's reflection in the pool while aiming for the eye of the fish. All archers fail but one, Arjuna, who wins Draupadi.

Arjuna takes her home and calls out his mother that he has a surprise. From inside the house, Arjuna's mother assumes that he means alms and tells him to share the surprise with his brothers. Draupadi then becomes wife to 5 men, who agree to exclusive use for a year at a time and to not interrupt another's time or go into exile.

The Pandavas come out of hiding for the wedding and take back half of their kingdom. But one night, a village man asks Arjuna to help to save his cattle from thieves, and Arjuna bursts into a room occupied by Yudhishthira and their shared wife to retrieve his bow. Arjuna saves the cattle from thieves and heads into exile as agreed. During exile, Arjuna marries other women, has children, and engages in adventures such as fighting his father Indra (the god of storms) for Agni's (the god of fire) right to fulfill his duty in burning down the forest. Arjuna also saves a man named Maya, an exceptional architect that builds a palace for the brothers and causes another issue for Duryodhana.

Duryodhana challenges the Pandavas to a dice game with stakes of 13 years of exile for the family that loses. Arjuna's brother Yudhishthira plays and loses, so they go back into exile before returning to demand return of their kingdom. Duryodhana refuses, so war is inevitable.

Both Arjuna and Duryodhana ask for Krishna's help as he is the wisest man in the land. Krishna offers them either his Army or his counsel. Duryodhana chooses the army. Before the battle, Arjuna asks Krishna to drive their chariot between the two armies and that scene becomes the *Gita's* dialogue. The following chapter summaries from the *Gita,* as translated by Eknath Easwaran, contain shortened quotes, with some verbiage regarding inequality purposely left out.

The War Within

"O Krishna, drive my chariot between the armies . . . seeing my friends and relatives present before me in such a fighting spirit, I feel the limbs of my body quivering and my mouth drying up. My body is trembling, my hair is standing on end, my bow is slipping from my hand, and my skin is burning. I am now unable to stand here any longer. I am forgetting myself, and my mind is reeling. I see only causes of misfortune. I do not see how any good can come from killing my own kinsmen in this battle, nor can I desire any subsequent victory, kingdom or happiness . . . of what avail to us are a kingdom, happiness or even life itself when all those for whom we may desire them are now arrayed on this battlefield? - when teachers, fathers, sons, grandfathers, maternal uncles, fathers-in-law, grandsons, brothers-in-law and other relatives are ready to give up their lives and properties and are standing before me, why should I wish to kill them, even though they might otherwise kill me? . . . Driven by the desire to enjoy royal happiness, we are intent on killing our own kinsmen. Better for me if the sons of Dhritarashtra, weapons in hand, were to kill me unresisting on the battlefield."

Self-realization

(Krishna) "This despair and weakness in a time of crisis are mean and unworthy of you, Arjuna. How have you fallen into a state so far from the path to liberation? It does not become you to yield to this weakness . . . There has never been a time when (those) gathered here have not existed, nor will there be a time when we will cease to exist . . . The Self of all beings, living within the body, is eternal and cannot be harmed . . .

Those who do not seek to serve are without a home in this world. On this path effort never goes to waste, and there is no failure . . . Perform work in this world, Arjuna, as a man established within himself – without selfish attachments, and alike in success and defeat. For yoga is perfect evenness of mind . . . Attachment breeds desire (which turns to anger). Anger clouds judgement; you can no longer learn from past mistakes. Lost is the power to choose between wise and unwise, and your life is utter waste . . . Use all your power to free the senses from attachment and aversion alike ...."

Selfless Service

(Krishna) "One who shirks action does not attain freedom; no one can gain perfection by abstaining from work . . . Selfish action imprisons the world. . . Do your work with the welfare of others always in mind . . . If I stopped working, I would be the cause of cosmic chaos, and finally of the destruction of this world . . . Perform all work carefully, guided by compassion . . . The senses have been conditioned by attraction to the pleasant and aversion to the unpleasant. Do not be ruled by them; they are obstacles in your path. It is better to strive in one's own dharma than to succeed in the dharma of another. Nothing is ever lost in following one's own dharma . . . Fight with all your strength, Arjuna! Control your senses, conquer your enemy - the destroyer of knowledge and realization. Arjuna, cut through this doubt in your own heart with the sword of spiritual wisdom. Arise; take up the path of yoga."

Spiritual union includes feeling the joys and sorrows of others.

(Krishna) "It is not those who lack energy or refrain from action, but those who work without expectation of reward who attain the goal of meditation . . . The will is the only friend of the Self, and the will is the only enemy of the Self . . . The Supreme Reality stands revealed in the consciousness of those who have conquered themselves. They live in peace, alike in cold and heat, pleasure, and pain . . .

Select a clean spot . . . and seat yourself firmly . . . then still your thoughts. With senses and mind constantly controlled through meditation, united with the Self within . . . the mind is unwavering like the flame of a lamp in a windless place. In the still mind, in the depths of meditation, the Self reveals itself . . . having attained that abiding joy beyond the senses . . . They see the Self in every creature and all creation in the Self . . . When a person responds to the joys and sorrows of others as if they were his own, he has attained the highest state of spiritual union."

(Arjuna) "O Krishna, the stillness of divine union you describe is beyond my comprehension. How can the mind, which is so restless, attain lasting peace? . . . Trying to control (the mind) is like trying to tame the wind. What happens to one who does not attain success in yoga? Will he lose the support of both worlds like a cloud scattered in the sky?"

(Krishna) "No one who does good work will come to a bad end . . ."

Wisdom from Realization

"I will give you both jnana and vijnana (spiritual wisdom and practical knowledge). When both of these are realized, there is nothing more you need to know. Earth, water, fire, air, akasha (space), mind, intellect, and ego – these are the 8 divisions of my prakriti (everything that is not the soul). But beyond this I have another, higher nature . . . I am the taste of pure water and the radiance of the sun and moon. I am the sacred word and the sound heard in air, and the courage of human beings. The state of sattva, rajas, and tamas come from me, but I am not in them. The gunas make up my divine maya, difficult to overcome. But they cross over this maya who take refuge in me . . . everywhere and in everything . . .

There is merit in studying the scriptures, in selfless service, austerity and giving, but the practice of meditation carries you beyond all these . . . I am the true medicine . . . I am what is and what is not . . . Those who worship other gods with faith and devotion also worship me . . . I look upon all creatures equally; none are less dear to me and none more dear.

I am in the heart of every creature . . .
I am the sun, the storms, the moon, the ocean,
the Himalayas, the Ganges, the sound Om,
time, the spring, the sages, and poets.
I am consciousness itself.
(Krishna)

The Cosmic Vision

Krishna appears with an infinite number of faces, ornamented by heavenly jewels, displaying unending miracles and countless weapons. Clothed in celestial garments and covered with garlands, sweet-smelling with heavenly fragrances . . . the source of all wonders, whose face is everywhere. If a thousand suns were to rise in the heavens, the blaze of their light would resemble the splendor of that supreme spirit.

(Arjuna) "O Lord, I see . . . every kind of living creature . . . embodied in every form . . . the cosmos is your body . . . shining like a fiery sun blazing in every direction. You are the refuge of all creation . . . you touch everything with your infinite power . . . The multitudes of gods, demigods and demons are all overwhelmed by the sight of you . . . My heart trembles; I have lost all courage and all peace of mind . . ."

(Krishna) "Even without your participation, all the warriors gathered here will die. Therefore arise, Arjuna; conquer your enemies . . . "

The Way of Love

Knowledge of the knower is true knowledge.

"As for those who seek the transcendental reality without name, without form, contemplating the unmanifested, beyond reach of thought and feeling, with their senses subdued and mind serene and striving for the good of all beings, they too will verily come unto me. If you cannot still your mind in me, learn to do so through the regular practice of meditation. If you lack the will for such self-discipline, engage yourself in my work, for selfless service can lead you at last to complete fulfillment. Better indeed is knowledge than mechanical practice. Better than knowledge is meditation. But better still is surrender of attachment to results, because there follows immediate peace . . . Not agitating the world or by it agitated, they stand above the sway of elation, competition, and fear; that one is my beloved.

139

The body is called a field, Arjuna; the one who knows it is called the Knower of the field . . . Knowledge of the field and its Knower is true knowledge. . . The field is made up of the five sense organs and the five organs of action: the three components of the mind (manas- the mind that stores sensory impressions, buddhi - intelligence, ahamkara - self-will), and the undifferentiated energy from which all these evolved . . . Those who know truly are free from pride and deceit. They are gentle, forgiving, upright, pure, devoted, filled with inner strength . . .

Know that from Prakriti come the gunas and all that changes . . . Purusha, resting in prakriti, witnesses the play of the gunas born of prakriti . . . see the Lord the same in every creature . . . do not harm (self) or others . . . As the sun lights up the world, the Self dwelling in the field is the source of all light in the field. Those who, with the eye of wisdom, distinguish the field from its Knower and the way to freedom from the bondage of prakriti . . . Clay, a rock and gold are the same to them . . . alike to friend and foe"

Faith and Freedom

(Krishna) "The deluded do not see the Self . . . They do not see the Self enjoying sense objects or action through the gunas . . . Bound on all sides by scheming and anxiety, driven by anger and greed, they amass by any means . . .This wealth is mine and that will be mine too . . . I enjoy what I want. I am successful. I am powerful. I am happy. I am rich and well-born. Who is equal to me? . . . Bound by their greed and entangled in a web of delusion . . . they miss the goal of life; miss even happiness. Our faith conforms to our nature . . . To be steadfast in self-sacrifice, self-discipline, and giving is sat (that which is) . . . But to engage in sacrifice, self-discipline and giving without good faith is asat (that which is not), without worth or goodness . . . I give you these precious words of wisdom; reflect on them and then do as you choose."

140

Gita Conclusion

The *Mahabharata* continues the battle story for 18 days. Most soldiers are killed and the Pandavas take back the kingdom to rule for 36 years before retiring to the Himalayan mountains where they die, one by one until only Arjuna's brother, Yudhishthira, is left with his faithful dog.

Some Puranas written after the *Gita* translate the poem as a thesis for new religions; however, the practice of ancient yoga renders judgement of any faith form as right or wrong as a distraction that promotes separateness. If one feels more connected to their essence, pure and free from fear, by worshipping a particular faith form . . . then that wonderous experience of spiritual connection is complemented by yoga.

And while some have taken the *Gita* as a call to arms. Others, like Mahatma Gandhi, saw it as a way to gain higher perspective on conflicts within that we all face. The Gita's message includes 4 types of yoga.

1. Jnana Yoga – yoga of knowledge
   (not identified by body, mind, or senses – but the Self)
2. Bhakti Yoga – yoga of devotion (faith in a higher power)
3. Karma Yoga – yoga of selfless action
4. Raja Yoga – yoga of meditation

Becoming Golden

I wanted to go to the child
and the woman in pain
and breathe golden light into her and say,
"you can no longer deny the truth,
you are golden."

When I took a job in Northern California and made my way across the country with what was left of my purged belongings at age 49, most of which fit neatly into a Nissan Versa hatchback, I flashed back to my 7-year-old self sitting in the backseat of car in the dark on the side of Hwy 13 in Nebraska. But this time I was both my mother and the child.

In California I ordered everything my apartment needed to be a relaxing sacred space including meditation cushions and African drums. But nothing changed except my décor. So, I focused on work, faked smiles, swallowed vitamins by handfuls and ate fermented foods. At night I drifted off to sleep after 2 cigarettes and wine, but woke myself up screaming, "I hate you!".

The Senior Center nearby offered classes to people seemingly much wiser than me or at least determined to survive since they were still alive. So, though I'd never done Yin or Qigong, I signed up for both. In Qigong class, visually frail elderly people glided around like fairies while I couldn't softly sway left or right. And in Yin class, a woman 20 years older than me put us in torturous poses, clearly unaware that her blissful messages were entirely lost on me due to my own brain's messaging of "maybe you can survive another 5 minutes if you count every second".

But since I knew that my body had been exiled from my mind for decades, Yin and Qigong gave me something new to work with. And back in the comfort of my apartment, amid the meditation cushions and drums, I dove into research about both philosophies and sciences.

Qigong is a part of Traditional Chinese Medicine (TCM) and is the foundation of Tai Chi. Qigong utilizes Yin and Yang concepts. Yin represents earth qualities related to dense filtering organs of the kidneys, spleen, and liver that rise up the front body and insides of the legs and arms. Yang represents sky or heaven qualities related to lighter organs of the large and small intestine, and bladder that descend the back of the body and outsides of legs and arms.

Qigong practice is known to improve health and longevity through the focus on Qi, or vital life force, and it is adaptable to any person or situation. Though it is typically not part of a curriculum for yoga teacher training, it is included here as a fluid way to be imperfect, and another way to promote harmony between mind and body. Yin is approved curriculum for registered yoga teacher programs, though I personally find the practice of Yin less inclusive and accessible for students unless it is taught differently than per the fundamentals of the practice.

Yin is a relatively modern practice that also has origins in Taoist principles and Traditional Chinese Medicine. The formulization of practices into something labeled Yin began with Paulie Zink, a westerner, who trained for 10 years under a Kung-Fu and Taoist yoga master from Hong Kong and then won the International Karate Championships in the early 1980s, crediting his abilities to his master's flexibility training. After his success, Zink taught a combination of Hatha Yoga with Taoist Yoga, as well as postures, movements, and personal insights that he called "Yin and Yang yoga" to martial arts practitioners. His Yin portion included long-held poses, and the Yang portion was a typical asana flow practice.

Paul Grilley, a yoga teacher focusing on Ashtanga and Bikram practices, studied with Zink. In the late 1980s, Grilley went on to meet Hiroshi Motoyama, a Japanese scholar and yogi who focused on the physiology of the meridians and the qi (or Chi) and the parallels of the nadis, chakras and prana of yoga. Grilley took what he learned from Zink and Motoyama, what he knew from anatomy and Hatha yoga and developed a fusion of sequences with aims like that of an acupuncturist.

In Yin yoga, Yin is associated primarily with moon energy that is stable, immobile, feminine, passive, cold, and downward movement that relates to the connective tissues (tendons, ligaments, fascia). Yang is associated with the sun, or energy that is mobile, masculine, active, hot, and upward movement that relates to muscles and blood. The practice of Yin yoga is a targeting of connective tissues, which occurs in a cold body and cool environment. Yin must be practiced before muscles are warmed up, because when muscles are cold, more stress is transferred to connective tissue, which is the fundamental practice of Yin.

Moving between Yin postures must be done slowly so as not to break the connective tissue, but to gain elasticity. Inside of each Yin pose, the focus is on loading joints, then relaxing and softening into the pose to move closer to the bone. Yin poses, done in accordance with Yin principles which include long holds (usually a minimum of 3 minutes), can penetrate into connective tissue to expand flexibility while invigorating energy centers to release blockages and increase energy flow.

After guiding the class into Yin poses, Yin teachers may explain the physiology and anatomy of poses, tell traditional stories, recite poetry, sing songs, or reflect on a theme. However, as with leading any yoga class, dharma or spiritual talks must not turn into a sermon while people in class are a somewhat captive audience.

Many Yin poses can cause injury when not guided and approached slowly and safely, especially for those with degenerative changes in their joints and bones. According to Ayurvedic principles, Yin is not generally beneficial for Vata - people with more air/flexibility in their joints, or Kapha- those with earth energy/slowness of metabolism. So, Yin is most beneficial as a counter to Yang, or heat (Pitta constitution or Pitta excess). Since I am a small framed Vata with bone density issues, Yin was not beneficial for my body's structural integrity. So, I use Yin sparingly to connect with my body as in meditation.

On the other hand, I dove into formal Qigong training to embody the treasures of awareness, focus, and presence in nature. After every Qigong practice, whether it was a few minutes or an hour, I felt completely connected to life and the harmony within myself. At the end of a short Qigong class that my brother Wyatt, the E.R. doctor/yoga teacher, taught at a retreat in Guatemala, he said

"Tune into the sensations in your hands."

"That's your Chi (Qi)."

Everyone in the group present seemingly became golden as we noticed the positive energy we created ourselves without much effort.

Since then, I have often fused Qigong into group classes to offer the feeling of being golden on the inside from cultivation of harmony and vitality, and I've witnessed the transference of my own Qigong practice into my relationships with everything in life.

Going Dark to Discover Light

Qigong and Yin practices can increase one's sense of inner wisdom in either stillness or harmony in motion. So both can support another of the *Yoga Sutras* 8 limbs of yoga – Pratyahara - the conscious drawing of awareness away from the external world, including one's own senses, and into the internal self.

In the *Gita's* chapter on self-realization, Krishna tells Arjuna, "Use all your power to free the senses from attachment and aversion alike." He goes on to explain that this is like a turtle drawing in its limbs from the external to control distractions and gain autonomy of one's own wisdom.

While on-the-mat practices can ease withdrawal from the outside world long enough to realize your inner self, the practice of Pratyahara off-the-mat is likely now exponentially more difficult than it was when the *Gita* and *Yoga Sutras* were written. For example, even a few decades ago, if your home phone number was unlisted, you were unreachable by those you didn't give your number to. Now, widespread internet connection means that if you want to be unreachable, you must turn off your apps or your whole device.

Now "going dark" is a commonly used term that means taking a break from social distraction at your fingertips. But you needn't go dark to practice Pratyahara, you can start with what's easiest for you. For example, is there a sport you play, or craft, or anything that you love to do so much that you can tune out the world while doing it?

Decades ago on a drive to Alaska, I stared out our minivan window at hikers readying their gear at trailheads and jealousy, or perhaps disdain, came upon me. I had come to the last frontier to succeed at business and motherhood, so the hikers both irritated and intrigued me. Then the first winter descended and gray covered the earth and sky in one solid mass. I watched fellow Alaskans react to hibernation with drugs, alcohol, sex, gossip, work, etc., until summer came and everyone woke to hope, including me.

Then one early summer day on the banks of Deception Creek, I stood mesmerized by King Salmon swimming in the clear water. My family left to fetch supplies, but I refused to budge – preferring to stay with the fish and grizzly bears. Suddenly I understood why fishermen angled for hours, and how unattended children playing along the edges of the raging water without episode. Being in the wilderness surrounded by towering mountains and the all-encompassing sound of a rushing creek made normal distractions impossible. Soon thereafter, I was on a bush flight enroute to a remote camp with my sister.

Upon arrival we boarded a boat, where the engine and waves obliterated the voices in our heads. Cold saltwater spray, clear blue sky, soft blue water, emerald green shores and mountains filled our senses. In this pristine wilderness just off of Shelikof Straight, there was no concept of time except for the low hanging afternoon sun. Our guide Steele had sold his Harley to buy the fish camp and build a cabin where all supplies came by barge or float plane.

Every moment was magic, even the cold-water bucket baths. Though there was cause for concern of grizzly bears, Steele quelled our fears with one of many dark satirical lies that abound in the wilderness to shut people up hailing from controlled concrete worlds. The only problem was that the trip couldn't be long enough due to family, work, and finances. But on our last day, the mainland was socked in with a heavy fog, and no planes could fly in or out. We spoke in whispers of hope of no departure and shared insights about how our life choices could be broadly categorized as blatant refusal to accept anything less than perfect distractions.

Freedom from stress, fear and guilt would come at a price, and we wanted to pay it. Steele could see our internal dilemma, so he suggested kayaking in the rain. That we did, and just off the Bering Sea, in the rain and fog, our senses simultaneously turned on and tuned out in time to the only artificial sight and sounds that existed - paddle blade strokes.

When the skies opened up and a plane's engine could be heard in the distance, we voluntarily headed to the landing strip with our soiled packs and clothes, our slight smiles telling of a deeper wisdom discovered, the place where minds were free of clutter that could be returned to no matter where we roamed. When my family and I moved to Kansas 3 years later, I became a kayak guide to share this floating freedom with others.

Pratyahara is not shutting distractions out so you can think more, it is shutting out distractions so you can experience life more. Finding what works for you both on and off the mat to support this practice can pay huge dividends for your brain health and increased enjoyment of life. Though at first it might feel like pushing a train up a hill; once the initial resistance gives way, pratyahara gains its own steam and becomes a superpower in the world we currently live in.

Train your mind to free your spirit.

Heart Opening Devotion

B*ackbends*
I have come to view the *Gita* as a journey of the heart through battles of the kleshas - ignorance, egoism, attachment, aversion, and fear of death-and the heart's guides through these battles as the Yogas of meditation, knowledge, service, and devotion.

Backbends are a category of poses that can also be journeys through tightly held beliefs, fears, and previous hurts toward the wisdom of the heart. In Sanskrit, the heart chakra is Anahata, meaning unstruck, unhurt, or unbeaten. In yoga, backbends are often referred to as heart-openers. These poses can stretch one's torso, while increasing circulation, stimulating glands and organs, and decreasing fatigue and tension. Practitioners may also experience emotional releases during or after backbends from expansion of the heart's energetic balancing point.

In the chakra system, the heart acts as an intersection where dense subtle energy - the right to be here, to feel and to act – meets lighter subtle energy - the right to speak, to trust and to be connected. The *Chandogya* and *Katha* Upanishads talk about this phenomenon as "small space within the heart" where the whole universe is contained. This space is also called the cave of the heart, and in it is said to exist the luminosity of compassion, intuition and knowing beyond knowing. Heart-opening backbends can feel like a sanctuary of spacious wholeness that is unbreakable.

Unfortunately, misalignment in backbends can be common in tense bodies with recognized or unrecognized avoidance stemming from trauma, grief, and heartbreak. Taking small steps to warm up the spine, hip flexors, chest, and shoulders, as well as to practice alignment essentials can support both safety and progression. Step progression in backbends is also important because opening the cave of a guarded heart can feel akin to walking through an internal battlefield of suppressed emotions.

Big Exhales   During and after big backbends, some students make loud audible exhales as a natural release of emotion or stress. Open mouth exhales and/or audible sounds on exhales are another way to unlock emotions stored in organs. For example, in Qigong, the heart can hold emotions such as grief and sadness; and releasing these emotions from the heart can be supported by exhaling the sound of the heart - 'aaahh.'

In Kundalini, cannon breath (also called 'o' breath) can include both open mouth inhales and exhales with the mouth in the shape of an O to move a lot of air in your lungs and abdomen with a marked effect on thought driven emotions. Cannon breath can support digestion, lung mucus movement, and nervous system resilience.

Lion's breath is another open-mouth exhale that offers similar benefits and seems to energize and transform practitioners into happy and wild lions – especially when placed near the end of class. Another powerful open mouth exhale technique is Breath of Joy that is so uplifting that it can feel like flipping a switch from a state of mental and physical exhaustion and disconnection to a state of whole being clarity and joy.

This book's companion, *Body as Teacher*, provides a Backbend section that includes cues, images, and variations of back bending poses, as well as breathing techniques for emotional release.

Krishna   Backbends and open mouth exhales remind us that the heart's natural state is luminous, open, warm, wise, and joyful for no reason, reminiscent of stories of Krishna prior to his role in the *Gita*. Krishna is also known by the name Gopala, protector of the cows. One mantra referencing Krishna is the Maha (Great) Mantra found in the *Kali-Santarana* Upanishad that was written around 500 CE.

The Maha mantra is said to vibrate and resonate in such a way that higher levels of consciousness and divine realization can be experienced.

150

This mantra is practiced daily by devotees of ISCON (International Society for Krishna Consciousness), also called the Hare Krishnas. It is included in the George Harrison (of the Beatles), "My Sweet Lord."

Swami Prabhupada, originally from India, took a translated text of the *Bhagavad Gita*, and the *Bhagavata Purana* (a text of worship to Krishna near the year 1000 CE) and combined them as doctrine for ISKCON. He then travelled to the U.S. in the late 60s to spread the message of the Maha Mantra as a way to experience the joy of devotion. ISKCON devotees repeat this mantra silently in Japa (with prayer beads) as well as out loud in Kirtan (call and response).

While I am not a devotee of ISKCON, I embrace that which uplifts and elevates human spirits and consciousness, and in my experience, this mantra can do just that.

*"If you want to change the world,
lay down your inner war,
your righteous anger . . .
and love."*
– Lisa Citore

Shadow Work at The Edge

"The only way out is through"
— Robert Frost.

On the first night of my yoga teacher training in Sacramento, students had to stand up and announce to everyone why they were there. Some wanted to teach yoga, others wished to deepen their practice, some (like me) didn't know why. No one said they were there to awaken smothered demons and teach them how to help us.

We remained unaware of this endeavor until about halfway through training, a weekend referred to as the Edge. Rumor had it that the Edge nearly killed people. Even my hairdresser, whose shop was 20 miles away from the yoga studio, had heard horror stories. I took it all with a grain of salt, after all I'd survived dancing on command, proclaiming raw emotions, staring into eyes of strangers, tons of homework, volunteering on weekends, and of course, teaching yoga.

I was wrong. The Edge weekend was harder than all the other stuff put together. That weekend helped me understand that to teach yoga effectively, you could not be in your own way.

The Edge exercises offered here are altered to reveal the ground, the fire, your power, and the openness of your heart to not only walk across to the other side, but also to be present for the gifts that are part of your purpose. It is recommended to move through these exercises in no more than 2 days. Standing in a fire is not beneficial to coming out stronger.

In other words, the Edge exercises this chapter's self-study are a sort of "coming to Jesus moment" where you can take what you've revealed so far in inner work, bring it to the surface, open the cave of your heart, and shine a light in dark corners to expose your superpowers. Repeat this self-study whenever you'd like to see what might be in your way, what might be creating distractions from your inner wisdom and most meaningful life.

From my personal experience, I have never met a person who does not have perceived limitations that are not currently true. And this is where the work of yoga can hold some of the greatest untapped benefit.

After all, according to the *Yoga Sutras*, the soul/inner seer/witness. looks out at the world of prakriti (everything else including our bodies) through the citta (layers of the mind) where samskaras (pre-conditioning, both positive and negative) show up. When the citta is clear, we suffer less.

If possible, do the Edge work with others who can hold space for your revelations as to what lies underneath your go-to explanations of life events and limitations, such as a therapist. Then, once you have shined a light on what is in your way, put your insight into practice to regroove the negative samskaras not serving you into grooves that do.

Teaching yoga works well as regrooving practice as it can incorporate all aspects of yoga in both preparation and delivery. But there are many other ways to put deep insights to work for your sustained expansion. Your inner wisdom will always show you the way when you listen closely.

Self-Study

Deriving concise statements with simple truth can be challenging.
If you get stuck, review your Ayurveda and Chakra answers.

⊠ Do not name others, objects, jobs, houses, etc. in your statements.

⊠ Concise statements reflect deep drivers of a need, choice, or action.

⊠ Feelings will overlap, reduce words by choosing those at the core.

1. The Edge, the Backstory, and the Cost.
   I.   I am doing the work in this book because _____.
   II. I ____ (shortened answer to #I) because _____.
   III. I ____ (shortened answer to #II) because _____.
   IV. I ____ (shortened answer to #III) because _____.
   V.   I ____ (shortened answer to #IV) because _____.
       a) My Edge is (#V in present tense): _____.
       b) My edge has cost me _____.
       c) If it continues _____.

2. The Truth. Our edges, or negative samskaras, can disguise the truth of who we are. So now that your edge and its cost are exposed, it's time to uncover what is far more powerful than that. Most always, your truth will reflect your edge – the other side of the negative conditioning that empowers you and drives a purpose within you and shows up at times when you felt elevated, glowing, or authentic.

   During those moments, what did others say about you or what they witnessed? How did you feel during those times (regardless of whether anyone else noticed)? In those moments, what was the overwhelming knowing beyond knowing that you experienced?

   When I feel elevated, glowing, my most authentic, etc., others describe me as _____.
   I could describe myself as _____.
   The Truth is, I am _____.
   The Truth is, I am (in one word) _____.

EXAMPLES

Statement I, my journal might include - I *moved to Sacramento after a divorce. My children were adults and lived away, my work environment was toxic, my beloved dog died. Chronic pain and depression were the worst they had been. Then I found hope at a yoga studio and a teacher asked me if I'd like to sign up for teacher training.*

I: I AM DOING THE WORK BECAUSE YOGA HELPED ME FEEL BETTER.

Statement II, my journal might include - I *needed healing because a relationship ended badly because I didn't know how to be in a healthy relationship and neither did he. We grew individually and shrunk together. I pushed him to prove he would love me forever. The answer was no. I also needed healing because of a hostile work environment had turned everyone against me, and because my daughter was suffering in dysfunctional relationships, and because my son was in the Navy on a ship as a rocket launcher and I feared for him, and because intense neck pain prevented me from experiencing normal enjoyment of activities.*

II: I NEEDED HEALING BECAUSE MY MIND & BODY FELT BROKEN.

Statement III, my journal might include. I *was broken because it felt like my first marriage broke me mentally, emotionally, and financially. I didn't know the right decisions to make next. Years later, my 2nd marriage was eclipsed by a business.*

III: I FELT BROKEN BECAUSE I STAYED IN PAINFUL RELATIONSHIPS.

Statement IV, my journal might include why I chose unhealthy relationships. *I chose relationships that hurt me because I felt disconnected. As a child, I was alone a lot. As a young adult in the Army, I accomplished more than I ever believed I could but was hurt badly. Then I left everything to move 2000 miles to sit in self-inflicted fear of loss realized*

IV: I CHOSE PAINFUL RELATIONSHIPS BECAUSE I DIDN'T TRUST MYSELF.

Statement V, my journal might include why I didn't know, trust, or love myself. *I didn't trust myself because I felt abandoned by people that I thought would protect me.*

V: I DIDN'T TRUST MYSELF BECAUSE I DIDN'T KNOW HOW TO FEEL SAFE.

a)   I fear that I will face this life alone.

b)   It has cost fulfilling relationships, even with myself.

c)   I will create and feel more pain. I will be alone.

Others have described me: INSPIRING HOPE, COURAGE, CONNECTION.

I could describe myself as JOYFUL, RADIANT, INFINITELY HELD.

The truth is that I am NEVER ALONE AND DEEPLY LOVED.

The truth is I am UNITY.

3. If you were offered $1M or the counsel of someone very wise, which would you take and why?
4. What are your limitations to doing your purpose in the world and why are they limitations?
5. How might releasing things beyond your control change your life?
6. If your field was free from attachment to the senses, memories, impressions, intelligence, self-will, disdain or states of change, what would it look like?
7. Name something you love doing that doesn't involve electronics, other people, self-gratification, drugs, or sleep. Try doing this for one hour total where you don't reach for distraction while doing it.
8. Chant, say or sing the Maha mantra or another affirmation to remind you that compassion for self and others expands wisdom and joy.

Hare Rama Hare Rama; Rama Rama Hare Hare
Hare Krishna Hare Krishna; Krishna Krishna Hare Hare
Translation: Calling on the source of wisdom to remove illusion.
Meaning: Honoring the qualities of devoted compassion, love, tenderness within.

11. Dharma

The Work of Sacred Service

Seva is Sanskrit for selfless or sacred service. But what is selfless, is there any such thing? Does our humanness allow us to truly give to another without any thought of reward? Can one assist another person, community, or group without expectation of what goodness may arise?

Most major religions hold Seva or something like it, as a key component of spiritual well-being. The word Seva itself is often associated with the religion of Sikhism, which originated with the founder Guru Nanak during the 1500s in the Punjab region (now India-Pakistan) during a time of religious persecution. Its beliefs include faith and meditation on one creator, unity, and equality of all or "Ek Onkar" (oneness), engaging in selfless service, striving for justice for the benefit and prosperity of all (even when that means resistance from oppression), and honest conduct and livelihood while living an active householder's life based in truthfulness, creativity, self-control, and purity.

In my personal experience, Seva has helped me to get out of my own way and live my truth as much as teaching yoga. But seva challenges us to look at ourselves differently and is bound to spotlight negative samskaras that may show up in our perceptions, such as caring for others out of a perceived obligation, or an underlying comparison of another's human condition, or even judgement of the seva's level of success.

Seva is service without attachment, and while aspects of it may include monetary or other resources, that is not what it is at its heart. Selfless service liberates the purest aspect of us within that wants to give. For example, in *Tuesdays with Morrie* by Mitch Albom, Mitch asks his coach if he can visit him weekly. During that time Morrie shares stories and insights on life such as, "Taking makes me feel like I am dying. But giving makes me feel like I am living." One of my stories of giving follows in hopes it may provide insight into your journey. Some names have been changed due to respect for loved one's privacy.

157

The Work – Part 1

"Anyone can love babies and puppies, the real work is with that which is hard" — *AMK.*

I felt certain as I paced back and forth in my office, the swish of my wide-legged dress pant bottoms accompanies my thoughts of how there is no other way. After 8 years of working above and beyond for this organization, I will speak my truth and trust my boss will honor it.

My office, adorned with the sign, "Procurement Analyst," symbolizes that commitment. What this position was before me is not what it is now. I wanted more, so I gave more, and it became more. True, I was the only one in the organization who left the country frequently and ended the year with no vacation, but now more was not enough.

I wanted it all.

I stepped out of my office and fixed my gaze on the motivational posters affixed on either side as I made my way down the hall. Some were soldiers and others of nature. All had captioned inspirational messages that I agreed with wholeheartedly. Finally, I stood at attention outside of my director's door, waiting to be called in. Perhaps what I was most concerned about was disappointing him. I'd had a lot of great bosses in my previous jobs, in fact it seemed that each had been more courageous, more expert, more inspiring and more caring than the last. But Mr. Wild had been the first to expect me to do more than he had, no matter that I was a woman and relatively early in my career, and he gave me the autonomy to prove it.

"Sir, I'd like to stay working here. But I need 2 weeks unpaid leave a year to volunteer or I'll join the Peace Corps".

He smiled at me from across the large, polished desk and granted my leave. I may have seen a tear welling in his eye. He was a deeply religious man and knew enough about me to realize that I was on a spiritual quest.

158

Coloring in the Margins One year prior, my extended family and I had embarked to a tourist destination chosen to suit everyone in our group – hiking, museums, cultural heritage sites, beaches, and boating. A week before departure from the states, I recalled that a child I was sponsoring also lived in Guatemala. A query to the foundation revealed she lived at one of villages around Lake Atitlan that was included in our jam-packed itinerary. With a great sense of trepidation I could not understand, I asked if it were possible to meet her.

Being a child's sponsor was something I hadn't meant to be after a childhood of overhearing adults speculate about such scams. But during mass one Sunday, a guest speaker told us of a need for donations outside of the church. This annoyed me. Routines and rituals at Catholic Church had provided momentary fulfillment that belonged to me after rousing my unwilling family to put on clean clothes and frantically rushing to town in search of a parking space in an overfilled lot with people clamoring to feel better. It was an unwritten contract really.

Yet photos of seemingly devastated human beings lined the exit of the church, so my children and I stood with the rest of the parishioners, stuck. One picture, a girl around my daughter's age, with almost the same birthday, drew us in. Since then, $30 had left my account every month, and colorful letters with margins full of hand-drawn flowers, sun and mountains from a girl named Petra arrived in my mailbox frequently.

So when I found myself pacing the shores of a small village on Lake Atitlan, I silently condemned myself for opening pandora's box. A translator and social worker would accompany Petra by boat from her village to the dock I studied, where people with dark hair in brilliant clothing moved about oblivious to my fears.

When Petra, her parents and her entourage arrived, we went to a private room at our hostel to expose what we were there for. Petra's Mom, Rosa, spoke Tz'utujil, and was mostly silent. Emilio, her dad, spoke Spanish and delivered lengthy statements of gratitude that his

159

daughter could go to school past the 1st grade because of me. I placed the glitter pens and journal in Petra's hands and also said thank you a million times as it seemed we were all moving toward closure. Then, at the last second, Emilio invited us to their home, crushing my plan for a superficially fulfilling experience that still allowed time for sightseeing.

Soon, this small Mayan girl sat silently next to me on one of the lake's many open passenger boats as we glided across crystal blue waters lined with massive volcanoes. 20 minutes later at another dock, we piled into 3-wheeled tuk-tuks decorated glamorously with prayers to Jesus for protection and bumped down rutted roads to the village of San Iglesia, with no doors promising to keep body parts inside. By the time we arrived at their house, my very existence had been transported to an alternate universe never before in my realm of my memory.

At the entrance of Petra's home, a tiny structure held together with dirt, cornstalks, rocks, and rusty tin smaller than my bedroom, something within me broke open. The curtain lifted, and Petra beckoned me inside with a bright smile in a dark doorway. After my eyes adjusted to this space with no windows, no doors, and no floor where three girls, ages 3, 8 and 12 lived with their parents and ate meals from an indoor campfire.

Tears welled as my heart grew outside of its chest.

Petra's Dad repeated his appreciation that my small monthly donation, which was more than he earned working hard physical labor in the same timeframe, had brought such opportunity to their lives. And then everyone else went outside except for me, Petra, her mother Rosa, and my mom. I assumed that Rosa's display of stoicism all day was due to a mother's understandable distrust. But her hard jaw softened, eyes watered and hands shook as she motioned for me to sit next to her on the bed. As Petra placed a handmade bracelet on my wrist, Rosa thanked me and God through body rocking sobs that needed no translation. Our tears mingled as we held each other like sisters.

160

When at last I stepped outside to the bright glare of the sun, the difference between the light was one thing. The fact that I had changed while the world remained the same, was quite another. Petra touched my hand and searched for words in Spanish to ask when I would return. To my surprise, my reply rolled off my tongue without a 2nd thought.

"Próximo año".

As we walked back to Santa Cruz on a narrow dirt trail through the mountains, a large group approached us. They were led by a little boy of no more than 4 years old, all of them carrying a large load of wood on his or her back. The little boy met my eyes as he passed, flashing the happiest grin I'd seen on a toddler in recent memory, exclaiming "Hola, Hola!" Though poverty, lack of health care and education were normal here; so was fresh air, working together as a family and trusting that each day was a blessing. Days after returning home, my thoughts turned over possibilities of what and how, as much as of why not. And so it was, the time to really do the work that I most needed to do was at last upon me.

My church led me to volcanoes
over blue waters a mile deep,
all of it awaiting my sacrifice.
Then the universe paused
to witness my soul awakening.

161

The Work – Part 2

With my 2 weeks of unpaid leave granted, from my couch in Kansas I began enlisting help to navigate permissions and masonry requirements from a non-profit performing construction near Lake Atitlan. Letters were mailed and a social media fund-raising campaign posted. Not only did we raise enough money for Petra's family to get a concrete floor and cinderblock walls with rebar and a door, but there was also enough for more floors and concrete stoves to flute cooking fire smoke outside.

Soon thereafter, my parents, daughter, and friends descended once again upon the "Wild West," the nickname for San Iglesia La Laguna that denoted more extreme poverty and lawlessness than its sister villages. We were armed with work gloves and dreams of basic shelter.

I stepped off a tuk-tuk again in front of what used to be Petra's tin shanty home in San Iglesia La Laguna that was now leveled in preparation for a new floor, walls, and roof. Petra slipped an embroidered traditional Mayan blouse over my head in a moment that seemed too great for a single lifetime. Tears streamed down my face and into crevices of century old cobblestone under my sandals, marking my passage into the most transformative spiritual journey of my life thus far.

Squatting on dirt that had been the foundation for all humankind's homes for longer than any of us would breathe air in my lifetime, amidst mounds of fine gravel mixture next to Petra and her older sister Estafania, I settled into waterproofing cinder blocks with bare hands. Petra was now 9 years old, tall for her age and very slight, with a quiet and careful demeanor. Estafania was 13, already developing into a woman's body, with evident wisdom and courage. Their long black hair often came untied from high braids and hung in long ponytails on their backs. But their long skirts, wrapped multiple times around their waists and held securely with long weaved belts, never looked less than perfect. We sang the ABCs in Spanish as it was the only common language any of us had basic knowledge, and I wondered,

"Am I here for these girls, or are they here for me?"

My parents hailed from a generation of farmers and ranchers who had toiled with whatever resources could be scavenged to produce shelter, water, and a patch of ground that might yield life for not only a family, but a whole community.

I grew up observing that a new pair of socks was a luxury and learned carpentry skills needed to repair my own home when money wasn't available to pay others. And when I set off for the Alaskan frontier with my young daughter and son, I took odd jobs on boats in exchange for a hindquarter of deer.

Still, none of us had constructed a home like this . . . hauling cinderblocks from the boat dock by hand and wheelbarrow, painstakingly sifting rocks through a screen, stirring massive mounds of refined sand, rock, concrete, and water by hand with a hoe, and bucketing recycled plastic food containers full of hope onto a dirt patch as towering volcanoes and quetzals looked on.

There were no bathrooms or running water nearby, and it was more than 90 degrees in our cramped work areas, yet everyone involved seemed to be experiencing the best day of their lives.

Hours later, Petra's younger sister, Paloma, claimed my daughter and her friend for playmates. Paloma was the most powerful 4-year-old I'd ever met. Her heart was so big, even her little chest curved out. She was a warrior in the making, no doubt. Dozens of children converged and street games commenced, inducing resounding echoes of laughter.

The next morning as the sun rose over San Iglesia, families with small concrete floors laid yesterday were offered a finish choice of red, blue, yellow, or green to complete the transformation of their previously dark spaces. A man in his 70s had lived his entire life on dirt and today was the first day the sun reflected brightly on a cheery red floor that he would find much easier to keep free of parasites. Another man, his family's new floor also in place, put down his construction supplies and picked up his bamboo to continue making loveseats for a profit of $.50 per day.

As the day went on, my mother radiated brighter with each passing moment. She had worked hard to shed expectations common in her generation and was a force of good and right unbreakable feminine power and wisdom transcending far beyond my world. At 62 years old, Mom had been a guest speaker at my last woman's retreat in Kansas, where she spoke of even when she'd had nothing except 3 kids to raise, she'd always had choices - to give up, conform, or seek a new way. She had navigated many landmines to forge new ground on the hard path to the easy life, and she believed that we all possessed the same resilience.

When Rosa, Petra's mother, arrived later in the day with a stack of wood she had hand cut, worthy of a young man in his prime with a chainsaw, I asked, "Can you teach us something?"

A neighbor granted us entry to her fire, and we joined in a circle on a dirt floor around a large ball of dough. The Mayan women and girls present corrected our mistakes in attempts to let us to save face, but it was humbling to know that this relatively simple act to feed a family was so challenging to do well. The indoor fire's smoke permeated every pore of our bodies, so it was fitting that soon the tears started until each of us was sobbing in sisterhood for all the beauty and suffering of creation.

Estafania, with wisdom beyond her years, saw the moment as not one of an ending, but one of a beginning. She suggested we walk to the beach, leaving Emilio standing in the street scolding Rosa as we walked away. Sitting on the rocks, staring into the crystal blue waters, I pulled out my journal and made columns for English, Spanish, and Tz'utujil. We learned greetings and practiced them wholeheartedly. "Kinbana, goodbye. Siaq'ara, good day. Utzaguach, hello. Piox, thank you.

Estafania added another word - ruguaxikin in Tz'utujil. Then she removed the earrings from her ears to place them in mine. "You are blood sisters now," Mom declared.

Releasing pre-conditioned expectations
can fill the heart with so much love
There isn't room for anything else.

164

The Work – Part 3

Our struggles differ. But our quests for love and purpose are very much the same.

Each time I returned to the giving ground of San Iglesia La Laguna there were some of the same friends and family, and some that were new as there was never a lack of people desperate to experience the glow they had witnessed unfold in me under Mayan magic.

On one visit, Estafania was 17 years old, and though she was an excellent student, she had recently dropped out of her first year of sponsored college and now asked me to build her a home. I said no and suggested that she go back to school, but she was devastated by my refusal to give something that seemed so easy for me to do in her eyes.

The non-profit that I'd been partnering with had strict rules about choosing benefactors for schooling and for construction, one being that the person needed to be actively attempting to better their own life. Besides, I was in the middle of a divorce and a move across the country to try to salvage my broken heart and questionable financial decisions.

To further complicate matters, Petra wore an air of entitlement, refusing to join in on school activities we took part in in another remote village. Rosa told me that Petra was the target of her father's alcoholic rage, leaving this little girl seemingly with the weight of the world on her shoulders . . . perhaps partly since she was "chosen" through sponsorship.

On a day off from construction projects, we were about to embark on a trek up the towering volcano San Pedro when Alex, a local guide who had become a close friend over the years, pulled Estafania and Petra aside at the trailhead as the first rays of daylight beamed through the rain forest and began speaking to them alone in Tz'juhil. For the rest of the hike, the girls bolted ahead of our group with happy smiles the rest of the day. He had put them in charge of their own attitude, their own care and the care of several white people ranging from the ages of 48 to 73.

Hours later, after climbing through prehistoric wonderland, Estafania, Petra, Mom, and I sat on the summit in silence.

Knowing that I couldn't intervene in abuse tortured me. Women and children did not have the same rights here as men, and any attempts at changing the justice system on my vacation would make things worse. So, I silently prayed that the girls could carry the strength, courage, and independence they exhibited up the volcano into the rest of their lives.

Yet even as I prayed for them, guilt crept through me . . . guilt for letting my insecurities, fears and hurts prevent me from achieving anything I'd ever dreamed of. After all, for women especially, regardless of other details, birth in the U.S. meant winning a lottery. Even though I'd had hurdles in my life, every one of them paled in comparison to these girl's hurdles to the point of utter insignificance.

Also on the hike that day were my aunts, Janet at age 73 and Sharon at age 62. After the first hour of hiking upward, our group rallied for a break at a vista point where people from another group decades younger than my aunts announced they could not continue the strenuous trek. Alex guided us to a private area to share a story of Guatemalan history while rechecking everyone's food and water situation. Then he gave each of us a respectful choice to stay at the lookout or continue upward. My aunts insisted on continuing, and so Alex made a pact with them.

Earlier in the week, Janet had taken perch on a cinderblock in the mid-day heat next to a Mayan woman who looked to be around her age. Janet began searching her bag for a snack to share when the woman peered into her eyes, smiled, and gently touched the rim of Janet's eyeglasses. Janet's shoulders relaxed as her smile broadened with deep understanding, and she removed the reader glasses from her face and placed them in the small, calloused hands of a women she only knew at the deepest level of her soul. The woman's look turned incredulous as if Janet had handed her a million dollars, so Janet coaxed her to try on the glasses to experience a part of life she previously assumed outlived.

Now it was Janet's turn to turn the clock back with a stranger's help.

The incline of the volcano was grueling and often required desperately grasping for centurion tree roots. About halfway up, it was customary to take your own journey at your own pace, lest you try to do this hard thing for anyone else and kill yourself. So, we hadn't seen Janet and Sharon in hours. Just when Mom could no longer bare not knowing, we saw Alex's hands held high in the air coming round the last bend of the trail before the top. He held Janet's daypack and Mom cried with relief, knowing her sisters were going to make it. Alex delivered Janet's pack to Mom and turned swiftly to cheer the determined women up the crux of the volcano.

Sharon appeared first, though she stopped just below the summit, transfixed. We clapped and motioned for her to come the rest of the way, but she was motionless in this moment toward freedom after climbing many mental and physical obstacles in her life. Janet and my sister appeared behind her then, and the moment of a lifetime was held suspended like a miracle unfolding under divine timing. The beautiful human spirit amidst suffering and triumph is an awe-inspiring mystery.

On the journey down, Janet held onto Alex for support while we all sang "Amazing Grace." Sunset turned to darkness behind volcanoes as we bumped down the long road back on tuk-tuks. When our feet hit the ground of our hostel, we made a bee line to the sound of a strumming guitar, where a young man sang lyrics telling of choices made. We toasted to journeys up and journeys down, and to men like Alex and girls like Petra and Estafania who shared the same quest for love and purpose.

The Work – Part 4

The next couple of years saw 3 more trips to Lake Atitlan and these years would hold the most danger of what I was most not ready for. One trip hadn't been planned at all, but as I hummed along with "Unbreak My Heart" in Spanish at a café in the middle of Mexico on my self-enrolled week of Spanish Immersion, an urge came over me to hop a bus down to Guatemala. The 12-hour overland route would cost less than 2 meals at that very café, and I could still be back at work on Monday. Soon I was at Petra's rebuilt home once again, this time ready for a "coming to Jesus meeting" about school.

A month earlier, the nonprofit organization that I'd been working with to sponsor Petra's private school tuition reported that she rarely showed up for classes. It didn't appear she would complete the criteria for passage to the next grade. The organization advised me to donate for the schooling of another student that valued an education.

Petra had not only been receiving my donated school sponsorship, but her family had also been receiving a monthly stipend for food and other household needs from my church donation. And it wasn't only Petra, now the youngest sister Paloma was also skipping out on her sponsored education paid for by a friend of mine.

Everyone's mood was somber as I walked with Rosa, Petra, and Paloma past rows of coffee plants up to a waterfall adorned with petroglyphs. Once our feet were in the water, I blurted out,

"How come you didn't go to school?"

Petra said she had been sick and Paloma had learning difficulties.

"But I want to go to school. I want to be a teacher."

I explained that organizational rules had been broken and now I wasn't allowed to pay for either of their schooling through the program – but I could pay school funds directly. And I asked,

"What about the other money I send?

Which is more important if you need to choose one?"

168

Rosa said that the money for school was most important, so I paid it and cancelled the other. Within weeks, I received pleading messages to pay the other donation again as it had been providing necessities. And news came that Estafania had delivered another baby promptly after her husband left her, so she was without school, work or shelter. I suggested they seek out women's coops near their home.

Months later I was again back in Guatemala for more projects, but it seemed nothing could go smoothly. One morning before sunrise, our collectivo (shared public van) drove through a roadblock of flames that leapt several feet in the sky. Later, our chicken bus lost its gears as we headed straight up a mountain.

None of it seemed to phase Petra and Paloma, their frustration with me remained fresh. I must have seemed especially lost because a young boy named Pablo took it upon himself to take care of me. His family had very little, but he insisted on sharing everything he had with me.

Before leaving, our group spent the day with Alex again, who took us to a village on the lake we had yet to explore, Santiago Atitlan. Alex put his arm around me and grinned widely, "I'm taking you to see Maximo. He came here to change the people, but instead the people changed him."

We found Maximo, along with two assistants (since Maximo was not alive) feeding him cigarettes, holding audience for a man who had pilgrimaged to seek faith in his family's strength and prosperity. The pilgrim knelt in front of Maximo while Maximo's assistants brushed the man as if trying to remove dust or debris before giving him guidance,

"Your pilgrimage and request are noble.

But you must wipe off the past to go forward with good luck.

The blessings you request need space to allow them."

Holy Season   Another year then passed before I returned to Lake Atitlan, this time for a different kind of trip… to stay in the jungle for a month and do nothing but self-care and write. For 3 weeks, I also thought of my local family every day, after all they were just a boat ride or tuk-tuk away in the next village. I wanted to see them badly but didn't wish to subject myself to more anger.

The small budget I was on only allowed eating out in the village except for once each week while I was there, and even then, it would need to be a small meal. A woman staying near me in the jungle to recover from an Ayahuasca retreat in Peru told me I was crazy for even thinking of going to see the family and that I was asking for trouble.

Then one day I ran into Emilio at the village square picking up trash and tending to a garden. I was still angry with him, but gentleness seemed to emanate from his body. He asked me to sit on a bench next to him amidst white orchids, or White Nuns, with blooms that reminded me of many Catholic nuns I'd spent time with growing up, but here marked the beginning of Holy Season and signified Guatemalans love for the rich culture, purity, and beauty of their country. Emilio was in an alcohol rehabilitation program and wanted to tell me that he was sorry for hurting me. Then he asked me who was caring for my heart.

So, on a Thursday that happened to be Thanksgiving Day in the U.S., I headed to Petra's house with a chicken and an apology.

"Knowing you has changed me. Before, I did not feel that I was doing enough. When we met, I started to understand my own choices and felt more closely connected to God. But all the time, I feared doing the wrong thing and possibly hurting instead of helping. I know now that none of our actions will ever be perfect, but we all have something needed in this world. I am sorry for any pain that I caused you. Thank you for allowing me in your life. I will always love you."

They reassured me that they loved me, even without any money. It had been hard, but after my donation had run out, Rosa found a way to send Petra to private school.

Rosa stood up and placed her arms around me,

"We are grateful for everything you have done. And for you.

We will always be family."

Then Petra placed a newly made friendship bracelet on my wrist.

Every year I return to the lake and spend time with my family there. And I search every street in every place I roam for even a glimpse of Pablo's generous soul.

Through this imperfect Seva attempt, I saw more of my soul and more of others than was possible in my lifetime otherwise. And I received far more than I gave.

*Selfless service can
present a clear
reflection of one's
inner journey.*

Soul School for Living True

An essential aspect of Ayurveda includes following your dharma because living in alignment with one's dharma allows universal harmony. When dharma is not aligned with actions in life, harmony is disrupted.

Dharma is often referred to as purpose or soul's mission. This book's approach to Dharma is self-discovery founded upon what we were born with (body and mind) and what we experience through karma. Karma means action, word or deed; or cause / effect. One event causes another, action creates reaction, and everything is connected.

Most people will experience a level of great discomfort or suffering (not the same as major or clinical depression) that brings elevated awareness after a signifigant traumatic event, or after realizing that attaining desired success did not offer true fulfillment or happiness.

This is similar to what is referred to as the dark night of the soul in a poem by San Juan de la Cruz over 500 years ago. Conflicts can be catalysts for mind, body and spirit growth as impacting the world positively is more difficult if you have not experienced suffering that allows you to feel, see and know on a deep level. Darkness, heaviness, hardness of tamas is calling for space to feel so you know what is calling you out of the door. Your soul is asking to be heard above your ego.

Victor Frankl writes of being a prisoner in concentration camps during the Holocaust and how purpose is tied to meaning and suffering, explaining that without meaning, suffering becomes a crisis creating an "existential vacuum". In many societies, the prison's form looks different and challenges to one's purposes can be difficult to identify.

According to the *Yoga Sutras*, our perceived limitations have to do with negative samskaras. But for many, it can seem there isn't enough time to find their purpose, let alone live it. During my years of navigating Seva in Guatemala, another personal journey emerged – one of discovering what living true to one's self means. I hope that my story of "Living True" may provide insight into your own journey.

172

Living True

That night, Carlos, the owner of a sturdy open-air restaurant built out of rocks and concrete mixed by hand, separating the jungle from the end of a rugged cobblestone street, swung his resonator steel guitar over his shoulder and sat next to me. He performed a raspy blues concert as if for me alone, drinking my wine in between songs.

After he felt ready, he leaned in to answer my unasked question.

"I never felt free until I was. People have a passion inside them, maybe music, maybe science, writing, building things, whatever . . . but feel guilty for taking time away from commitments, so usually spend no more than a short time, if at all, every day on their passion. It takes at least 10,000 hours to master a skill. But most people don't spend that much time, and many don't even have time to discover what they are passionate about."

Our conversation drew in others until many were in heartfelt discussion of what was most important to each of us. Couples from Canada, Australia and Portlandia were enthralled at the idea of volunteering but unsure how to begin – so I messaged a friend and within minutes they were set to arrive at a construction site the next day.

Conversation then turned to the political scene in the U.S., and I excused myself – making my way outside to smoke. A French couple was under a canopy of lemon trees doing the same. Soon we were in lively conversation about life, dreams, daring, loving, and holding onto something much greater than money. When they discovered I was leaving already because of limited vacation days from work, the woman glanced at me with disappointment,

"So, you're not living true."

That night under my thatched roof, I tossed and turned, wondering what really does define living true. Hell, I'd travelled the world, risked my life to find out its meaning, and even now – I'd travelled deep into the Mexican mountains solo and hitched a ride to stand on the doorstep of a family that had lost hope and blamed me for it – just to tell them I loved them. How was that not good enough to prove I was living true?

Then I saw what I was doing right now in this sleepless night was no better than the woman who judged me for not giving myself fully to life. And suddenly it was clear, a knowing came over me . . . living true has as many ways to show up as there are people on the planet, birds in the sky, animals on the prairie, trees in the fall, experiences of life, birthplaces, and so much more. And it is as universal as the power that holds it all together.

At sunrise the next morning, a small open boat sped me across the lake surrounded by volcanoes. I breathed in deeply as if to hold onto the smells of mountain highland fruits and nuts, along with fresh baked bread and live chickens that my seatmates, traditionally dressed Mayan women, were hoping to sell at another village that day. After the boat ride, I took the only open seat in a collectivo van filled with people from Israel, Germany, Russia, and Mexico.

As we headed north for our border crossing, the song "I Want to Break Free" played dozens of times. A rider strummed along with his ukulele, and it all mixed perfectly with the wind from so many open windows whipping amongst us - mingling all of our experiences into a plethora of connection. On the three flights back home, I had $2 in my jeans that hadn't been washed for a week, and shoes that smelled of chickens.

I was glowing.

It is better to strive in one's own dharma
than to succeed in the dharma of another"
- The Gita.

3 years later

On the collectivo from Guatemala city, a Canadian man shared how he turned his life around. "I went to Tikal 40 years ago. I was crazy back then. I fell asleep on top one of the pyramids and before morning, I heard the most terrible noise. The devil was after me for all the things I had done. I ran through the jungle for hours. That straightened me out."

For this trip, my intention was to straighten out what was left of the screaming monkeys my body stored in the form of chronic pain. This meant self-study and massages every day, most were self-massages, except for two that I carefully selected. The first paid massage was with an English therapist who worked into muscle groups and joints, saying,

"We keep trying to get something from 'out there.'

It's not possible, the only way to what makes you whole is in here."

The second was with a Mayan woman licensed as a general doctor and doctor of Ayurveda, who performed an abdominal massage on me in her garden, which provoked pain to release unaddressed trauma in my organs. Then she placed a singing bowl on my heart and said to repeat after her.

"I give you permission to feel."

Bang, she hit the bowl, and vibrations went into my heart and body.

"I give you permission to heal."

Bang. Tears flowed.

"I give you permission to give love and compassion to yourself."

Bang. Heavy sobs wracked my body.

But it wasn't enough. She knew I stopped letting emotion move.

I whispered,

"I am still afraid to trust."

My last paid self-care item was a tarot reading with a one-eyed woman in an actual pyramid. I didn't care to learn things about my future, but I did long to trust. Paulina looked at me closely out of one eye.

175

"If you feel free, you will trust."

Each time I walked solo down the long foot path to and from the village and my jungle casita, I practiced letting everything be a part of my life, not my death. On one of my last walks, I ran into Roberto, the man whose life changed 40 years ago in Tikal when he thought the devil was after him, but it only monkeys in the distance. He claimed to finally know what he wanted most out of life.

"I've got to find someplace where there is a community of happy people where I can raise food."

I smiled and handed him a bliss ball from my paper bag,

"Well, I hope you find what you are looking for. I won't see you again. I'm heading back to Kansas."

His hopeful expression turned to one of terror,

"Oh no! You can't go back there. They are not ready for you."

I smiled again and took my leave. Everyone was ready to have a home, be happy and live true. This much I knew. It is also true that it is far easier to look either at one's own unresolved backstory and/or to others for purpose and truth, to blame unhappiness and limitations. Unravelling backwards is easier than breaking cycles. Being fully present in a new cycle may be the most significant challenge we share as humans. There is refuge in knowing we are not alone in our suffering and that together, we can unlock suffering to create space for all to live true.

Not everyone is ready to receive or is desiring of what we wish to offer. That's okay. According to yoga, liberation is not selfishness, it is the opposite. Freedom begins with self if it is to take hold in the world, and no time spent living your Dharma is ever wasted.

Living True is the practice of awareness, feeling, knowing, and acting on what is true instead of that which is distorted.

Liberating Adjustments

"If you have come here to help me, you are wasting your time. If you have come because your liberation is bound up with mine, then let us work together"
— Aboriginal saying.

Years ago, as a new student in Buck's class in Northern California, I felt equal amounts of anticipation and shock as Buck walked through the packed class placing his hands on and giving personal attention to the 60+ people present. While I'd experienced a teacher helping me figure out a pose before, I'd never witnessed such intimacy amongst strangers. It didn't take long for me to settle into soothing touch that offered heightened body awareness and acceptance.

Around the same time, I also frequented another studio where teachers offered basic adjustments but also had class assistants who never spoke and were in stealth mode except when stopping at individual students to provide lingering assists. Not knowing where assistants were at any given time felt unnerving to me initially, but after a few classes ended in unexpected head and neck massages by people I had felt but not seen, I was curious as to what motivated these miracle workers.

During training at another studio, our curriculum required attendance at public Ashtanga classes. The combined effect of the sequence, focused ujjayi breath, heat, and length of the class meant that many bodies could contort unusually well – but not my body, which resisted seated series forward bends and pretzels shapes. Hands-on adjustments were also offered, and during the seated series my tense body was like a magnet for well-intentioned teachers and assistants. I knew that any forcing of my body, gentle or not, in these seated Ashtanga poses was an awful idea, and I was afraid. Rather than helping, adjustments in these poses resulted in my resistance and agitation.

Adjusting, also called assisting, is used here to describe both methods used for correction of misalignment, encouragement of body awareness, physical engagement, or relaxation. Throughout years of asana practice as a student in various public classes, I've experienced great adjustments, and some that resulted in never returning for repeat treatment.

My bad experiences occurred after informing the teacher before class not to offer adjustments when I was practicing a modified version of a pose as that could create problems for me. During these classes, these teachers forgot or didn't care and put their hands on me exactly when and where it was the most unwelcome. One teacher did this even after I said no loud enough for the whole class to hear. Unwelcome situations like this, and many others that are unwelcome for various reasons, dissolve trust and interfere with practice, both mentally and physically.

Earlier, this book discussed how yoga teacher-led space can cross lines from beneficial to harmful when a teacher uses their platform to foster dependence, insecurity, or fear in students. For many teachers though, harmful adjustments simply come from a desire to help combined with an inability to know what students are experiencing physically and emotionally. Lack of action can also cause harm. Neglecting to offer support to a student unaware of self-adjustments is not only dangerous, but also exclusive rather than inclusive.

The Yoga Alliance Code of Ethics includes many areas of concern for yoga teachers, but here in part and in summary are some that can help with creating a safer environment for everyone.

- ✓ Do no harm, intentionally or negligently, to students.
- ✓ Provide reasonable accommodation for people with disabilities.
- ✓ Obtain consent before adjusting students in yoga practices

Like Seva, adjustments can promote expansion of goodness when offered mindfully and ethically. And adjustments need not apply to only hands-on adjustments. Teachers can also adjust language to be more somatic or focused on vayus, as well as adjust energetic load through

178

props and pose variations. Use Warrior II as an example. Say that practitioner's joints appear misaligned, or for whatever reason they seem to be missing out on the pose's energetic and musculoskeletal benefits.

VARIATION OPTIONS
With all limbs:
5 Star, palms down, heel toe feet towards under hands, right toes turn to short edge of mat, bend right knee.
Without all limbs:
Chair or Prone Warrior II to align joints that are available.

SOMATIC/VAYU CUEING OPTIONS
With all limbs:
Feet corners press downward; inner arches lift.
Roots firmly ground as strength spirals upward to hips.
Energy gathers inward to midline and rises skyward.
Heart circulates through outstretched arms in front and behind.
Head centers over shoulders, shoulders align over hips.
Equanimity, all parts in balance, equal, connected to the whole.
Gaze at nothing and everything at once over front middle finger.
Without all limbs:
Review cues above and adjust body part references to retain energetic forces towards missing body part while engaging in chair or prone variation as indicated.

PROP OPTIONS
Dowel across shoulders or perpendicular to body for proprioception.
Teacher places hand on the mat to signify foot placement.

HANDS-ON ADJUSTMENT OPTIONS
Light touch on a hand to invite movement forward or back.
Foot on side of back foot to invite stabilization in back leg.
Light touch on knee and neck to invite flexion and rotation.
Palm on top of head to invite engagement upward.
Palms on shoulders, middle or upper back to shift alignment.

Embodiment of Jewels

Balancing Poses   Often, the most challenging part of balancing in life is overcoming mental gravity (negativity, judgements, comparisons, self-shaming, distractions, etc.) that can feel heavier than physical gravity.

One way to hack mental gravity on and off-the-mat is to expose the body and mind's natural elevating capabilities through small steps. For example, if you learned to ride a bike, you may have used training wheels or had someone steady the bike to develop confidence. Eventually you maintained your bike upright without assistance because with practice and adjustments, you developed the embodiment of balance within.

Balances are a category of poses that can also offer an experience of very real and present fortitude within while on your mat. These poses can increase spinal and core stability, circulation, coordination, concentration, brain and bone health, stamina, and increase energy.

Regardless of physical characteristics, all bodies can achieve balance through internal adjustments of energy, though not all bodies will look similar in that balance. Start by practicing variations closer to or on the ground, where your brain can learn to allow self-uplifting through a merging of both downward and elevating vayus at the same time.

Vibrating Breaths   Some breathing techniques can elevate energy upward while maintaining grounding effects. For example, both Humming and Whistle Breaths stimulate the vagus nerve and thyroid while promoting calm inner tranquility and can complement physical balancing.

Humming breath – sometimes called Bumble Bee breath – is done by placing your thumbs on the exterior part of your ear canals (or flipping your lobes inward with your thumbs) and then inhaling through your nose and exhaling in a humming sound with your mouth closed. You can also place your index fingers over your eyes, middle fingers on your nostrils, ring fingers above your top lip and pinky fingers below bottom lip. Humming breath can stimulate digestion and promote a sense of contentment. Try experimenting with different frequencies to note how they may change your inward experience.

Whistle breathing is done by puckering your lips on an inhale and then closing your mouth on the exhale. Alternatively, you can inhale through your nose and exhale through puckered lips. This movement of air and sound can stimulate both the vagus nerve and thyroid to promote tranquility within that can translate to a sense of levitating equanimity like the embodiment of a bumble bee.

Buddha   Embodiment used here means to absorb, assimilate, incorporate, or integrate yogic teachings and practice that promote equanimity and inner peace. In Buddhism, this principle is often expressed in terms of - "Be like the Buddha" or "Buddha is everywhere."

Some Buddhist mantras and chants overlap with other tradition's chants, as in the Mahayana sutras which correlate to both ancient Vedic texts and the rise of Buddhism. The Buddhist mantra, Om Mani Padme Hum or the "jewel in the lotus," can settle the mind, open and uplift the heart, and promote embodiment of practice that can transform ordinary thought and actions into exalted ones like that of a Buddha. This transformation from ordinary to exalted is the embodiment of crossing the threshold from past karma to Living True.

Embodiment –
Absorb, assimilate, incorporate, or integrate teachings and practices that promote equanimity and peace

Self-Study

1. Dharma Statement

   Use concise answers (you already know the backstory).

   a) My body is seeking _____,
      My mind is seeking _____,
      My spirit is seeking _____.
      What I don't want is _____.

   b) If you had 10,000 hours of free time, what one passion would you use to spend it learning or practicing?

   c) If you had a 2nd 10,000 hours, what else would you choose?

   d) What have you known to be true about yourself since you were a child – without other's input?

   e) Review your Chakra reflections. List 3-5 potent insights.

   f) Review Enneagram type/wing's gifts/healthy levels (optional). List 3-5 words that resonate.

   g) Review your Dosha's qualities. List 3-5 words that resonate.

   h) Review your Truth answers (from the Edge exercise). List 3-5 words that resonate with you.

   i) Write a Dharma statement to guide you through any important decision by using the words you wrote that feel most potent to your soul and/or summarize answers into more potent words.

   j) Consider how your soul would most like to serve others, or what the thousands coming after you or before you in your lineage would ask of you if they could. Review your word list and add any that are missing from what your soul might say.

   k) Practice arranging the words into one or two sentences that are specific enough to guide you, and general enough to cover every aspect of your life. Say your sentence(s) out loud and make changes until a version lights up your whole being.

      Example: I unite through service of love, compassion and truth to expand joyful authenticity, belonging, prosperity, and wellness amongst all beings seeking harmony, including myself.

2. Seva
   a) Part 1, The Work - Reflect on Seva Choice.
      ✓ What do I desire to give freely of the deepest part of me?
      ✓ In what ways can I give this service without attachment?

   b) Part 2, The Work - Reflect on Consequences.
      Consider the unintended consequences that may arise, such as those of culture and race. For all of time it seems, one religion, race or culture has been attempting to change another religion, race, or culture . . . often citing the benefits of goodness for all but inflicting something entirely different. And, as complex as religion, culture and race considerations are, perhaps even more complex is the consideration of what abuses individuals you are offering Seva have suffered. It can be beneficial to consult experts prior to setting forth on your Seva to help mitigate unintended harm arising from ignorance.
      ✓ How much do I understand who is affected by my Seva?
      ✓ Who can help me to understand how to share my Seva?
      ✓ Can I be present for what unfolds that was not anticipated?

   c) Part 3, The Work - Reflect on Control.
      A time will come when your ego wants to judge your Seva results. It may arise as pride, frustration, anger, or heart felt pain that your intentions did or didn't obtain results deemed "good."
      ✓ In my Seva, how can I surrender when necessary and let others and/or the universe/God unveil the rest?

   d) Part 4, The Work - Reflect on Time.
      Short durations of practice of service without attachment do not often reveal the complexities that evolve with service over time.
      ✓ Knowing that true contemplation and revelation takes time, how long will I devote to this Seva?
      ✓ How can I plan ahead for the time needed for this service?

3. The work of service. Put your answers to work.

4. Consider ways to assist people with somatic and vayu focused cues.

   a. What are concise somatic and vayu focused cues for these poses considering practitioners with all limbs?

   Half Lift

   Upward Dog

   b. What are concise somatic and vayu focused cues for these poses considering practitioners without use of lower limbs?

   Downward Dog

   Warrior 1

5. Chant, sing or say Om Mani Padme Hum or another affirmation that promotes a sense of embodiment of both grounding and elevating at the same time. Try this for 3 minutes.

Om Mani Padme Hum

Translation: The jewel is in the lotus.

Meaning: Honoring embodiment of equanimity and tranquility in mind/body.

12. Revelation to Revolution

Inner work provides valuable insight into why we show how we do and so informs our form and the foundation, not as assumptions without merit, but as causation and cause for meaningful differences in life

Similarly, the subtle energies of the Chakra system, Enneagram wisdom, Ayurvedic science, Dharma, Seva, and mastering the external through Pratyahara brings the foundation of yoga to life for action towards individual meaning and purpose.

However, the unveiling of layers can reveal a depth of wisdom that may feel overwhelming at first. After all, most people have lived much of their lives within their samskaras (pre-conditioned thoughts and actions), and opening doors previously inconceivable can feel paralyzing.

Decades ago, when I began what I hoped to be a new cycle of life; I instead experienced a subtle liminal place between freedom and self-constructed limitations that felt like a hard barrier to change. Though events forced me through those barriers, I was a willing participant because going back to wearing blinders would feel like death.

During this liminal unraveling, I picked up a handsaw and set out to blaze a new trail through the woods. Each day after work, rain, snow, or heat, I went to the forest to forge a new path I named the Liminal Trail.

When outer work meets inner work, actions must channel that inspiration and fear across boundaries and into a revolution for mind, body and spirit that evolves old samskaras into new possibilities. This process can be messy, but breaking barriers for long-term impact requires a surrender of assumptions of what a path might look like.

Channeling you will feel chaotic. Let it be there - alongside the mess. The revolution of samskara and samsara happens there.

Part 3 of this book integrates the foundation of yoga with the personal revolution of inner work to offer a perpetual evolution of goodness.

Part 3 – Unity

I released the birds to fly,
The brightly colored wild ones.
Winged hearts and voices of aspects of me.
Yet they clung to the open cage door.
Peering out, bound to artificial by might.
Who might be.
How might be.
What might be.
In time, revelation came upon them,
that might was the cage itself.
And that true freedom lay waiting.
Looking in.
Who is in. How is in. What is in.
And in that way, to that holy drumbeat,
at last they lifted.
In joyful song of revival.
Evolving into infinite possibility.

13. Channeling

After another surgery that didn't fix my chronic pain, I questioned that maybe my pain really was all in my head. Some health care providers had implied just that, but their theory defied logic in my view. For a decade, I'd consistently practiced on and off-the-mat yoga, Qigong, and exercises given to me by physical therapists and trainers.

How could I have achieved an all-time high in mind-body connection without my brain somehow getting the message to rewire itself? Why did my body still tense if I wasn't mindful of releasing tension? And how come some body parts couldn't release tension no matter what?

If chronic tension and pain did stem from learned responses in my nervous system, then maybe I could hack those unwelcome messages going straight to my nerves to wreak havoc. So I took Emily Dickinson's advice, "If your nerve denies you, go above your nerve."

Understanding Nervous System basics can help identify where to aim when looking for physical channels attached to grooved painful samskaras.

After death, well-meaning sighs echo in unison.
"at least they are no longer in pain."
There is so much more to death
than being out of pain.
And there is so much more to life too.

Yoga and the Nervous System

Your nervous system tells your heart to beat, your breath to breathe, your stomach to digest food, your brain to learn and remember, body parts to feel and move, sleep to happen, and wounds to heal. This system's coexistence and communication with other bodily systems is genius. It often performs like a silent hero with as long as it receives maintenance.

Maintenance includes nutrition, exercise, injury protection, care for conditions (injury, infection, or diseases), avoidance of toxins (environmental hazards, pesticides/artificial additives, certain drugs), prolonged blue light exposure, and prolonged stress.

Each component of your nervous system tells a specific story about what and where issues may arise. Diving into these areas can also help pinpoint which self-care method supports that component's health.

Nervous System Major Components

1. Central Nervous System *(CNS)* = *brain* and *spinal cord*
2. Peripheral Nervous System *(PNS)* = *nerves* branching from CNS

The PNS has 2 parts:

Somatic nervous system *(SNS)* = *voluntary* movements

Autonomic nervous system *(ANS)* = *involuntary* movements.

The ANS has 2 main parts (the 3rd is embedded):

Sympathetic Nervous System (*fight* or *flight*)

Parasympathetic Nervous System (*rest* and *digest*).

Enteric Nervous System (*gut brain*)

CNS, Brain

The Central Nervous System (CNS) includes one of our major organs – the brain - which consists of distinctive parts working together.

The brain's frontal lobe houses personality and cognitive processes such as emotional expression, problem solving, memory, language, judgment, and sexual behaviors. The frontal lobe lies just behind the forehead and includes the prefrontal cortex, which is not fully developed until young adulthood. Our prefrontal cortex helps with high level memory, attention, and emotion regulation.

The limbic system exists deep in the brain's center and is often grouped in what is called the reptilian brain. It manages primal responses for survival, reproduction, and social needs, and is also a home for of our body's previous experiences.

Some limbic structures are:
- ✓ hippocampus (memory)
- ✓ amygdala (emotions based on memory)
- ✓ cingulate gyrus (processing unpleasant experiences)
- ✓ basal ganglia (voluntary movements and rewards)
- ✓ hypothalamus (regulating body temp, hunger, homeostasis)

Brain structures can change shape in reaction to negative experiences, injury, and stress. This is called brain neuroplasticity – the brain's ability to adapt given new information. For example, psychological trauma and prolonged stress can cause durations of anger, depression, chronic fatigue, and anxiety that change brain structures and chemical balances, such as in depression, PTSD, and neurodegenerative diseases.

Brain structure can also change due to positive experiences, learning and treatment, including some yogic methods. Even as far back as the 1930s, psychiatrist Carl G. Jung lectured in Zurich, Switzerland on the psychology of Kundalini yoga, which includes unusual movements known to stimulate the brain.

CNS, Spinal Cord

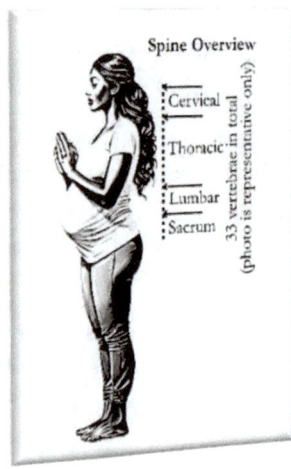

Spine Overview

Cervical
Thoracic
Lumbar
Sacrum

33 vertebrae in total
(photo is representative only)

Our spinal cord connects to our brain in a band of tissues, nerves and cells that signal sensations and movement in other body parts. It is divided into regions that work together – the cervical, thoracic, and lumbar.

Damage to the spinal cord includes injury, illness, and/or compression, leading to limited nerve messaging and subsequent mobility and sensation limitations or other changes.

Restricted function of the spinal cord often results in anxiety, depression, fatigue, loss of muscle mass and referred chronic pain. Pain can become a cycle of prolonged psychological and physiological focus on avoidance of pain which can lead to more pain.

Pain experienced can be:

*V*isceral (from *internal organs,* can be *felt but not rationalized*)

*S*omatic (from *skin, muscles, joints,* can *emphasize symptoms*)

*N*europathic (from *nerve damage* or *dysfunction*)

Spinal cord health benefits from a good mattress and posture, limited time in one position, core and back strengthening exercises, and movement of cerebrospinal fluid. Yoga poses can improve posture, strength, and spinal cord fluidity, especially when adapting or modifying poses to improve spinal alignment.

Practicing off-the-mat yoga can also compound benefits of poses and breathing techniques, as can physical therapy, massage, chiropractic care, acupuncture, and mental health therapy.

PNS, Somatic (SNS)/Voluntary Responses

The Peripheral Nervous System (PNS) is made up of nerves that travel from your CNS (brain and spinal cord) carrying messages as electrical currents to and from other body parts to call for a somatic response (voluntary) or autonomic (involuntary) response.

The Somatic Nervous System (SNS) includes sensory nerves that help us react to feedback our brain receives from touch, taste, sound, smell, etc. It also includes motor nerves for conscious direction of our muscles as well as some involuntary reflex responses. Damage can occur from inflammation, autoimmune conditions, diabetes, Lyme disease, shingles, chemical exposure, injuries, tumors, and genetics. Prolonged damage can result in neuropathy (weakness, numbness, and pain).

Psychosomatic conditions can also be influenced by our body's previously stored responses to past trauma that can present similarly as other damage to the somatic nervous system, including muscular pain, compromised immune system, fatigue, bruxism, tremors, heart palpitations, GERD or IBS, dizziness, insomnia, and fight or flight response to unexpected sounds, movement, and touch. Physical and emotional stored trauma responses can override natural brain feedback loops, meaning support for lasting recovery may require multiple forms.

Our somatic nervous system's health benefits from exercise, good sleep, a healthy weight (which varies according to Ayurveda), and vitamins such as B12 and B6. Other treatments can include spinal injections, nerve ablation, physical therapy, acupuncture, chiropractic care, ART (Active Release Technique), and mental health therapy.

Studies have reported positive impacts of the somatic practice of yoga on neuropathy as well. The somatic practice of yoga focuses on mindfulness about where body parts are and what sensations are experienced (other than sight) to connect mind and body. Somatic practice can also include pranayama (breath regulation) and guided meditations, such as those in Yoga Nidra.

191

PNS, Autonomic (ANS)/Involuntary Responses
Sympathetic & Parasympathetic Nervous Systems

Part of the Peripheral Nervous System is the Autonomic Nervous System (ANS) which acts as a conduit from your brain to most organs to regulate processes outside of conscious control, like salivation, tears, sweating, heart rate, and blood pressure. For example, when you are hot, your body sweats; and usually your breath keeps you alive.

The ANS includes the Sympathetic Nervous System (SNS) which helps you react to perceived danger without conscious thought. Threats to well-being lead to brain messaging of fight (face), flight (escape), freeze (become still), or fawn (comply) as survival responses meant to be temporary. Long term heightened sympathetic responses can arise from infections, chronic stress, and trauma that can lead to constant distress like PTSD, depression, migraines, digestive issues, and insomnia.

Optimizing function in the SNS includes practices and treatments to manage automatic trauma responses, including vagus nerve stimulation that can trigger calming neurochemicals. Breathing techniques that target vagus nerve activation include Ujjayi (introduced in Part 1 of this book), as well as Breath of Fire, among others. To do Breath of Fire, start by panting like a dog with your mouth open. Place a hand on your abdomen to feel where the panting is felt. Next, close your mouth and recreate that breath by inhaling through your nose naturally and exhaling rapidly.

Breathing techniques that activate parasympathetic responses include Durga breathing (covered in Part 1), as well as the Caliber of Life breath that is done by inhaling through your nose for 5 seconds, exhale for 5 seconds, and then suspending your breath out for 15 seconds. Mantras and meditations can also strengthen the PNS, many of which are included in this book's companion, *Body as Teacher.*

You can fight.
You can hide.
You can shut down.
You can comply.
You can also breathe.

192

ENS, Brain in the Stomach

The term gut health is commonly used to describe how well our esophagus, stomach, small and large intestines, liver, gallbladder, rectum, anus, and pancreas are working together to break down and absorb nutrients from what we eat and drink, and discard what isn't needed by our bodies. Since digestion usually occurs automatically, it can be taken for granted, but it is an all-consuming process.

By the time we notice a problem with our digestive processes such as bloating, constipation, diarrhea, IBS, leaky gut, GERD, heartburn, etc., our Nervous System is already impacted because what happens in the brain shows up in the stomach and vice versa. The brain and stomach partnership is explained as the Enteric Nervous System (ENS), the millions of nerve cells in the gastrointestinal tract that communicate with the ANS on continuum.

Digestive processes are primarily a parasympathetic response, so digestion happens best when we rest, and because of the ENS-ANS connection, this rest applies to the brain too. Mindful eating may feel difficult on days that require much multi-tasking, but eating in a rush has a negative impact on digestion and our mental state because our ANS recognizes our hurried stress as something to prepare a flight or fight reaction to which puts us on edge, rather than in a state of relaxation needed for optimum digestion, absorption, and metabolism.

When it comes to supporting a healthy brain-gut connection, small changes go a long way. For example, a few slow long deep breaths in the lower abdomen before eating takes no more than a minute but is enough time to engage the parasympathetic nervous system for rest and digest even when we are in a hurry. Poses that place additional pressure on the abdomen can also promote digestion.

Yoga can be so effective in calming the brain in the stomach that most yoga teachers recommend separating practice about 2 hours from mealtimes to ensure enough time for digestion if possible.

Taming Monkeys to Focus Resources

Years ago, I was part of a 4-person team in a "Cowboy Tough" competition, a 360-mile unsupported race through Wyoming backcountry that involved trekking, mountain biking, rock-climbing, white-water rafting and canoeing across a course we traversed with map and compass. Months prior, I announced to my team that I needed to drop out as my physical pain was unbearable, and it threatened to seep into my race thoughts and actions. But my teammates promised to help.

It was true that our team was adept at mountain biking through ravines and over boulders, rappelling off cliffs, paddling through thunderstorms, orienteering through snakes and poison ivy, eating packaged food while changing clothes on a dead run following the needle on our compass. We were also surrounded by superhuman teams who could somehow do all we could do in less time.

Nearing 30 hours into the race with no sleep and having suffered significant setbacks, our team's pace crawled close to quitting. We had only practiced similar beat downs together on terrain with less elevation and shorter durations. And now, it didn't matter if our bike frames were composite, titanium or aluminum. Without focus, it would all fall apart with the collective resonance of a trainwreck. And it did.

Though I was typically practical, playful, and curious, I became a demanding, insensitive, adversarial escapist. Another teammate who normally offered reassurance, trust, and vision became catatonic, passive-aggressive, and ambivalent toward everything except conflict avoidance. A third teammate who was naturally funny, optimistic, and the glue of the team, turned panicky, defensive, and suspicious. The last teammate's usual warmth, affection, and humility became critical, resentful manipulation.

Had we spent as much time practicing laser focus as we had preparing gear - our natural gifts and actions may have better empowered the team.

We finished with buckles, but none of us were proud.

"You are taming a monkey. Once it is tamed, it will listen to you" — *Sri Swami Satchidananda.*

2000 years ago, Patanjali likely knew that focusing was a challenge for most people and provided Dharana as one limb of yoga for consistent practice. Dharana is single-pointed focus that offers deep internal wisdom and connection. And while many activities can help us feel we are in a state of Dharana, such as exercise (including poses), time in nature (hiking, swimming, gardening, etc.), massage, etc.; unfortunately, it can take a while doing these before thoughts of other people, places, things, and memories fade enough to focus on what is occurring in the present. Other focus tools often used are coffee, energy drinks, and certain drugs. But what if increased focus was available everywhere for free . . . even in the backcountry without sleep, water, food, or emotional support?

Nadis

Many breathing techniques act as focus tools, like channel breathing using the 3 primary nadis/channels that fall into the category of subtle anatomy. The Ida subtle channel is left of and parallel to the spinal column, relating to cooling (also called Moon or Yin) properties and parasympathetic nervous system. The Pingala subtle channel is to the right of and parallel to the spinal column, relating to heating (also called Sun or Yang) properties and the sympathetic nervous system. The Sushumna energy runs along the spine, relating to the CNS.

Surya Bhedana, or Right Nostril, is a breathing technique that utilizes the Pingala channel to stimulate the sympathetic nervous system for increased energy,

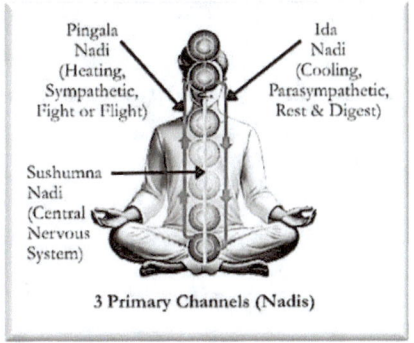

Pingala Nadi (Heating, Sympathetic, Fight or Flight)

Ida Nadi (Cooling, Parasympathetic, Rest & Digest)

Sushumna Nadi (Central Nervous System)

3 Primary Channels (Nadis)

195

circulation, energy, clarity, body temperature, metabolism, and blood pressure. This breath is done by lightly blocking your left nostril with your thumb or finger, then inhaling through your right nostril. Next lightly block your right nostril with your thumb or finger, and exhale through your left nostril. Continue inhaling through your right and exhaling through your left.

Chandra Bhedana, Left Nostril, is a breathing technique that utilizes the Ida channel for soothing and cooling effects on metabolism and blood pressure. This breath is done exactly opposite from Surya, or Right Nostril breathing, and can stimulate your parasympathetic nervous system to soothe anxiety and promote better sleep.

Both of these breaths typically also use breath retention, as does Nadi Shodhana, Channel Clearing Breath, which can help balance nervous system parts. All are included in this book's companion, *Body as Teacher*, along with other breathing techniques for nervous system focus.

Tara   Green Tara in Buddhism is a bodhisattva that chooses to lift sentient beings out of difficulty though she represents the mother of success, achievements, and liberation. Chanting the Green Tara mantra supports awareness of the eight great spiritual fears we have as humans: lack of knowledge, arrogance/ego, jealousy, rage, greediness, mistaken ideas, desire, and distrust. This awareness, coupled with equal awareness of our innate human resources of intellect, humility, equanimity, tranquility, altruism,

 action, contentment, and trust, can provide a tremendous sense of mind and body connection and protection.

The awareness of our fears,
coupled with awareness of our resources,
empowers both self-protection and achievement.

196

The Heart's Highest Intention

POV: When your ego gives you an ego boost for being so egoless.

Inversions are a category of poses that impact the components of your Nervous System via inverting your brain relative to your heart. They are also a great on-the-mat practice of Dharana, or laser focus because they involve hand placement, spinal alignment, core and bandha engagement, controlled breathing, specific relaxation points, and controlled ascents and descents.

Inversions can strengthen the entire body, improve balance, boost positive energy, and heighten self-awareness so long as they are done safely. However, inversions can also expose parts of your ego still seeking to validate self-worth at the expense of your body and brain.

Decades ago, my party trick of standing on my head felt like acting out a sequel of Green Eggs and Ham - I could do a headstand on a boat, with a goat, in the rain, on the train, in a box, on a surfboard, etc. Fortunately, by the time I began a consistent practice of yoga, I no longer wished to continue by Green Eggs headstand sequel. Instead I wanted all the benefits of feeling weightless without thought, sort of like a paranormal experience, in less demonstrative and dangerous variations. So, I chose to learn variations of inversions in workshops in small steps.

Turning of things upside down for new perspectives with laser focus on safe progression offered more than my party trick ever did . . . the feeling and knowing that reining in genius powers of the nervous and musculoskeletal systems can make what seems impossible possible.

Savasana

Experiencing this levitating supernatural space of brain inversion prior to stillness can greatly enhance your readiness for lack of efforting. So inversions are often done near the end of asana practice prior to Savasana, also called final rest or Corpse pose, which typically lasts 5 to 10 minutes. Savasana allows practice benefits to integrate in your mind and body.

Savasana can also be the most challenging pose of the class. Laying on your back on a thin mat over hard floor, in stillness, next to people you may not know in the dark can be the opposite of a blissful state. So preparations for the most benefit in Savasana include:

- ✓ Options for seated, legs up the wall, or laying on one's side.
- ✓ Comfortable room temperature.
- ✓ Low lighting to promote internal experience without preventing sight and eye pillows for those who want darkness.
- ✓ Props (bolsters/blankets for pregnancy, pain, temperature).
  - o Eye pillows on eyes/forehead, in palms of hands.
  - o Folded blankets under body or on abdomen for security.
  - o Rolled blankets under shoulders (armpit to armpit).
  - o Unfolded blankets to cover body (tucked under feet).
  - o Bolsters under knees or used for side-lying as needed.
- ✓ Calming sounds (either no music, nature sounds, or music without lyrics or words in calming pitches, tones, and rhythms).
- ✓ Neutralizing scents to limit overload of the trigeminal nerve.

Head massages can offer deeper relaxation if students grant permission.

- ✓ Use clean hands and a hypoallergenic lotion.
- ✓ Quietly kneel near one's head and rub lotion in your hands. Gentle smells/sounds let the other person know you are there.
- ✓ Place hands under their head and use fingers to stroke upward from neck base on either side of the vertebra to the skull's base. Repeat 3x, ending with thumb pressure at the skull's base.
- ✓ Gently anchor thumbs near the hairline next to temples. Place your index or middle fingers at point between eyebrows. With light pressure, fingers sweep upward over the forehead center and to opposite sides of the face, ending at your thumbs. Repeat this double U shape motion.
- ✓ End with slight pressure in a circular motion at the temples.
- ✓ To finish, hover hands, palms down, then rise quietly to leave.

198

"Perfecting posture is relaxing, relenting effort and allowing attention to merge with the infinite"
- Yoga Sutras 2.46.

Guided body scans can also support relaxation. However, talking through savasana can lead to less brain rest rather than more, unless the intention is a Nidra state.

Coming out of Savasana occurs best without sudden movements, sounds, or lights. Allow time to bask in a moment of presence before a need for action. Alternate language and movements so that coming out is natural. The sacredness of coming out into a refreshed state of consciousness can promote a new learned/automatic relaxation response wherein the pose is sacred regardless of details.

Once the full benefits of Savasana are experienced over a period, some find they can lay on the hard ground anywhere and experience bliss. The brahmin monks I witnessed in India that slept on cobblestone streets, with only their orange robes between them and the dirt and rock, seemed to always rise with a smile and peaceful light in their eyes.

*N*idra

Yoga Nidra can also be done while in Savasana. The practice of Nidra is derived from the *Mandukya* Upanishads outlining of differing states of human consciousness, including a fourth state that combines the first three. Later Tantric traditions formalized the formula that is now called Nidra. Kundalini Yoga calls this last state transcendental consciousness. Nidra is an effortless experience of awake awareness of what is true and is the practice of the 4th state of consciousness.

Upanishads States of Consciousness

1. *W*aking
2. *D*eep Sleep
3. *D*reaming
4. *N*idra or Transcendental Consciousness

199

Yoga Nidra is guided deep relaxation that is practiced while lying down for approximately 30-45 minutes. Guided meditations, or Nidra scripts, are systematic rotations of consciousness through layers of the koshas in a subconscious (awake) state which can promote clarity with old thoughts, behaviors and habits, and a renewed sense of self, a coming home. Many Nidra scripts are available on-line with these steps:

1. set-up
2. turning inward
3. sankalpa (heart's highest intention)
4. body scan (rotating consciousness)
5. breath awareness (connecting mind and body)
6. opposite sensations or emotions (stimulating homeostasis)
7. visualization (initiating sensations of lightness)
8. reaffirm sankalpa
9. coming back/return to breath and body

Many studies have been conducted on Nidra, including one at Walter Reed Army Hospital in 2004 where Robin Carnes led Yoga Nidra based on a book written by Dr. Richard Miller, a student of T.K.V. Desikachar. Dr. Miller's book integrated nondual wisdom teachings of yoga, tantric practices, Advaita, Taoism, and Buddhism with Western psychology.

Regular practice of yoga Nidra was found to counter stress, reduce anxiety, normalize irregular sleep patterns, improve cognition, boost creativity, and memory, enhance overall energy. A 40-minute practice of Nidra may be experienced by the brain as 3 hours of sleep.

The study at Walter Reed also found Nidra had positive impacts on PTSD and chronic pain in soldiers. Army leadership renamed the protocol of Nidra as iRest. iRest programs or Nidra classes are also used in hospices, senior facilities, prisons, yoga studios, and more.

"Bliss relaxes the atma, the inner self; Yoga Nidra is the doorway."
— Swami Satyananda Saraswati.

Self-Study

1. Which nervous system condition interests you the most?
   Research studies on the impact of yogic methods on that condition.
2. Make a diagram that lists parts of the Somatic Nervous System, Parasympathetic and Sympathetic Nervous Systems.
3. Try out some or all of the extra elements for Savasana for yourself while you listen to a recorded Nidra script.
4. Chant, sing or say the Green Tara mantra or another affirmation that helps you feel protected from lack of knowledge, arrogance/ego, jealousy, rage, greediness, mistaken ideas, desire, and distrust.

Om Tare Tuttare Ture Svaha
Meaning: Tara — star; Tuttare — healing from 8 fears;
Ture — liberation; Svaha — let this embed in me

14. Flow

Sutras Pada 3 - Absorption

The *Yoga Sutras* refined yogic teachings into an 8-Limb science of methods one can use to live a more meaningful life. Pada 1 defined yoga, the obstacles, purpose, and the importance of practice. Pada 2 outlined Karma, Kriya yoga, Ashtanga yoga, and six of the Eight Limbs. Pada 3 covers the last 3 limbs of yoga and what arises.

Sutras 3.1-3.15. Samyama is considered advanced and internal practice of the 3 final limbs of yoga.

+ *D*harana (*focus*/concentration)

+ *D*hyana (*meditation*)

+ *S*amadhi (*bliss*/transcendence/absorption)

= *S*amyama (*deep understanding*, self-control/knowledge)

Sutra 3.1. Dharana is deep concentration, shifting the diffused light of the mind into single-pointed focus. In Dharana, the mind is fixed on or bonded with one thing like your breath, a flower or tree, flame, or a picture. When Dharana is established through practice, the flow of meditation is possible.

Sutra 3.2. Dhyana is an unbroken effortless flow of knowledge and communication to and from an object of focus. After long stages of Dharana, this flow becomes easier, and Dhyana feels like timeless spaciousness.

Sutra 3.3. Samadhi cannot be practiced; it can only be experienced. Samadhi cannot be derived from blissful experiences from nature, bodily sensations, ideas/aha moments, or ego. It is something entirely different.

Sutras 3.4-3.8. Samyama practice is a threefold evolution that results in discovery of truth covered by human experiences. Practice of the first 5 limbs allows for these to unfold with time.

Sutras 3.9-3.15. Stages of unknowing/knowing will occur during this unfolding of Samyama.

Sutras 3.16-3.50. Samyama results in vibhutis (abilities) and siddhis (powers). Included in Patanjali's explanations are knowledge of past and future; the sun, stars, moon, all animal sounds, organs, knowledge of past life and other's minds; karma that is coming soon and coming later; the strength of an elephant and lightness to walk on water; being indestructible by mastery of perception; and omniscience. It is interesting that these abilities and powers have been mentioned in many spiritual traditions, though I don't personally know any yogi's who exhibit them.

Sutras 3.51-3.56. Kaivalya (independence) comes by not attaching to vihbutis and siddhis. When the mind is clear, Purusa experiences itself in absoluteness.

When the buddhi (intellect) becomes clear,
consciousness reveals itself and siddhis (abilities) are experienced.
When all of this has occurred in discernment without attachment,
liberation from suffering is possible.

Yoga and the Endocrine System

It's easy to make assumptions. And usually, they are wrong.

At 40 years old, a doctor advised me that a pacemaker was necessary to speed up my heart.

I stared at her blankly.

She assured me that pacemakers were common and sent me on a month's long journey of tests to prove her theory. After her tests were completed and no issue was identified, a nurse encouraged me to reduce my stress and eat more salt and protein. Another nurse encouraged thyroid and hormone tests and fixing my heavy periods. And when another doctor's recommended bone density scan revealed that my bones were 20 years older than they should be, I was told to take drugs and start yet another weight training program. I did almost everything recommended and also signed up for Kundalini yoga teacher training where I learned more about the endocrine system that I had in my previous fifty years.

Your endocrine system works with your nervous system to deploy messages through your bloodstream to regulate metabolism, circadian rhythm, mood, reproduction, and more. Dysfunction in the endocrine system can result in thyroid conditions, acne, menstrual disorders, and osteoporosis, as well as contribute to diabetes, infertility, obesity, cancer, and more. Disrupters include high levels of stress, some cosmetics and home products, plastics, pesticides, cigarettes, etc.

Understanding endocrine functions can help identify yogic methods that may support endocrine health in addition to nutrition, hydration, exercise, sleep, limiting disrupters, and medical care. In addition, some organs outside of the endocrine system work so closely with it that they must also be considered in endocrine health and function.

Endocrine Components and Yogic Support

The pineal gland regulates melatonin, a hormone that regulates circadian rhythms. Melatonin production benefits from natural light and practices that support CNS health, such as meditation and mantra.

The hypothalamus is a conduit between the nervous and endocrine systems, relaying signals relating to temperature, thirst, hunger, stress, and attachment behaviors. Yogic methods that can support the hypothalamus include breathing and focus techniques, and meditation.

The pituitary, also called the master gland, responds to signals from the hypothalamus to produce and/or release hormones, such as TSH (thyroid stimulating hormone), prolactin, and oxytocin. Yogic methods that may support pituitary balance include 3rd eye gaze, bowing poses, and mantra.

The thyroid receives messaging from the pituitary to regulate metabolism, body temperature, and energy. Yogic methods that may support thyroid health include poses and breathing techniques that stimulate the throat or neck, such as Ujjayi and Jalandhara bandha.

Adrenal glands respond to stress by producing cortisol, adrenaline, etc. that impact blood pressure, metabolism, and electrolyte balance. Yogic methods that can support adrenals include restorative yoga, Nidra, and breathing techniques that support the sympathetic nervous system.

The gonads (testes and ovaries) produce reproductive hormones such as estrogen, progesterone, testosterone, and others that impact growth and reproductive health. Yogic methods that can be supportive are those that increase pelvic circulation such as Kundalini frog and bridge pose.

The pancreas produces insulin that impacts blood sugar and food breakdown. Yogic methods that support digestion can support the pancreas, such as breathing techniques for digestion and poses, such as Cat, Cow, Cobra, and knees into chest.

Adipose, fat tissue, produces hormones impacting insulin, inflammation, and metabolism. Yogic poses, breathing techniques, and off-the-mat stress management practices can support metabolic health.

The kidneys, digestive tract and liver are also involved in hormone regulation. The kidneys influence blood pressure and electrolytes; the gastrointestinal tract produces hormones relating to hunger and digestion; and the liver metabolizes excess hormones. Supportive yogic methods for these organs can include breathing techniques and poses that place gentle pressure on them (such as backbends, twists, and right sided bends).

Endocrine system and nervous system components work hand-in-hand for your overall health. Positively impacting any component of either one can have a ripple effect into others. On the flip side, endocrine and nervous system issues are so interconnected that it can be difficult to know precisely where to aim supportive methods for the most benefit. Nonetheless, if you consistently feel a marked positive change after specific methods, they may be offering you benefits that are measurable.

Kundalini, Merging and Radiance

Recognize that the other person is you.
There is a way through every block.
When the time is on you, start, and the pressure will be off.
Understand through compassion or you will misunderstand the times.
Vibrate the Cosmos. The Cosmos shall clear the path.
(the 5 Sutras of the Aquarian Age)

Kundalini energy practices to move one's dormant energy upward along the spine and through chakras had interested me for many years. But after practicing Catholicism most of my life, the idea of awakening dormant energy for it to flow through into life sounded like black magic.

But, after years of painful injections into my lumbar and cervical spine for pain relief that rarely worked, I began looking deeper into Kundalini practices and ways to test my assumption for myself. After an introductory Kundalini training and a handful of practices, I experienced a boost of positive energy and sense of overwhelming connection that seemed to flow into all aspects of my life. It did indeed feel magical.

There was, however, darkness in the form of Yogi Bhajan – the man widely credited with bringing Kundalini Yoga to the U.S. from India. Bhajan had committed decades of abuses against students and teachers, and vile actions have traumatized many in the Kundalini community.

So, I embarked on all women led Kundalini training in the hopes of landing in a safe space in which to create more magical feelings in my life – which is exactly what happened. Now Kundalini kriyas add a dimension to my yoga practice that would not feel complete without them. Kundalini yoga is considered the yoga of awareness.

The history of Kundalini yoga starts long before Bhajan. Kundalini philosophy originated around 3000 years ago in the Upanishads and later developed more formally through Tantra and Laya yoga (considered the yoga of absorption). Kundalini practices were initially restricted to selective castes or lineages in India, which kept them relatively esoteric for centuries. During the Tantric era, Kundalini practices became more accessible to Indian householders, those people engaged in family life and everyday work. Then in the 1930s, awareness of Kundalini grew when psychiatrist Carl G. Jung lectured in Zurich with a group of scientists and doctors on the psychology of Kundalini and chakras.

Both Kundalini kriyas shared by Yogi Bhajan and Laya yoga practices combine mantra, poses, breathing techniques, and mudras in practice. And, both Kundalini and Laya yoga include Tanta's philosophy of energy movement emphasizing Shakti (the ability to experience change through energy). This weaving together of Bhakti and Raja yoga often differentiates Laya and Kundalini practice from other schools of Hatha yoga.

Laya mantras are primarily in Sanskrit. But Bhajan claimed to be a practicing Sikh, and he combined Sikh mantras in Punjabi written in a Gurmukhi script into the kriyas he taught However, Bhajan's abuses of others are not in alignment with the philosophy of yoga or Sikhism.

In 2020, the Olive Branch organization reviewed Bhajan's teachings and collaborated with the Kundalini community resulted in the revision of some of Bhajan's teaching methods. Though the trauma of this now dead teacher's actions is still fresh, this transparent partnering means that basic Kundalini teachings were not lost even though the teacher was.

In fact, legacy indoctrination that kriyas must be "as taught by Bhajan" can limit awareness of personal experience. For example, there are no wrong mantras to use in kriyas. And covering your head with a white turban is not necessary to practice Kundalini – though many Kundalini practitioners still wear white clothes with natural fibers and cover their head and hair to positively impact energy frequency or aura.

Kundalini kriyas are set sequences for specific outcomes. They typically include poses, breathing, mudras, meditations, and mantras that can impact both nadi (yoga's energetic pathways) and meridians (Traditional Chinese Medicine's energetic pathways). Because of kriya's focus on specific outcomes, their use of nadis and meridians, and because hundreds of set kriyas exist (for the nervous system, endocrine system, immune system, etc.), kriyas can appeal to those desiring heightened control of practice outcomes. Some kundalini movements are even in use in neuro health programs.

A 40-day sadhana includes practicing a specific kriya every day for 40 days in a row, as this is the time believed to be effective at making a marked change. However, as with all schools of yoga, yoga off the mat is as important as physical practice.

A daily kundalini sadhana is a daily routine that includes practice, as well as Ayurvedic daily routine essentials. One daily practice is eating only until full as well to protect the akasha, or cosmic space for energy to flow, within your digestive system. Another practice is short cold showers to build resilience and stimulate circulation, those this type of cold exposure is not recommended during menstruation, late term pregnancy, or for those with certain health conditions.

Kundalini kriyas typically begin with specific opening and closing chants. Sat Nam is usually the final closing of a Kundalini practice as an intentional upward momentum of energy. The two words together translate to "truth is my identity/name." Though both Sat and Nam appear in the same contexts used in this mantra as in ancient Vedic texts, the mantra's use in this way likely originated with Guru Nanak, founder of the Sikh tradition. When practitioners say Sat Nam to one another, it is a recognition of truth and the practice of truthfulness (Satya).

When we are truly ready to receive, then what we need will become available."
— *John Gray.*

I wanted to share kriyas in my small-town Midwest studio. But kundalini kriyas can include poses, breathing techniques, gazes, bandhas, mudras, and mantras that many people are not accustomed to — especially those who are more comfortable thinking of their bodies as muscles and bones rather than energy flowing through matter. So, I added descriptors to a weekly class for transparency about added energy work, and to my surprise, this class became one of the best attended classes at the studio.

Turns out, I was the one with the problem. Sequencing fusion classes with kriyas couldn't follow the format I used for other classes — a format including opening, presence, engagement, flow, edge, release, and savasana that is outlined in the next chapter. Adding the kriya to the flow or edge section of class and following it with savasana and then mantra would best extend benefits of the practice into life, but that left no place in class for musculoskeletal release after active physical work.

Recalling how vayus work from previous chapters, cooling down and stretching muscles after a kriya may disperse the energy momentum intended by the kriya. I wasn't ready to sacrifice energetic benefits, nor was I ok with sacrificing physical benefits, so it took a year of practicing different kriyas to discover the solution is based on vayus in each kriya.

Understanding vayu directions and how to balance joint actions and opposing muscle groups, combined with consistent and varied practice of Kundalini kriyas, can catapult your clarity of what, where, when and how to merge kriyas into a practice that is sequenced for functional wellness -while still optimizing vayus intended in the kriya.

For example, in my Kundalini training, a teacher introduced a pose that Yogi Bhajan called Ego Eradicator. My teacher reframed the traditional pose name to Radiance Charger, believing that better described the felt experience of the pose.

Radiance Charger requires holding both arms up at 60 degrees from your torso with fingers curled inward to knuckle pads on wide palms with thumbs up, while gazing internally toward your 3rd eye and doing Breath of Fire (BOF), usually for a minimum of 3 minutes. The BOF technique was introduced under the previous Autonomic Nervous System section.

Radiance Charger with Breath of Fire was hard at first, but after witnessing the practice of it transform my own facial appearance into some semblance of a fountain of youth, it became easier. Radiance Charger quickly became my go-to breath for a quick wake-me up at work, before public speaking or any other important creative or social endeavor.

Still, I knew functional sequencing for joints and muscles was necessary to physically sustain safe access to Radiance Charger's detoxification effects, increased energy, and laser focus.

To find a solution that met my desire for more energy flow without sacrificing musculoskeletal stability, I took the problem apart. I named the primary joint and muscle actions of Radiance Charger that could be destabilizing over time - shoulder joint flexion and abduction, and upper torso tension and spinal flexion. Then I looked for poses I enjoyed as much as Radiance Charger to offer opposite joint and muscular actions (counterposes), which were Camel, Reverse Plank or Table, Cow Face arms, Standing Seal, Qigong Spreading Feathers, and Shoulder Rolls.

The missing link then was vayu direction. Since this pose, along with Breath of Fire moves energy inward and upward through the chakra system and circulates outward toward the hands, its primary vayus are Prana, Udana, and Vyana. So, if one is to retain momentum after Radiance Charger, Camel, Shoulder Rolls and Cow Face Arms would complement this energy while stabilizing tense upper torso muscles.

211

The other counterposes I had picked out, Qigong Spreading Feathers and Standing Seal, release energy downward and balance energy (Apana and Samana vayus) so those could be included in my sequence prior to Radiance Charger and would complement stabilization of the root chakra, opening of the heart chakra and decompression of the Sympathetic Nervous system so Radiance Charger may even be more effective from the start of the pose.

Teaching Radiance Charger and most Kundalini kriyas also involved explaining the importance of physical alignment, mudra, and breath to increase possible endocrine and nervous system benefits. Short well-timed explanations were necessary to be effective, but concise and clear language can be challenging with such intricate systems. I was eventually able to do this by understanding how the Nervous and Endocrine systems work, as well as my own experience of kriya effects through consistent practice.

Since most kundalini kriyas have specific times for each pose, there is often time to interlace a short motivating story and Radiance Charger always reminds me of *The Little Prince*, the French story where a boy cleans a volcano every day, so it won't erupt in destruction. When performing Radiance Charger, it can feel exactly like cleaning stuck physical, energetic, and mental layers to access our wisdom (Vijnanamaya kosha) more easily while also practicing Pratyahara (mastering the external), Dharana (single pointed focus) and Dhyana (meditation).

Radiance Charger and several Kundalini kriyas are included in this book's companion, *Body as Teacher*, along with variations for health conditions and cautions, so that everyone present can safely clean their volcano.

If the volcano is cleaned every day, there isn't any eruption"
— *The Little Prince*.

212

Steering to Inward Prosperity

According to Yoga and Ayurveda, harmony in life is possible when we are in alignment with our inner self. While external-internal alignment is a felt experience, sometimes it can also be outwardly visible, such as when a practitioner seems to glow after practicing Radiance Charger.

Likewise, the alignment of our spines is integral to ease in life, though our spinal alignment or misalignment is typically not visible without imaging equipment that more closely displays how lifestyle patterns, injuries and health conditions have impacted spinal structures. However, when someone is "in" a Revolved pose, also called Twist, in the way that is best for their spine, often a sense of inner peace can radiate outwardly.

The act of steering oneself inward in Revolved poses can support digestion, balance, and spinal health, and promote a sense of internal alignment and prosperity. However, when it comes to these poses, what one's back should look like cannot be found by looking at the teacher or others. In fact, oversteering or forcing parts of your spine into a twist can reduce inward energy needed for mind, body, and spirit flow according to Tantra and Kundalini, and counter harmony according to Ayurveda. So, to achieve maximum benefit, progress into your own revolution.

+ *S*tabilize the spine by *aligning shoulders over pelvis.*

+ *L*engthen spine on inhale to *maximize space* between vertebrae.

+ *T*wist on an exhale from the level of the *navel and up.*

+ *F*inish into the twist as *gaze follows.*

= *R*evolved Pose spinal *alignment*

Some practitioners have difficulty understanding how to twist from the level of the navel, so after stabilizing and lengthening, try hinging forward 45 degrees before twisting to engage the thoracic spine more naturally, or start with progressive variations to learn alignment before adding deeper twists into a practice.

While revolved poses/twists do compress and stretch digestive organs, they do not rid your body of toxins. Clean water and food, healthy activity, limited exposure to environmental toxins, and good sleep are necessary to lower toxicity levels and reduce bodily system blockages for mind and body radiance and prosperity.

Guru Gaitri   *W*hen I began focusing on preventing further degenerative changes in my spine, I found ways to modify poses for my structural integrity while also increasing my felt experience of optimum vitality. Around the same time, I also adopted the Guru Gaitri (also spelled Gayatri) Mantra (a.k.a. magnificent mantra in 3HO based Kundalini) as my new mantra practice to heighten inner guidance, radiance, and sense of internal prosperity.

This Gurmukhi mantra includes eight words for divine energy actions that when translated mean sustainer, liberator, enlightener, infinite, destroyer, creator, nameless, and desireless. When these words are chanted together with the navel pulled in on the word Har and the "r" in Har is pronounced with the tongue to the palate, the pituitary gland is believed to be stimulated, as is a sense of inner radiance and inner alignment.

ਗੋਬਿੰਦੇ ਮੁਕੰਦੇ ਉਦਾਰੇ ਆਪਾਰੇ
ਹਰਿਆਂ ਕਰਿਆਂ ਨਿਰਮਮੇ ਅਕਾਮੇ
Gobinday Mukunday Udaaray Apaaray
Hariang Kariang Nirnamay Akaamay

Whether it was a placebo effect or not, I experienced measurable positive changes in mind, body, and career, while also feeling an internal flow of happiness in a new way.

214

Self-Study

1. Research studies on yogic methods for an endocrine condition that interests you.
2. Create a diagram that lists: Pineal gland, pituitary gland, thyroid, adrenal glands, hypothalamus, gonads, pancreas, kidneys, stomach, small intestine, and liver. Label each part with its related hormonal functions.
3. Chant, sing or say the Magnificent mantra or another affirmation that promotes inner guidance.

Har Har Har Har Gobinday
Har Har Har Har Mukunday
Har Har Har Har Udaaray
Har Har Har Har Apaaray
Har Har Har Har Hariang
Har Har Har Har Kariang
Har Har Har Har Nir-naamay
Har Har Har Har Akaamay

Meaning:
Gobinday – Sustainer
Mokunday – Liberator
Udaaray – Enlightener
Apaaray – Infinite
Hariang – Destroyer
Kariang – Creator
Nirnaamay – Nameless
Akaamay – Desireless
Har – Infinite or God

15. Fusion Method

"First we do hard, then we do easy" — AMK.

Creating a yoga practice that promotes body, mind and spirit wellness is quite an endeavor. Even if you are experienced across many different disciplines, it can be challenging to create sequences that are physically and energetically beneficial, promote mental health, and leave space for self-discovery and one's inner wisdom.

In my first yoga teacher training, we were told that figuring out how to do all that meant teaching six yoga classes per week for a sustained period. I took that recommendation as absurd as I also had a family, full-time job, home, and planned adventures . . . and what I most wanted was a simplified way to create great classes that impacted all of life positively.

Nonetheless, I taught several times a week. Each month got maybe 1% easier since planning sequences for body, mind and spirit wellness felt like tackling a master's level capstone project. Eventually, I came up with a simplified and reliable way to sequence mental, physical, and energetic wellness that also continues to offer creativity, increase my sense of agency, and grow my love of daily practice. If these details feel tedious, there is a template at chapter's end for simplified reference.

<u>This fusion method involves 5 parts.</u>
1. Identify an authentic focus area (what needs attention).
2. Create substance using the Koshas (layers of support).
3. Add musculoskeletal basics (physical functionality).
4. Categorize your substance (organize choices).
5. Sequence #4 into a Fusion Framework (sequence and test).
If desired, choose music or instruments either before or after this process.

Steps #1-#4 can be done quickly with practice. The last step takes a bit longer as that is where theory transforms into practice. This book's companion, *Body as Teacher*, outlines yogic methods that can help.

216

Authentic Focus

Start by asking yourself what you want to focus on. What does your heart say, what does the season say, what does your body say, is there any dissonance around you? In every training I lead, some students are surprised to hear me say that developing your personal practice and sequencing for others can both relate back to self.

Focusing on what you know to be true, rather than on assumptions about others, is a practice of the Yamas and Niyamas that yields realness. Classes taught from a genuine need can be far more empowering for others than teaching to what you think "they" might need or expect. And chances are that the challenge you are facing will resonate with others.

Let's say you have a current need for lower back strength.
#1: Class Focus = lower back strength/stability

This first step helps you know where in yoga's koshic model that your goal most obviously fits. Our example of lower back strength/stability fits well into the physical layer. But while many yoga classes go straight from the goal to sequencing around that goal, the Fusion Method uses the class focus as the beginning of inquiry – what else influences this outcome?

For example, suppose you want to build muscle, so you embark on a weight training program and hit the weights and your goal successfully. If weights were the extent of your strength program, your sense of inner resilience may not feel like it had the gains that your muscles did. Unfortunately, working on one area of our lives may not impact the long-lasting changes we desire.

So, step #1 of choosing a focus for your practice is important, but what follows that focus is what creates the depth that can positively impact multiple aspects of life . . . and potentially shift grooves of negative samskaras (pre-conditioning) - the most meaningful work of yoga.

217

Create with the Koshas

As above, so below.
As inside, so on the outside.
As to my left, so it is to my right.
It takes more energy to maintain a division.

After determining your focus, next go to Ayurveda's Koshic model (physical, energetic, mental, wisdom and bliss layers of being) to brainstorm yogic techniques that can contribute to that focus.

#2: Create Substance with the Koshas
The model below uses our example of lower back strength/stability.

1. Physical Layer
The physical layer of our body is easy to see and notice. So it is often where symptoms of endocrine or nervous system conditions show up. Positive changes here can assist your energetic layer and body's messaging system.

✓ Physical Focus (body part/area and goal for that body part/area)
   Ex. lower back stability
✓ Poses (to support your physical focus)
   Ex. Mountain, Plank, Side Plank, Locust, Warrior 2, Reverse Plank
✓ Pose Variations (building blocks)
   Ex. Reclining Mountain, Table, Cobra, Gate, Knees Down Plank, Reverse Table
✓ Breathing Techniques (for physical focus)
   Ex. Durga breath
✓ Limit or Avoid (poses contrary to physical focus)
   Ex. limit Forward Bends

2. Energetic Layer

Our energy can influence both our physical and mental states and can positively impact the tone of your practice. Sometimes, changes to our energy can originate in the endocrine system. Poses and energetic aids (breathing techniques, bandhas, chakras, mudras, doshas, etc.) can benefit this layer, while also impacting other layers and group dynamics.

✓ Energy Theme (vayu, chakra, and/or Endocrine focus)
   Ex. inward, downward, balancing, root chakra right to be secure
✓ Energetic Poses and Practices (other aids for energy focus)
   Ex. root chakra poses (Easy Pose, Low Lunge), bandhas, Buddhi Mudra
✓ Breathing Techniques (for energy focus)
   Ex. humming breath
✓ Limit or Avoid (energy directions contrary to energy focus)
   Ex. limit those that are not centering

3. Mental Layer

Our brains are a symphony of geniuses directing our life, but they can get stuck on difficult tunes and echo interference into our lives. Sometimes this sense of interference can be related to Nervous System dysregulation. Theming with the Yamas, Niyamas, Pratyahara and chakras can help to re-groove thought patterns. Kundalini kriyas, Nidra, and mantras can also help with clarity. When discord in this layer turns to symbiotic connection, those positive shifts also impact the energetic, physical and wisdom layers.

✓ Mental Theme (promoting thought or Nervous System part)
   Ex. inner strength, equal parts strength and surrender in practice
✓ Mental Practices (Yamas, Niyamas, chakras, mantras, kriyas, etc.)
   Ex. Sita mantra, root chakra, Kundalini Stretch Pose
✓ Breathing Techniques (for mental focus)
   Ex. Ujjayi breath
✓ Limit or Avoid (contrary to class mental focus)
   Ex. cues or distractions contrary to inner strength and stability

4. Wisdom Layer

Dharana and Dhyana offer space to merge from mental processing to witnessing a larger picture. Yogic stories can affirm positive attributes we possess. Study of the Gita can support discovery of various yogic paths. And Seva serves to expand wisdom. Since wisdom is subtler than all other layers except bliss, it helps to first to move through blockages in other layers that may be in the way to our inner wisdom.

- ✓ Wisdom Theme (messaging that promotes mental or physical focus)
  Ex. body as a great teacher
- ✓ Wisdom Practices (meditation, yogic story, Gita/Sutra wisdom, etc.)
  Ex. Sita's alignment, Gratitude meditation, reminder of Gunas
- ✓ Limit or Avoid (contrary to wisdom focus)
  Ex. narrative around body comparison that implies ideal strength

5. Bliss Layer

The bliss layer and the limb of Samadhi are discovered not by doing, but as the result of practice and/or pureness of faith according to Patanjali. Some practitioners experience glimpses of this transcendence during savasana or meditation when all other layers of being have had a work-out/work-in in the previous moments. Bliss can be a result of practice and be experienced by anyone, regardless of faith form or non-religion.

- ✓ Space for Bliss (where is this?)
  Ex. Savasana of at least 5 minutes
- ✓ Limit or Avoid (contrary to the experience of bliss)
  Ex. uncomfortable room temp, other intrusions to deep relaxation

Add Musculoskeletal Basics

Now review the poses and/or kriyas you used for the physical, energetic, and mental Kosha layers. Our example of low back strength included *Mountain/Reclining Mountain, Plank/Knees Down Plank, Side Gate/Side Plank, Locust, Warrior 2, Easy Pose, Table/Reverse Table, Stretch Pose, Runner's and Low Lunge, Revolved Low Lunge.*

Next, add poses to balance joint actions and muscle groups for structural integrity, and add transitional poses you plan to use. When choosing these, remember the vayus you selected for your focus.

#3: Add musculoskeletal basics to your substance.
Choose poses below that are not already included in those you chose in your Koshic model. All poses should complement your chosen vayus.

✓ Transition Poses
   Ex. Downward Dog, 3-Legged Dog, Standing Seal, Half Lift, Runner's Lunge, Seated Staff (can use these to focus on learning bandha engagement)

✓ Poses to balance Joint Actions
   Cobra, Bridge, Star, Goddess, Balancing Table, Sphynx, Balancing Half Moon (added these because poses selected did a good job of all shoulder joint actions, but were limited in spinal and hip extension actions)

✓ Poses or Props to Strengthen Focus Area
   Forearm Plank, Side Plank with leg lift, Table Tiger
   Blocks between thighs in Mountain, under hands in Down Dog/Runner's Lunge.

✓ Poses or Props to Soothe Focus Area
   Cat/Cow, Reclining Pigeon, Spinal Twist, blanket under sit bones in Easy Pose and bolster under knees in Savasana.
   (reduce pelvic tension that may aggravate the lower back)

Categorize Substance

Next categorize what you've included so far into baskets that will be more manageable to use for your class framework (on the next page).

Lower back strength example:

✓ Focus/Themes/Cues
Lower back strength, inner strength, inward and downward energy, body as teacher, Sita's strength regardless of challenge, equal parts will and surrender, the temporary states of Gunas, root and sacral chakra right to be secure and feel.

✓ Poses and/or Kriyas
Koshic Model: *Mountain/Reclining Mountain, Plank/Knees Down Plank, Side Gate/Side Plank/Balancing Half Moon, Cobra/Locust, Warrior 2, Easy Pose, Table/Reverse Table, Runner's/Low Lunge/Revolved Low Lunge*
Musculoskeletal Adds: *Downward Dog, 3-Legged Dog, Half Lift, Cobra, Bridge, Star, Goddess, Balancing Table, Table Circles, Reclining Pigeon, Spinal Twist, Forearm Plank/Forearm Side Plank, Table Tiger, Sphynx*

✓ Breathing Techniques
Ujjayi, Durga, Humming

✓ Energetic Aids
Kundalini Stretch Pose, Bandhas

✓ Meditation
Gratitude meditation

✓ Mantra(s)
Sita Ram mantra

✓ Limit or Avoid
Most Forward Bends, cues around favored body shape, intrusions to relaxation

✓ Props
Blocks between thighs in Mountain, hands in Down Dog/Runner's Lunge. Blanket under sit bones in Easy Pose and bolster under knees in Savasana.

Fusion Framework

The last step is placing your substance from #4 in a framework and testing it out to know where to move things around and change poses as needed. You can also add music if desired (music copyright information comes after this framework). You will know when your sequence works by your own experience. Using the minimum time for each section results in a 40-minute practice; using the maximum time results in an 80-minute practice. Adjust sections lengths for the overall time you desire.

Tuning In *(1-3 minutes)*
Tune in to acknowledge a transition from external focus to self-care.
Music/Sound: Om, another mantra, or no sound and inward intention.

Presence *(3-5 minutes)*
Establish presence with a breathing technique and simple movements that help prepare joints and establish energy to expand upon.
Music/Sound: Simple rhythms that complement breath are ideal. Music here can introduce the overall class theme but should not detract from present moment awareness.

Engagement *(5-10 minutes)*
Engage mind and body towards your focus in functional and somatic ways. Pose variations as building blocks usually work well here.
Music/Sound: Reinforce mental focus with music expressing universal challenges (different than songs with lyrics that promote triggers or attachments).

Flow *(15-30 minutes)*
Flow refers to energy momentum and need not mean Vinyasa. For example, when sequencing for Yin, flow refers to linking poses together with the least amount of physical adjustment from one pose to the next.

If vinyasa is used for Flow, start with basic poses that link easily and are held for 5 full breaths each (both sides if applicable), providing time for concise cues and an experience of healthy alignment. In subsequent repetitions, 1-3 new poses can be added each time. All repeated poses are synced to breath, and all new poses are held for 5 inhales and exhales the first time through for cueing and body connection. Transitions between poses are fluid and synced to breath to maintain energy. A flow may be 2-5 progressive rounds with transitions that are fluid.

Music/Sound: Increase sense of inner agency. If Vinyasa, rhythms are a slower pace in longer held poses and faster as movements become linked by breath. If a kriya is used, music may be fast or slow depending on kriya movements. If Qigong is used, music with nature sounds and without words is the most complementary.

Edge *(5-10 minutes)*

The edge offers a challenge to move past perceived limitations, such as a peak pose, or a short, challenging kriya. Not all classes need an edge.

Music/Sound: Music uncommon for other parts of a yoga class fits well. This is also a good time to encourage playing of instruments or making audible sounds.

Release *(5-7 minutes)*

Decompress physical tension built during practice and allow wisdom to rise to the surface. Repeating basic elements included in presence or in engage a meditation or mantra, and targeted musculoskeletal soothing can round out class focus and allows a sense of full-circle.

Music/Sound: Slow and simple music or mantra can support decompression and space for inner wisdom. Lyrics used reinforce your theme in a positive, universal ways.

Savasana/Rest/Integrate *(5-10 minutes)*

Time for being rather than doing. Preparations for comfort have occurred prior for seamless transition to the subtle experience of bliss.

Music/Sound: Slow and simple with minimal, if any, words. Lyrics that bring up a problem and tense, fast or loud sounds can interfere with a good experience.

Closing *(1-3 minutes)*

Acknowledge being present for oneself. Certain schools of yoga offer closing mantras. Other classes end with Om, or a moment of gratitude.

Music/Sound: Acknowledges completion of a practice, like a short mantra or a few hums of a singing bowl are great options.

Symphonies for the Universe

Yogic practices can be done with or without music. However, music and sound (the science of Naad) can elevate nervous system benefits, as vibrational frequencies and rhythms also exist in the human body. I find music helpful to remind myself where I am as far as timing in a sequence.

As a new studio owner, I was unaware of music copyrights until stumbling upon a social media thread talking about protection from legal and financial liability for music copyright infringement. I doubted any of it was applicable to my small studio with 2 to 15 people in a class. Besides, I paid for a few different music streaming services, so I wasn't stealing but rather uplifting many artists by introducing them to people who would likely not have been aware of them otherwise.

However, additional research led to a plethora of responsibilities around playing music for others in yoga classes including obtaining written consent from artists or paying a music licensing service (or multiple services) if applicable. Fees start at a few hundred dollars a year up to thousands depending on many factors. You can research music copyright infringement laws to make choices about various streaming services options, artist permissions, and music copyright protection services.

Even if you choose not to play music in yoga classes for others, you may find it an invaluable source of inspiration for yourself in creating classes. Regardless of how much yoga one has learned, practiced, and integrated, the complexity of life has a way of rendering us at times with a sense that we still don't know what to do next. Many musicians have an uncanny ability to see right through life triggers to the source of disease and universally offer a validation and antidote that can feel unexplainable, and yet there it is . . . exactly what you need to see the next step.

Recommendations for music or sound within the Fusion Framework are helpful reminders, but not all generalities apply to all classes.

*S*araswati   In the *Mahabharata*, Saraswati is the mother of the Vedas who composes a symphony for Brahma's creation of the universe (until she eventually divorces him so she can focus on her passions). Saraswati first appears first in the *Rig* Veda, as an avatar goddess endowed with the power of abundant water. In her arms, she holds a book (the Vedas, universal, eternal, knowledge, and learning), a mala (meditation, inner reflection, and spirituality), a water pot (purifying power to separate right from wrong), and a veena (expressing how knowledge creates harmony).

Saraswati symbolizes our innate capacities to learn, create and express our inner truths. The Gayatri mantra is also known as the manifestation of Saraswati and is often referred to as the mother of all mantras.

*"I wake up to the sound of music.
Mother Mary comes to me.
Speaking words of wisdom.
Let it be"*
— *The Beatles*

Fusion Method Template

#1: Class Focus   _____

#2: Create Substance with the Koshas

    1)   Physical - Poses and breathing
            Body part/area and physical goal focus

            Poses (to support your physical focus)
_____

            Pose Variations (building blocks)
_____

            Breathing Techniques
_____

            Limit/Avoid (categories of poses contrary to physical focus)
_____

    2)   Energetic – Poses & energy aids (breath, bandha, mudra, drishti)
            Energy Focus (vayu, chakra, or Endocrine focus)

            Energetic Poses and Aids
_____

            Breathing Techniques
_____

            Limit or Avoid (energy directions contrary to energy focus)
_____

    3)   Mental – Yamas, Niyamas, Pratyahara, kriyas, mantras
            Mental Theme (promoting thought or Nervous System part)

            Mental Practices (Yamas, Niyamas, chakras, mantras, kriyas)
_____

            Breathing Techniques
_____

            Limit or Avoid (cues contrary to class mental focus)
_____

    4)   Wisdom Layer – Dharana, Dhyana, Yoga Stories, Gita, Seva
            Wisdom Theme (promotes mental or physical focus)

            Wisdom Practices
_____

            Limit or Avoid (cues contrary to wisdom focus)
_____

    5)   Bliss Layer - result of practice
            Space for Bliss (usually Savasana) _____
            Limit or Avoid (distractions contrary to bliss experience)_____

#3 Add musculoskeletal basics to your substance

Transition Poses

_____

Poses to balance Joint Actions

_____

Poses to Strengthen Focus Area

_____

Props to Strengthen Focus Area

_____

Poses to Soothe Focus Area

_____

Props to Soothe Focus Area

_____

#4 Categorize substance (place some or all answers from #1-#3 here)

Focuses (body part, energy, mental, and wisdom focus or theme)

_____

Poses and/or Kriyas (from Koshic model and musculoskeletal additions)

_____

Breathing Techniques

_____

Other Energetic Aids (mudras, mantras, drishtis, bandhas, doshas, chakras)

_____

Meditation

_____

Mantra(s) or Theme Sounds

_____

Limit or Avoid

_____

Props

_____

#5 Fusion Framework
Place your items from #4 where they best fit. You will likely need
additional space than what is provided in this template.

Tuning In
    Duration   _____
    Intention or Mantra _____

Presence
    Duration _____
    Concise theme introduction _____
    Breath technique to prepare mind _____
    Simple pose(s) to connect mind-body _____

Engagement
    Duration _____
    Cues for concise theme expansion _____
    Breath/energetic aids to build energy _____
    Engage joints/muscles/alignment _____

Flow
    Duration _____
    Cues - concise theme reinforcement _____
    Breath/energetic aids for class focus _____
    Type (vinyasa, yin, chakra, dosha, etc.) _____
    Poses (with transitions to link poses) _____

Edge
    Duration _____
    Cue - concise theme reinforcement _____
    Breathing technique(s)/energetic aids _____
    Peak pose or kriya _____

Release
    Duration _____
    Cue - concise theme affirmation _____
    Breathing technique/energetic aids _____
    Poses to soothe tension _____
    Meditation or mantra _____

Savasana/Rest/Integrate)
    Duration _____
    Preparations for comfort _____

Closing
    Duration _____
    Closing method and/or mantra _____

Total duration = _____
Note: Determine if accessibility considerations and plans are necessary prior to offering
the class you prepared to others.

Example Fusion Class

Options include pose variations to increase physical ease or effort.

Tuning In (3 min)

Blanket under tailbone for alignment of spine and low back stability

Tune into self-care with OM

Presence (5 min)

- ✓ Cue inner strength, inward/downward energy, and body as the teacher
- Easy Pose Durga breath (hands on abdomen)
- Reclining Mountain *(block between thighs - engage glutes inward and downward)* add humming breath on long exhales

Engagement (10 min), 5 Ujjayi breaths each pose

- ✓ Do right side first, then left side.
- ✓ Blocks for spinal alignment in Down Dog, Rev Side Angle, Forward Bend
- ✓ Cue hasta/pada bandha, rights be secure/feel, Buddhi mudra's clarity
- Table – Ujjayi Breath (learn - lean forward on inhale, lean back on exhale)
- Table / Cat-Cow / Bal Table-Tiger / Side Gate / Gate (leg lift option)
- Table / Low Lunge Buddhi mudra/ Rev Ext Side Angle *(align with blocks)*
- Table Circles / Down Dog / 3-Legged Dog (or Table) / Down Dog
- Forward Bend / Tall Mtn / Mountain Gratitude Meditation /Half Pyramid

Flow (25 min), Vinyasa breath to movement

- ✓ Slow to 5 Ujjayi breaths in new, revolved poses, locus, standing balances
- ✓ Do right side for all first, then left side
- ✓ Blocks for spinal alignment in Runner's Lunge
- ✓ Cue inner stability, authenticity; Hasta, Pada, Uddiyana, Mula bandhas.

Flow Round 1

- Tall Mountain / Standing Seal / Half Lift
- Plank (option Knees Down) / Side Plank (or Gate option) / Cobra
- 3-Legged Dog (or Bal Table) / Runner's Lunge (or Low Lunge)
- Rev Ext Side Angle (variation)/Runner's Lunge/High Lunge Buddhi
- Warrior 3 (or ½ Pyramid) / High Lunge / Star / Warrior 2 / Rev Warrior
- Step to Mountain (front of mat), repeat on other side

Flow Round 2

- Tall Mountain / Standing Seal / Half Lift
- Plank (option Leg Lift) / Side Plank (or Gate) (option Leg Lift) / Locust
- 3-Legged Dog (or Bal Table) / Runner's Lunge (or Low Lunge)
- Rev Ext Side Angle (variation)/Runner's Lunge/High Lunge Buddhi
- Warrior 3 / High Lunge / Goddess / Warrior 2 / Triangle / Rev Warrior
- Step to Mountain (front of mat), repeat on other side

Flow Round 3

- Tall Mountain / Standing Seal / Half Lift
- Forearm Plank (or Plank) / Forearm Side Plank (or Gate) / Sphynx
- 3-Legged Dog (or Bal Table) / Runner's Lunge (or Low Lunge)
- Rev Ext Side Angle (variation)/Runner's/High Lunge Buddhi mudra
- Warrior 3 / High Lunge / Star to Goddess / Warrior 2 / Triangle
- Reverse Warrior / Bal Half Moon (or Gate with leg lift) / Warrior 2
- Step to Mountain (front of mat), repeat on other side

Edge (5 min), use 5 Ujjayi breaths each pose
- ✓ Cue equal parts strength and surrender in practice
- Transition to Seated Staff (option Ashtanga transition) – *engage Mula Bandh*
- Reverse Table / Seated Staff / Rev Table / Staff / Rev Plank / Staff
- Stretch Pose (variation for back conditions), 2 minutes

Release (10 min)
- ✓ Cue equanimity within (Sita Ram mantra)
- Bridge / Reclining Pigeon / Spinal Twist (gentle low back variation)
- Gratitude Meditation

Rest/Savasana (7 min) - *Blanket under torso and bolster under knees if desired.*

Closing (3 min) - A moment of gratitude for inner strength followed by OM.

Note: Determine if accessibility considerations and plans are necessary prior to offering the class you prepared to others.

Variations for Accessibility

If you are offering a sequence to a group of people with mixed physical needs (those who do not want modifications and those that need them), additional steps prior to leading your sequence are recommended. It is my experience that it is easiest to develop your practice without pose variations first. So, after your class is created, you can add variations that work towards your desired outcomes. This may require some slight changes in order of sequencing, but often it does not.

Additional steps for inclusivity of benefits in group classes are:

1. Identify Potential Problematic Poses.

    Our Example Fusion Class is likely not accessible to those with knee conditions, those who are pregnant, recovering from surgery or injury, and those who have difficulty getting up and down on the mat primarily because of these poses: Table, Lunges, Warriors, Cobra, Locust, Downward Dog, Forward Bend, etc.

2. Prepare Variations for Problematic Poses.

    Use this book's companion, *Body as Teacher*, or another pose modification resource and choose pose variations that have the least impact on class pace or energy. Most of the problematic poses mentioned above can be fluid and beneficial if practiced in chair or in a standing posture.

3. Practice and Cue Variations.

    Explore variations yourself and note if props are needed, such as chairs, bolsters, walls, blocks, and blankets. Plan how you will prepare for and cue both groups of people at the same time. If it is not possible, consider how you will notify people with health conditions that your class is not recommended unless they are already familiar and comfortable with applying beneficial modifications for their conditions.

Self-Study

1. What is something you would like to focus on for a yoga practice?
2. Fill in the layers of the Koshas for that focus.
3. Review the poses you included in the Koshic layers and add poses to balance joint actions and muscle groups for structural integrity and add transitional poses you plan to use.
4. Categorize the yogic techniques you have gathered thus far.
5. Place your practice poses, breathing techniques, mudras, mantras, etc. into the Fusion Framework. Put it to the test on your mat and make changes as needed.
6. Add pose variations for accessibility of common health conditions.
7. Add music or sound to your practice.
8. Chant, sing or say the Saraswati mantra or another affirmation that helps you tune into your capacity to learn, create, and express yourself. Try this for at least 3 minutes.

Om Aing Saraswati Namah

Meaning: Salutations to Saraswati, truth, creation, memory, power, concentration

16. The Lotus

Free Yoga

When it comes to making money, yoga teachers can wrestle with an internal debate as to whether yoga as wellness service should be free. After years of sharing yoga with others, both with pay and with no pay, I agree that yoga should be free and also understand that free yoga does not achieve sustainable accessibility. If, as yoga teachers, we spiritually bypass this reality, liberation ground is lost rather than gained.

Consider what might happen if other wellness service providers such as massage therapists stopped charging fees for their services. Since money and time are required to educate, equip, and provide these services to others, and the providers themselves require shelter or food, the only providers able to offer free services would be those with previously accumulated wealth (thus limiting who can provide these services). When the pool of providers is limited, it can lead to a constriction between demand and availability where fewer people get served.

Another conflict of free yoga is that when we don't absolutely need it, we may not value it if it has no cost, regardless of intrinsic value. Nature provides a clear reflection of this paradox, as many people spend far more time caring for their automobile than their community park. However, when dollar signs accumulate, paying attention becomes easier. Rather than hoping that offering free yoga can solve a problem, the truer solution is that extensively studied wellness services proven to increase health outcomes, including yoga, could be covered by health insurance (which reduces cost but still does not render it free) to increase availability and diversity of offerings. But currently in the United States, though emergency health treatment is considered a right, wellness is not.

Mind Your Business

There is always a need for that which only you can create.

Embarking on business ownership is an opportunity and challenge. The idea of selling what you have to offer to others can be great motivation or great fear, or it might be both. If you have owned a business before, you possess facts and figures from previous endeavors that could send you running for the hills or support your sense of readiness to take on a new business, or it might be both. And other challenges arise when the perception of others (family, friends, students, etc.) is considered. It may feel easier to opine about what other businesses are doing right or wrong while delaying your venture.

Fortunately, yoga can offer massive flexibility as a business owner in that you could teach to one person or thousands at a time, open a yoga studio, teach at a gym or on-line or to your church. You could volunteer to lead wellness activities based in yogic philosophy at a local library, school, animal refuge, at a senior center or in hospice, etc., or write a book about a particular area of yogic interest or about all of yoga. Whether your initial investment is elbow grease and time, or those things and thousands of dollars, applying what you have learned and practiced can generate an intrinsic and/or financial return on your investment.

Other limitations are limiting perceptions, such as:

⊠ My physical location or on-line platform isn't the right space.

⊠ Someone already took my idea.

⊠ I need more training first.

⊠ There is a saturated market full of people more qualified.

The truth is that infinite space exists because of infinite human uniqueness. Yoga goes back thousands of years and touches all aspects of life, and each teacher is the only one on the planet with their lived experience. When you combine infinite formulas that exist, the market will never be saturated, and no one is better qualified than someone else.

Business Details

One way to understand accessibility constraints around yoga is to brainstorm a structure around what it takes to offer a service – because once you know where to start, uncovering particulars can be easier. The next few pages go into the details about owning a business. You may wish to skip or skim this for now if you are not interested or ready for business ownership. You can return to this anytime.

Business Arrangement

Working for someone else's business means that the space and tools to conduct business (website, accounting, marketing, taxes, insurance, waivers, etc.) are paid for and managed by that business. In return for your work using the business' resources, you get a paycheck for providing an agreed upon service. Being an employee generally means conforming your service to your employer's needs and structures, requesting permission for time off, and not marketing other outside offerings you may have to those coming in the door of the business you are employed by. Being a paid employee minimizes time and financial risk but also limits financial gain and personal choice. Being an employee also offers insight into how you might do things if you were the decision-maker.

Owning your business means that equipment, building, utilities, website, accounting, marketing, taxes, insurance, waivers, etc. are your responsibilities. While this arrangement maximizes your financial risk and behind the scenes work, it also offers autonomy for scheduling, marketing, your range of offerings, and price.

Independent Contractors (ICs) also provide services to businesses that have a space and platform. ICs are responsible for liability insurance and negotiating service and pricing terms, as well as use of the other business' resources.

Business License.

Prior to filing for a license, choose a business name and a business status (sole proprietor, limited liability company, corporation, etc.). The Small Business Administration provides free information on the various legal structures of a business. Registering a sole proprietorship through your state is usually free and on-line.

General Liability Insurance (GL).

If you own a business, liability insurance covers things like injury to others and damage to property. Should someone submit a claim for injury due to your services, regardless of whether that claim is substantiated, GL insurance also covers legal defense. Some yoga organizations offer registered teachers discounts. GL premiums average about $140/year depending on platform, type of yoga, and coverage. Applying on-line for coverage is fairly quick.

Liability Waiver.

There are many free templates on-line for liability waivers that further protect a business owner. Prior to providing services to someone, they can acknowledge risks and theoretically agree to "hold harmless" you and/or business. Waivers will not protect you from acts of negligence (things a reasonable person should have known better about). A waiver does not replace the protection afforded by liability insurance.

Facility.

Renting property to offer services means paying monthly rent, renters' insurance, utilities, and upkeep. As a renter, you may also be required to pay for repairs. Being a renter limits upfront costs and allows you to change your mind but means your payments won't build equity. If you choose to buy, an up-front build-out or renovation may be necessary, and in addition to mortgage payments, you'll pay property insurance, property taxes, utilities, repairs, and upkeep. To budget for utilities, it's helpful to call utility providers to get an estimate.

Platform.

Social media presence can draw interest in your services, but it is often a website that best serves people trying to make decisions about your services. You don't need to be a web designer to establish a website for basic services, many of which are free except for payment for your domain registration. Your website costs might average $1000/year (depending on features you want). Accepting payments via credit card can be done on your website or through other payment processors for a fee (about 3% for each transaction).

Marketing.

Businesses also must plan, manage, and pay for advertising other than a website such as signage, flyers, brochures, business cards, social media paid advertising, google listings, development of a logo, etc. Website platforms include features for marketing, sometimes for an additional cost. In-person events can also increase awareness of your services. To be effective, marketing efforts include identifying the people you wish to reach to direct your marketing efforts as such.

Taxes.

Businesses pay retail taxes, income taxes at the state and federal level, and payroll taxes if you employ others. State Dept of Revenue and the IRS sites offer criteria needed for tax reporting, so one can keep track of income and expenses prior to reporting.

Professional Organizations and Associations.

Many yoga teachers have upwards of $10,000 invested in training and education through registered programs and choose to register their services with recognized program directories. Many state and federal programs will pay only for services provided by teachers registered with Yoga Alliance or an equivalent organization. Belonging to other associations can offer perks too, such as a local Chamber of Commerce, but they all come with a price.

Music Licensing.

If your services include music, you likely need to consider subscribing to and paying for a copyright protection service. Annual costs are a few hundred to thousands of dollars.

Equipment.

In-person yoga offerings typically require mats, blocks, blankets, bolsters, shelving, and stereo equipment. Opening my small yoga studio required a $5,000 investment in this type of equipment. While on-line service offerings don't require similar gear, they may need an investment in good audio-visual equipment.

Supplies.

If your business is in-person, you will have expenses related to guest needs (like toiletries) and any consumable product you use to conduct business, like light bulbs.

Staff.

Small businesses often start out with one person wearing many hats as there isn't enough money to pay anyone else. When deciding whether to hire a cleaning service, marketing guru, front desk associate, web administrator, accountant, etc., budget is a consideration, and so is time and talent. Some yoga teachers enjoy cleaning their space but dislike the business side of things. Others like the business side of things. Only you know where your time is best spent. Hiring others adds payroll and reporting responsibilities.

501(c)3 Non-profits.

Businesses can be registered as a federally recognized 501(c)3 non-profit organization if services meet established criteria. The IRS.gov outlines criteria that includes organizations that provide "relief of the poor, the distressed, or the underprivileged," as eligible to apply for 501(c)3 status. Federally recognized non-profits are exempt from paying state and federal income taxes on eligible products and services. However, all costs previously discussed, except for income taxes, still apply to non-profits.

Pricing Structure.

If prices are too low, every feasible corner needs to be cut to continue offering services. If prices are too high, many people who want yoga services cannot afford them. Some widely used methods are calculating fixed and estimated costs plus profit, looking at your competition's pricing, positioning your business, and pricing uniquely based upon your brand benefits, or providing what you offer for free. Until such time as wellness services are covered by insurance, price determination is one of the hardest decisions to make in your wellness business. That decision is further complicated by what students seem to view as an acceptable amount to pay for services. However, business owners are in a great position to educate others on the value of wellness services. It is possible to charge a fair price for services that affords a reasonable standard of life, while also offering non-monetary or low-cost opportunities for those unable to pay.

In a nutshell, setting up and running a business is also a practice. Using basic parameters to guide you, your journey can yield greater awareness, presence and prosperity in ways that can and cannot be defined.

Walking Each Other Home

Many mantras in this book are derived from the *Samaveda*, one of the four ancient Vedas. Kirtan also arises from early texts as a call-and-response style song that tells a story. My first experience with Kirtan was in Ashtanga Primary Series class where a white female teacher in her forties led a long chant in Sanskrit, and dozens of mostly white students in spandex chanted back.

I was speechless.

That weekend I researched the chant's meaning and phonetics and set about practicing enunciation from the safety of my suburbia apartment. On Monday morning a co-worker shared interesting tidbits about his weekend while I sat smiling and nodding. Then the same co-worker, who didn't even know I was in yoga teacher training, asked me,

"So, what did you do this weekend, learn Sanskrit?."

Months prior I began joining in on the unison OMing before and after class, and now my eagerness to join in on chanting made even more sense. Growing up Catholic meant listening to stories of the bible during mass and repeating phrases to the priest or other reader throughout the story. Not only did these readings and responses help me listen more closely, but I also experienced my voice in community.

Years prior, as a soldier stationed in Europe, I attended Catholic liturgy in Rome at St Peters Square on Christmas Day. Snow fell gently and trumpets played accompaniment to the Pope's repetitive phrase in 26 languages that flooded warmth over my heart into a quilt of profound connection as masses of uniformed school children chanted in response.

"May this day live in your hearts forever."

"Papa, Papa!".

Fast forward to my Bhakti travels in India as part of a group, but more of a personal celebration of my yoga journey. On our first day, I picked my way through crowds in a celebration hall to watch others prostrate to statues and felt more disconnected than I had in years.

However, once the Kirtan began, all thoughts of past and future dissipated as I chanted and danced along with a thousand others, none of whom wore spandex. Near the end, millions of flower petals descended upon us in a crescendo of voices, huge smiles, and happy tears. No one partook in alcohol or drugs, yet every person present was high. The joy that reverberated from the ceiling, floor, walls, instruments, voices, and bodies penetrated every molecule of air until at last children lay on the floor covered in petals in absolute peace.

Our Bhakti group had weeks ahead of the same, and my joy from that first night turned day by day into a sense of entrapment. I had not fully understood what being with an ISCON group meant, so I found myself wrestling with judgement wherever we traveled. I was not critical of chanting the Maha mantra or of Krishna, both of which were beautiful. My judgements formed around daily sermons which opposed pervading love without form. This attachment of wrongs to disfavor with the divine felt like a tool for suffering I had chosen to put down a decade prior. The forced filtering of devotion made me want to smoke more, even though per our talks, cigarettes would lead to less love.

On one of our intercountry flights, I sat next to an Indian super model who asked what I thought of the afterlife and the mind's ability to experience heaven and hell on Earth. I asked for his thoughts on why some Indian widows could not remarry or earn a wage, leaving them no choice but to sit in a line of widows on the ground chanting all day in hopes of a coin in their bag or rice in their bowl, but men could not even be trusted to find strength to resist sexual desires at temples, even after chanting all their life. The man explained that all people have choice if they allow it, and that his choice is to marry a woman who is his equal, but first he must meet her. We agreed to pray for one another.

If my eyes are windows to the soul,
can I make that view from God?
Matthew 6:22-24.

"No mud, no lotus"
— *Thich Nhat Hanh.*

In our next city, we traipsed a mile of cobblestone in bare feet so as not to insult Krishna on our pilgrimage to a temple. I considered the pinworms and other parasites entering our bodies, as well as the stagnant water we splashed on ourselves as a form of cleansing, would certainly be more insulting. Then I realized that parasites could not be blamed for disturbing my peace. Only I could.

After this softening, I saw Krishna, Jesus, and heavenly saints everywhere with their arms wide open to me, even after smoking a cigarette outside the ashram gate with my adopted monkey. At another ashram famous for housing the Beatles, I sat in meditation in front of a graffitied wall proclaiming, "Love is my religion." And by the time I stared at the Taj Mahal, a world wonder built not for religion or money, but for love, I realized this trip had been perfect.

Ram Dass was a western spiritual teacher who spent time in India. His way of truth speaking cuts to the heart of yoga's journey.

"As long as you have certain desires about how it ought to be you can't see how it is." "We are all just walking each other home."

Kirtan can overlap with a drum circle, where people play drums and percussion instruments made up of simple household items, not for a performance, but for traveling to that deeper place of wisdom within each person and collectively. In a drum circle, whoever is leader will start the beat, then others will respond in kind with the same or similar beat. Like Kirtan, drum circles also don't require knowing how to play a drum. Anyone can join in. Drum circles are used as music therapy in recovery spaces, and Indigenous peoples across the world have used forms of Kirtan and drum ceremonies for thousands of years.

Krishna Das, another teacher who learned much in India, sums it up as . . . "It's like getting on a train. Even though you may be running in the opposite direction on the train, it still takes you to the destination. The destination is your soul."

243

Sacred Indigenous wisdom practices have also been in practice for thousands of years and can bring people together with no obvious commonalities besides being human, while simultaneously moving each person closer to their own essence – often using nature as a conduit.

Indigenous people are native to, or have ancestral history with, a geographical area prior to colonization, forced migration or subjugation. So, the term Indigenous can apply "to an estimated 476 million indigenous people in over 90 countries, comprising diverse communities with distinct languages, traditions, and identities" (tribal studies.com).

Growing up in South Dakota in the 80s, I learned little about the Lakota people who lived in nearby reservations after their tribes were displaced by my ancestors. Most white people in my area either seemed to hold an indifference and/or fear towards those who were brown and spoke differently. Eventually I left South Dakota, joined the Army, and later married a man of both Mexican and Native American lineage. Still, it took our children entering the 4th and 6th grade in Kansas for me to gain real perspective of the quest of generations to access what was taken from them through oppression and attempted eradication by the U.S. government and organized religion.

Non-Indigenous people and descendants of indigenous people may have little to no personal experience with Indigenous practices. While it is best to experience practices through those with lived experience and ancestral teachings, you can also familiarize yourself with some of these practices in this book's companion, *Body as Teacher*.

"I cannot think that we are useless or God would not have created us. "- Geronimo.

These sacred practices can further support your life journey. And when these practices are shared with others, you may experience a collective resonance through symbolism, storytelling, and belonging . . . and a knowing that we are more similar than different.

244

The Gift of BEing

Sitting with yourself without distractions from self… no phone, no TV, no computer, no book, no food, no movement… is a beautiful gift.

Two weeks before our last weekend of yoga teacher training, advertised as a celebratory retreat on the shores of Lake Tahoe, we learned that retreat activities would remain secret, but for sure alcohol, cigarettes and street drugs were forbidden. I hated surprises and wanted to share a glass of wine with people who, by this point, knew me about as well as God. To top it off, a rumor was floating around that last year's retreat included 24 hours of noble meditation. I fully understood what meditation was, we had been doing 15-30 min increments of it throughout training. AMK kept repeating all that was just practice and longer meditations were a form of true liberation. I could not buy in to this view. In the days leading up to the retreat, I cried at work in meetings and drove straight to an acupuncturist after work for anxiety.

After all the hype, the retreat's first activity turned out to be kayaking. All 45 students were relieved and happily sat in a circle on the floor with sunburns and hopeful grins waiting to be told about the next activity.

"We will begin noble silence after dinner. No speaking, no reading, no writing, no phones, no electronics, no eye contact with any other person and no touching for the next 36 hours. You will sit in meditation after dinner until bed and go to sleep without looking at anyone. We begin meditation in the morning again. If you have a health condition and think you may need a chair, ask for one. There are only 5 chairs, so be honest. You will have a few breaks during the day when you are free to walk around and observe nature, but no running, no exercising, no kayaking, nothing to busy your mind.

This is a beautiful gift."

At dinner I joked with people at my table about how lucky they were to be younger - they didn't have as many physical issues, husbands, adult children, jobs, places they've lived, deaths, etc. to face in the dreaded silent space where any possible distractions were stripped away. I comforted myself with all I had left - thoughts of communing with trees, insects, squirrels, rocks, mountains, and water during our breaks.

That night in a shared dorm that boasted one shower and two toilets for 20 people, an actual miracle unfolded. Our group followed all non-everything rules without issue, and we arrived promptly at 5am at the meditation hall without assistance of phone alarms. AMK sat elevated on some sort of alter in front of blankets with our names on them. My blanket was way too close to the front, which blew my plan of quietly low crawling for the bathroom when needed. But I remained hopeful she would at least guide us. Instead, she said the dreaded words.

"Our entire day of meditation is to not work on anything except for breathing and observing thoughts as they pass."

I was pissed.

It took all of 5 minutes before intense boredom owned my entire being. Then my mind decided to think about sex which could have been an interesting enough subject to pass the time, except that my physical pain was unbearable. I peeked around the room hoping to see someone else moving. I wanted a chair for my issues, physical and mental. Intense anger overcame me. Just when I was about to confront AMK in front of the whole class, a 5-minute break was granted to go to the bathroom and drink water in silence without eye contact. It ended far too quickly.

Back on the cushion, I started where I left off.

Anger at husbands worked until I realized they were hurt themselves. But could I ever trust again? Doubtful.

Was I willing to step out of pain onto a higher path? I might.

Did I just want out of pain to save myself? No.

The only way out was through.

My mind saw a door handle jiggle, and I grasped it and gave it a tug.

246

My husband's hand reached through to mine in the threshold.
We stood on either side of the door holding on tight.
Then we turned to face the stairway along the wall that separated us.
As we stepped up with hands clasped, the wall dissolved before us.
The wall remained solid at each step until we were on it together.

Ok, pleasure, pain, forgiveness, faith, growth – I was really getting somewhere, but in review of what had been covered, I found that if I were ever to be who I wanted to be, I'd have to get through my own barrier of guilt. Images went to holding my children as babies, hugging my dog Shilo, my Dad at his deathbed, and the best memories of growing up. I opened my eyes to see AMK staring into mine. The strength of these people was enormous. I was not alone.

After 15 hours of meditation, I felt fully alive.

It was truly a gift.

In yoga, you have achieved meditation, Dhyana, when you go beyond any concepts of time, space, or body. Practicing other limbs certainly helps one understand the value of meditation, but in my experience the only thing that makes meditation easier is meditation. There are various ways to prepare for it, such as guided meditation, but nothing can substitute for sitting still with yourself and connecting to your breath long enough to attain that which is otherwise unattainable. How long is long enough depends on how much you practice sitting with yourself in silence. The more it becomes a habit, the easier and quicker it becomes to experience this gift each time you begin.

"When to a man who understands,
the Self has become all things,
what sorrow, what trouble can there be,
to him who beholds that unity"
- Isha Upanishad.

Peace In, Peace Out

I am the light of my soul.
I am beautiful.
I am bountiful.
I am bliss.
I am.

The last chapter of the *Yoga Sutras* discusses the ceasing of karma, kleshas, and gunas, until all that remains is truth. And the last of Patanjali's 8 limbs is Samadhi, the state of transcendent liberation of suffering to profound connection and bliss. Patanjali's description of samadhi is akin to explanations by those who have experienced near death, such as those in the book *Proof of Heaven* by Eben Alexander, where body and mind may be in great danger, yet the spirit experiences joy - an unfathomable state unless experienced. Yet yoga says you don't have to almost die to experience life in this way while you are living.

Early on in my yoga journey, I aspired to enter a state of Samadhi and pretty much hang out there the rest of my life. Now I know that the very aspiring of such a thing pushes it away.

However, most yogic practices provide glimpses of Samadhi that in and of themselves are evidence that "peace on Earth" exists within each one of us. It is my deepest hope that one day, we can all meet ourselves, each other, and all of existence in that space of Sat Cit Ananda – truth, consciousness, and bliss.

1. What is unique about you that would show up in your offerings (pull from your dharma and truth statements, etc.)?

2. Is there a specific aspect of yoga (or other business) that inspires you?

3. What population do you want to serve and where are they located?

4. Write a mission statement that states purpose and overall intention. List key points from your previous answers and then play with concise sentences until you feel that your statement feels like a resounding yes.

   Example – 501(c)3 mission: *To ease distress through culturally diverse and layered approaches which honor ancient lineages of yoga to foster internal unity and connection to others. We are a wide-reaching platform for classes, quarterly publications, retreats, training, and education; uplifting events; and art and nature-based community projects.*

5. Biography. A bio helps people relate to you. Format of your bio.

   Name and Credentials. *RYT-200, E-RYT 500, specific types of yoga training, other relevant certifications, or education, etc.*
   Who are you as a person? *Give people a glimpse into your background.*
   How did you come to yoga? *Be honest, people want to trust you.*
   Why do you want to offer wellness services? *Name your why.*
   What is unique about your offerings? *What people might not know.*
   What can people expect to experience in your offerings?
   Type of yoga you like to teach and teaching style?

6. Chant or sing the Bliss Mantra or another affirmation that elevates your awareness of spiritual self and connection to others in the essence of their spirit. Try this for at least 7 minutes . . . or 15 hours.

   I am the light of my soul, I am beautiful, I am bountiful, I am bliss. I am. I am.

17. rEvolution to You

The foundation of yoga fused with inner work shines a light on individual meaning and purpose. Then, stepping across barriers can reveal a messy revolution to living true (acting on what is true instead of that which is distorted). Blazing a trail through dark corners and unknown lands to what living true means for you can mean diving deep into the nervous system and endocrine system, channeling Kundalini, applying focus through Dharana, and experiencing BEing in Dhyana.

In this hard path to the easy life, there will be many opportunities for change, stagnation, or evolution. For myself, the practice of living true becomes easier the longer I show up to do the work, and there is refuge in knowing that I am not alone. Each one of us holds a key. I continue to step forward knowing other hands will appear and collectively, we will create space for all to live true individually and together.

The evolution of you into awareness in action can show up in as many ways as there are people on the planet, birds in the sky, animals on the prairie, tree colors in the fall, experiences of life, and so much more. But allowing evolution requires allowing yourself mercy. In moments of self-sabotage, go to yourself like a frightened child lost in the woods and shine a light on your path brilliantly - not with force but with love.

One day, in savasana, she came to me . . . myself as a younger person. The present me embraced the essence of me as it leaned back in my arms and looked at me with profound grace,

"I'm proud of you. Thank you for helping me."

You were born for your evolution.

After all, the Guru is You.

www.ingramcontent.com/pod-product-compliance
Lightning Source LLC
Chambersburg PA
CBHW050924120626
46552CB00001B/28